Seasoned

Seasoned

A Memoir of Grief and Grace

Tom Zink

An Off the Common Book

Amherst, Massachusetts

ISBN: 978-945473-18-0

Edited by Janice Beetle

Book design by Maureen Scanlon

Cover photo by Julius Apus. Photographs in the book are from the author's collection and family archives, except as noted.

Biblical quotes are from the King James Version.

"The Trumpeter" poem, by Anne Springsteen, is reprinted by permission of Valparaiso University (thecresset.org).

This is a work of nonfiction. Some names have been changed to preserve anonymity, and some chronology altered to maintain narrative flow.

Printed in the United States of America by Off the Common Books, Amherst, Massachusetts; and in Canada by Beatty Printing, North Bay, Ontario.

For Steve

"I would appreciate it very much if you would write down for me some things you remember about him [Steve], both positives and negatives, ... and what his life meant for you."

From a letter written to the author and his sisters
by their mother, Charlotte Zink, in September 1977,
when Steve had been gone for as long as he had been alive.

Contents

ZINK AND ZUCKER FAMILY TREE

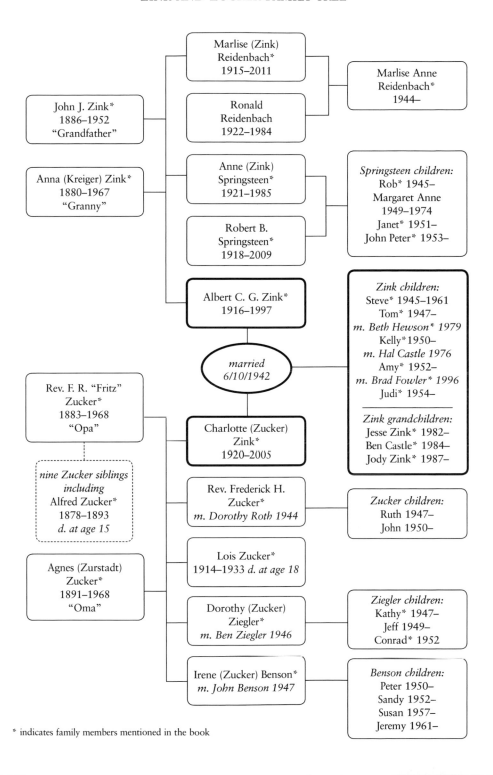

John J. Zink*
1886–1952
"Grandfather"

Anna (Kreiger) Zink*
1880–1967
"Granny"

Marlise (Zink)
Reidenbach*
1915–2011

Ronald
Reidenbach
1922–1984

Marlise Anne
Reidenbach*
1944–

Anne (Zink)
Springsteen*
1921–1985

Robert B.
Springsteen*
1918–2009

Springsteen children:
Rob* 1945–
Margaret Anne
1949–1974
Janet* 1951–
John Peter* 1953–

Albert C. G. Zink*
1916–1997

married
6/10/1942

Zink children:
Steve* 1945–1961
Tom* 1947–
m. Beth Hewson 1979*
Kelly* 1950–
m. Hal Castle 1976
Amy* 1952–
m. Brad Fowler 1996*
Judi* 1954–

Zink grandchildren:
Jesse Zink* 1982–
Ben Castle* 1984–
Jody Zink* 1987–

Rev. F. R. "Fritz"
Zucker*
1883–1968
"Opa"

nine Zucker siblings
including
Alfred Zucker*
1878–1893
d. at age 15

Agnes (Zurstadt)
Zucker*
1891–1968
"Oma"

Charlotte (Zucker)
Zink*
1920–2005

Rev. Frederick H.
Zucker*
m. Dorothy Roth 1944

Zucker children:
Ruth 1947–
John 1950–

Lois Zucker*
1914–1933 *d. at age 18*

Dorothy (Zucker)
Ziegler*
m. Ben Ziegler 1946

Ziegler children:
Kathy* 1947–
Jeff 1949–
Conrad* 1952

Irene (Zucker) Benson*
m. John Benson 1947

Benson children:
Peter 1950–
Sandy 1952–
Susan 1957–
Jeremy 1961–

* indicates family members mentioned in the book

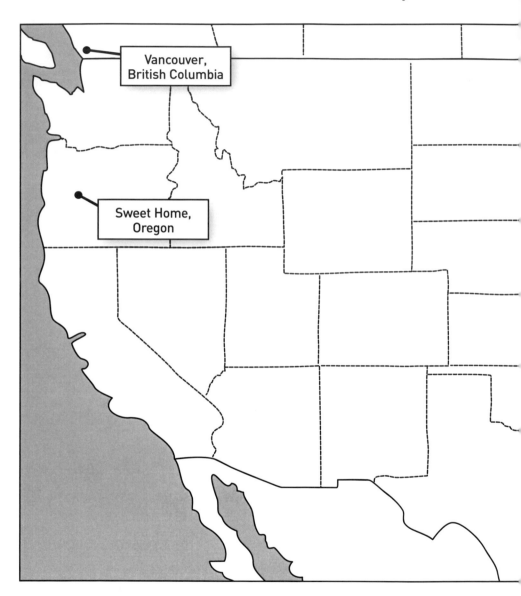

Vancouver,
British Columbia

Sweet Home,
Oregon

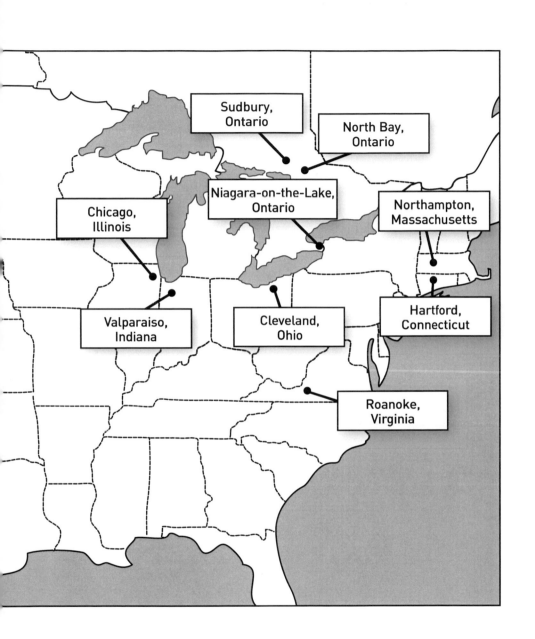

Sudbury, Ontario

North Bay, Ontario

Niagara-on-the-Lake, Ontario

Northampton, Massachusetts

Chicago, Illinois

Valparaiso, Indiana

Cleveland, Ohio

Hartford, Connecticut

Roanoke, Virginia

Prologue

"THERE'S ANOTHER bundle out there."

Those were the last words I heard my brother say.

He spoke them as he walked back into our garage, his hands clutching the wire wrapped around a bundle of newspapers. We were paper boys for the *Plain Dealer*, Cleveland's morning daily, published seven days a week. His words were a familiar morning refrain, a no-nonsense reminder to do my share.

I retrieved that last bundle and carried it into the garage. We snipped the wire and dropped the Thursday papers into the metal baskets that straddled the rear fenders of our bikes, like saddle bags you see on cowboys' horses on television. I grabbed one copy, quick-scanned the headlines, checked the Sports section, and offhandedly noted the date: Thursday, October 19, 1961. Off we rode in opposite directions to bring the news to our waiting customers.

Our house at the time was on a two-lane state highway, fifteen miles west of downtown Cleveland, running north towards Lake Erie and south into the next county. Columbia Road, as it was called, had gravel shoulders, rural mailboxes on posts near the roadway, and thirty-five-miles-per-hour speed limit signs.

Steve's paper route was on the highway, mine on Rose Road, a quiet side street that intersected Columbia a short distance from our house. It was a morning like hundreds of others in our twenty months as paper boys. But on this day, less than half an hour after we pedaled away from our home, my brother was killed on his bicycle, struck by a car that was trying to pass a slower-moving vehicle on Columbia Road.

I was the first in the family to hear of Steve's death. When Steve didn't return home shortly after me, I rode on my own, back along his route, and saw his broken bicycle on the side of the road, which had been closed by police who were still on the scene. After I identified myself, an officer bluntly delivered the news to me that initiated a transformation in my devout Christian family and in myself, one I would not understand for decades. From that moment forward, we all began to let Steve slip away, bit by bit, in the silence that masked our pain.

Within the confines of our German Lutheran heritage, death was perceived as the gateway to eternal life in heaven, a view that gave us comfort but effectively kept a lid on all of our feelings and questions. No one seemed to know how to talk to a teenaged boy whose older brother was dead. So I kept my own counsel and did my best to persevere. I lived by the myth that if I could just act as if nothing had happened, I'd be all right.

Over time, I lost touch with Steve—who I was with him, how we talked to each other, what his voice sounded like. In that brief part of my life when I had been his younger brother, we shared many things—riding bicycles, singing harmony, teasing, farting, telling lame jokes, wrestling, building models, playing basketball, studying, praying. I kept these memories and my pain to myself, mistakenly thinking this meant they mattered less and less. I shoved my initial emotional reactions into a deep freeze, where layers of ice, frost, and snow gradually accumulated to protect me. I learned how to drive a car, went away to college, traveled overseas with the Peace Corps, got married, had children, earned a doctoral degree, and managed, with my dear wife, to adequately provide for our family's needs.

As the years passed, my memories, my grief, and my love for Steve became encased in layers of impenetrable ice that kept me unaware of the cauldron that simmered below. On rare occasions, a smell, a phrase, or a song evoked a memory of those first fourteen years of my life, when my brother was alive, but I'd quickly retreat from naming the loss, understanding my grief, or facing the pain. An aching fear kept me from wanting to find out what lay beneath.

Then, one morning, thirty-nine years after Steve's death, I found myself in a church service in Ontario on a Canadian Thanksgiving Sunday with my sons, my wife, and her extended family. During the exchange of the peace, I watched my teenaged boys greeting their teenaged cousins, and for the first time was struck by the realization that Steve's death had snatched away my chance to bond with my own brother as a young adult. In that moment, it was as if a ray of sunlight began to melt its way through the permafrost that locked away my grief and my love. The revelation sent me reeling, and it marked the moment I knew I needed to follow that warm sunlight back into the past and set myself free.

As I began a mission to bring my brother, and my fourteen-year-old self, back to life and to fully embrace how I understood and coped with Steve's death, I also sensed I had a story to tell. I have discovered that the act of setting my words down in this memoir has become the key to opening myself to all the joy, sadness, laughter, and pain of remembering Steve. Telling the story shines a light into the past and has given me a renewed sense of grace and strength that I wish to share.

1 Beginnings

IN MAY 1920, a steamship bound for New York City made its way from Calcutta, India, around the Cape of Good Hope at the southern tip of Africa, bringing my grandparents, the Reverend Frederick (Fritz) Zucker, his wife, Agnes, and their three children back to the United States for a well-deserved home leave. Reverend Zucker, a third generation Lutheran missionary, had been preaching and teaching among the Tamil people in southern India since 1910 and was due for a break. Agnes, who worked in the dispensary, caring for the health needs of the Tamil community, was pregnant with their fourth child. My mother, Charlotte Zucker, was born on June 26, not long after the Zucker family arrived in Agnes' home town of Evansville, Indiana.

A year and a half later, Charlotte was carried in her father's arms onto a waiting ship for the family's return to India with a group of other Lutheran missionary families. In a photograph marking the occasion, Fritz, with his trademark mustache, wire-rim glasses, bowtie, and floppy fedora, is holding baby Charlotte in his left arm while pointing to the camera with his right. Agnes stands behind the three older children: Frederick and Dorothy, both squinting at the camera, and curious Lois, craning her neck to look up at her family's fellow travelers.

Reverend Zucker's mission work in India was sponsored by the Lutheran Church Missouri Synod, a conservative German denomination in the United States that formed a closely-knit, insular subculture determined to preserve and protect its own language, culture, and confessional beliefs. The Synod founders had emigrated from Germany to escape the encroachment of the German government on their religion. Once established in Missouri and other Midwestern states, a circle-the-wagons mentality developed to slow any assimilation into the rapidly changing American culture surrounding them. Preserving their faith meant that the fundamental beliefs of Martin Luther's theology in the sixteenth century were to be proclaimed without being altered, watered down, or modernized.

Central to the Synod's mission of proclaiming their fundamental beliefs was to establish Christian schools to train church leaders and educate the young. Within a year of their arrival in Missouri, a small group of pastors built a log cabin schoolhouse that became Concordia Theological Seminary in St. Louis, the training school for Synod ministers. My grandfather, Reverend Zucker, graduated from this seminary. His first call after graduation was as pastor for a church in Lakewood, Ohio, near Cleveland. Within a month, he opened an elementary school at the church and became the school's first teacher.

Many local Missouri Synod congregations throughout the Midwest organized Lutheran elementary schools. In the larger cities, like Cleveland, Detroit, and Chicago, churches banded together to found Lutheran high schools. These institutions have played a significant role in my family's story across the generations, from the Lutheran school that Reverend Zucker founded in Lakewood to the Lutheran elementary school my father attended in Baltimore, Maryland, to West Shore Lutheran School and Lutheran High School West, which my siblings and I attended in suburban Cleveland.

The Zucker family spent the next six years in India. The three older children, Frederick, Lois, and Dorothy, attended a boarding school for missionary children, high in the central hills of southern India, in a place called Kodaikanal. Here the tropical heat was less intense than along the coast, where the mission churches were located. When she was old enough, Charlotte joined her siblings at the school. Fritz and Agnes made frequent visits to the school to see their children. In a letter to her grown children years later, Agnes recalled one of those visits when Charlotte was five years old:

> Charlotte had become a good friend and playmate of little Margaret. They were such sweet little playmates that when, a few days before Christmas, a message came that Margaret and her mother had died suddenly of diphtheria, I was afraid to tell Charlotte, lest it might spoil her Christmas. When I mentioned it to her, however, I was relieved to hear her say, "How nice, then she will celebrate Christmas with Jesus in heaven." To me it has always been an example of the truth that Jesus emphasized, that we must accept the great truths of the Bible as humbly and confidently as a child trusts a trusted adult's word.

Fritz and Agnes' oldest daughter Lois had epilepsy, and treatment for her condition was not available in India. They decided to terminate their second mission term early and return to the United States to seek help. In early February 1932, Fritz traveled with Lois to New York for medical treatments that failed to provide any help. Father and daughter returned to join the rest of the family members, who were busy packing for the next move to Hoffman, Illinois, where Fritz had accepted a call to a Lutheran church in the small farming community about fifty miles east of St. Louis, Missouri.

By this time, the oldest Zucker child, Frederick, had left home to begin his post-secondary studies to prepare for the Lutheran ministry, as his father and grandfather had before him. During these years of the Great Depression, Charlotte and her sisters all learned valuable lessons in getting by, making do, and doing without—lessons Charlotte carried with her throughout her life. Family entertainment was simple and free. One of the Zuckers' prized possessions was an upright piano. Agnes would play while her daughters gathered around her and sang their favorite hymns and popular songs like "Home on the Range" and Gene Autry's hit "Sierra Sue."

Lois' epilepsy continued to be a concern, a medical puzzle with no clear remedies or treatments. One summer afternoon in 1933, when Lois was eighteen, she lay down for a nap and never woke up, apparently suffering a seizure and suffocating in her pillow. The shock to Agnes and Fritz and their four children must have been profound, even though all the Zucker family members were well aware of Lois' fragility. It was the second time that Fritz had experienced the sudden, unexpected death of a teenaged family member. When Fritz was eight years old in the summer of 1892, his older brother Alfred went for a swim with a friend just days after his fifteenth birthday, intending to cross the Maumee River near their home in Fort Wayne, Indiana. When Alfred's legs cramped up, his friend tried valiantly, but unsuccessfully, to save him and Alfred drowned. A family of faith that trusted in God's promises of eternal salvation in heaven, the Zuckers carried on, and the sudden loss of Lois became another reason for Charlotte to regard death as a blessing—an entry point to heaven—rather than an occasion for deep sadness.

Charlotte was an excellent student at the Lutheran elementary school in Hoffman and at Carlyle High School. She remembered talking with a boy in her high school geometry class after they had just taken a difficult test. He asked her, "Do you think you passed?" Charlotte thought, Passed? Of course I passed, you silly thing. But what she said was, "Oh, I do hope so." She was so accustomed to good grades that the thought of failing never crossed her mind. She graduated from high school in 1938 at the top of her class, with dreams of continuing her education as her older brother Frederick and sister Dorothy had done. She was delighted when she received her letter of acceptance and was awarded a scholarship to a small Lutheran college in Indiana called Valparaiso University. But she had to wait. Money was tight for the Zucker family so Charlotte worked for the first year after high school at the Hollywood Candy factory in nearby Centralia, Illinois.

ALBERT ZINK, my father, grew up the middle child and only son of John J. Zink, a noted architect who designed dozens of art deco movie theaters in and around Baltimore, and Anna Krieger Zink, a career woman who worked in Baltimore public schools for ten years before she was married to John in 1913. After their wedding, John and Anna lived in New York City while John studied theater architecture at the Columbia School of Architecture. There, they became fast friends with the family of their pastor, Reverend Karl Kretzmann, his wife, and their six sons. The Kretzmann boys were a fun-loving bunch. Serious about their faith and their religion, they also believed that the good Lord desired joy in believers. All six of them attended the Missouri Synod Lutheran seminary in St. Louis and became pastors, professors, missionaries, and writers with considerable influence within the Lutheran Church Missouri Synod. The Zink and Kretzmann families remained close even after John and Anna moved back to Baltimore in 1915.

Albert, who was also sometimes called "Al," and his two sisters, Marlise and Anne, grew up surrounded by music. Their mother was the church organist and choir director. Their extended family was a potpourri of musical talent: choir directors, singers, music teachers, organists, and pianists. On summer evenings, the aunts, uncles, and cousins would gather on John and Anna's front porch on Overland Avenue. Someone would say, "Hey, let's sing 'Sweet and Low'." As Marlise and her mother started the melody, the harmonies flowed in, family members finding their places in six-, seven-, and eight-part harmony, as Albert recalled, "with crescendos and diminuendos, no instruments, no leader." Late into the evening they sang—church hymns, love songs, and parlor songs. Jokes, quips, and laughter punctuated the music. The neighbors sat on their porches and listened. When Anna or John noticed the hour and said it was time to stop, a collective plea flew through the summer evening air from neighbors' porches: "Please don't stop! Keep singing!" The evening of harmony would then often finish with Brahms' lullaby, "*Guten Abend, Gut Nacht.*"

Albert loved to make things with his hands. At the dinner table, he would shape his mashed potatoes into mountains, pooling the gravy into lakes and rivers with pieces of lettuce and broccoli for trees and bushes. His mother's insistence on proper table manners soon put an end to his dinner plate designs, so Albert began building cardboard models of houses and churches. One year he fashioned a tiny scale model of his mother's baby grand piano for her birthday. The keyboard was only three inches long and inside the frame, he stretched about thirty pieces of thread for strings. Albert said Anna was "completely enchanted" with the piano model, and he was proud of it because, "It represented a tribute to my mother's musical legacy to her family."

Providing music lessons for her children was one expression of Anna's musical legacy. She arranged for a friend to give Albert his first piano lesson. Albert failed to arch his fingers properly above the keys, and the teacher rapped his knuckles with a wooden ruler. His first lesson proved to be his last, but Albert did inherit from his parents a finely tuned musical ear. Although he claimed to be unable to read a single note of piano music, he would, as an adult, be able to sit at our family's spinet piano and play hymns with both hands in impeccable four-part harmony with no music in front of him; always, he played in the impossible key of G-flat, which makes almost exclusive use of the black keys.

Albert's strong desire to please his parents and others in authority often competed with an inner urgency to do things his own way, no matter what. One day when he was a boy and his mother was away at the store, he got the bright idea to scrub the kitchen floor and surprise her. He filled a bucket with water and grabbed a mop. Just then his mother walked in the back door. "Albert," she said, as she set her grocery bag on the counter, "will you please scrub the kitchen floor for me?" He stormed off, refusing to do what he had planned simply because he'd been asked to do it.

Albert started delivering newspapers when he was about twelve years old. He took great pride in his ability to fold the paper in thirds, then in half, tuck in the loose end, and fling it from his moving bicycle onto front porches up and down Overland Avenue. One customer's cat, always perched on the porch, became a favorite target. His batch of newspapers came in a bundle wrapped with a piece of newsprint and a wire. His supervisor was very clear with his boys: take the wire wrapper home and dispose of it there; do *not* throw it down the sewer. One day, Albert couldn't be bothered to lug the wrapper and the wire home, so he kicked them down the sewer. Mrs. Angell, who ran the nearby hardware store, was watching, and word of Albert's indiscretion reached his supervisor. Albert was fired, his two dollars a week down the drain, or more accurately, the sewer.

John and Anna kept two decanters of wine on the dining room sideboard, one red and one white. On a Sunday afternoon when he was in his late teens, Albert was home by himself when his buddy Bobby Coles came over. Bobby saw the wine and said, "Hey, why don't we try some of that?" So they did. And then they tried some more. And some more. After Bobby left for home, Albert went upstairs to take a bath and get ready for a choir concert at church that night. He locked the door and fell asleep in the tub. The next thing he knew, his father was pounding on the bathroom door, "Hey! You in there?" No response. More pounding on the door. Albert woke up.

"Whatsa matter?" Albert said.

"What're you doing in there?"

"I don't know. Sleeping, I guess. Why? What's wrong?"

"Don't you know we gotta sing in the choir tonight? It's seven o'clock!"

Albert had been asleep in the tub for three hours. He made it to church in time with the rest of the family, but on his way up the stairs to the choir loft he stumbled and created a huge clatter with his lanky body, an unintended, unwelcome opening prelude for the evening concert.

Albert once described himself as a guy who "hates procedures. Ain't nobody gonna tell me how to do anything. I'll do it, and I'll get it done better than anybody else, but don't tell me how to do it." In memoir notes he wrote years later, he described himself as a "recalcitrant teenager." At the end of eighth grade, he felt no need of further schooling, figuring that "any more education would be a waste of time." The Baltimore school board and his parents had other ideas. He enrolled at the Baltimore Polytechnic Institute, known as "Polly," one of the toughest technical schools in the United States at the time, with hopes of becoming an engineer. His low grades forced him to repeat tenth grade. He managed to graduate from Polly then spent a dispiriting year at a dead-end job. His dreams of becoming an engineer were fading; he saw only a bleak future ahead. His father encouraged him to consider college, but that required a recommendation from the principal at Baltimore Polytechnic Institute. Albert's desperate plea to the principal and his signed promise to work hard to pass all his courses secured the recommendation, and he was admitted to the engineering program at Johns Hopkins University in Baltimore.

DURING THE YEARS that Albert was finishing high school and beginning his studies at Johns Hopkins, his older sister Marlise completed high school and continued her music studies at the Peabody Institute, also in Baltimore. Her strong, clear soprano voice made her a valued choir member at Baltimore's Bethlehem Lutheran Church, where she was also active in the Walther League, the Missouri Synod's national youth organization. Marlise aspired to further her education in music but was unclear what direction to take.

In the spring of 1938, at a Walther League convention in Pittsburgh, she found herself at the convention banquet seated at a table with four of the Kretzmann brothers, who were all now in their thirties and had remained close family friends with the Zinks. Dinner conversation settled at one point on the topic of Valparaiso University, a small liberal arts school in northwestern Indiana known affectionately as "Valpo."

In response to a growing call within the Lutheran Church Missouri Synod for post-secondary education for lay, or non-ordained, people, the Synod purchased Valpo in 1925. Because it was established by church people whose careers were in secular fields, Valpo became a counter-culture within the Synod. It served as a rallying point for the growing movement, led mostly by lay people who urged the Synod to move away from the closed mindset of its early years and to become more fully engaged in the dynamic social, cultural, and political changes in twentieth-century America.

All four Kretzmann brothers were part of this movement to modernize the church. Their support of Valpo and their enthusiasm for its mission within the Synod were palpable. Just two years later, the oldest brother, O.P. Kretzmann, would become Valpo's president. The conversation soon shifted to Marlise's conundrum: What college should she choose?

As dessert was being served, one of the Kretzmann brothers took a copy of the dinner menu, turned it over, and wrote on the back a sentence that would influence the course of Zink family history for decades to come: "I, Marlise Zink, do solemnly promise that I will attend Valparaiso University, starting in September 1938 OR ELSE." All four Kretzmanns signed the scribbled document, including Mick, who used his full given name, Martin Luther Kretzmann. Mick didn't bother to include his last name in his signature, and, years later, Marlise told me, with a chuckle, that she knew she could not disobey a warrant signed by "Martin Luther" himself, even if it was scrawled on the back of a dinner menu. And so it was that Marlise Zink went to Valparaiso, Indiana, in the fall of 1938.

Marlise enrolled in the university as a music education major. One year later, her younger sister, Anne, entered Valpo as a freshman. The two sisters lived in a women's dormitory called Altruria Hall, where they soon met and became good friends with a new student, the daughter of a Lutheran pastor from southern Illinois, Charlotte Zucker. The friendship between these three young women blossomed. They sang in the university choir. Charlotte and Anne worked together on the school newspaper, *The Torch*, and formed an especially close bond. Anne began signing notes to Charlotte with "KS" for "kindred spirit."

IN THE SPRING OF 1940, Albert received permission from his father to visit Marlise and Anne in Valpo, provided he lived up to his promise and passed all his courses at Johns Hopkins. Prior to his visit, Albert wrote to his sister Anne and asked her to set him up with a different blind date for each of the five evenings he would be in Valpo. As Albert's train arrived in Valpo that June day in 1940, standing on the platform with his sisters Marlise and Anne, was the first of Albert's blind dates, the preacher's daughter from Hoffman, Charlotte Zucker. One can only speculate whether Anne chose her own "kindred spirit" for Albert's first date, hoping for some special magic between her brother and her dear friend.

Albert's self-professed "love of fun and frolic" and his innate sense of mischief surfaced quickly on his first date with Charlotte. He asked her to repeat a tongue-twister: "I slit a sheet, a sheet I slit, and on the slitted sheet I sit." He wanted to see, he recalled years later, "if she knew what she was talking about." For a preacher's daughter, the challenge was a verbal minefield, but Charlotte was game and gave it a go.

Recalling this first date years later, Albert remembered that he was "mesmerized" by this "indescribably beautiful" young woman. He told Anne to cancel the rest of his scheduled blind dates; he only wanted to spend time with Charlotte. The two rented bicycles the next day, and when Charlotte demonstrated her cycling ineptitude, they returned the bikes and rented a bicycle built for two. One evening, they walked through campus and talked about their families, their faith, their lives. Later in the week, they sat together at a piano and sang. Albert's ease on the keyboard captivated Charlotte as much as her clear soprano voice charmed him, and in those moments, Charlotte first thought to herself: This is it!

After Albert returned home, letters traveled back and forth between Baltimore and Hoffman. The word "love" appeared more and more often. Charlotte lived for Albert's letters in that summer of 1940. Albert was somewhat embarrassed about his handwriting, so he used all upper-case letters, creating a tidy, draftsman style. One day, the Zucker family stopped at the Hoffman post office for the mail. Charlotte, sitting in the front seat of the car, ripped open the letter from Albert and began reading his tender, loving words. From the back seat, her mother said, "Oh, he printed it so clearly, I can almost read it from back here!" In a flush of embarrassment, Charlotte quickly hid the letter to keep the sentiments private. The smitten couple arranged occasional visits—a Thanksgiving weekend in Baltimore one year, a summer break in Hoffman the next, and a Christmas visit in Baltimore, where Albert proposed and Charlotte accepted.

Albert and Charlotte were married by Charlotte's father, Reverend Zucker, at Trinity Lutheran Church in Hoffman, Illinois, on June 10, 1942, two years after their blind date. Albert's sister Marlise sang a solo during the ceremony, and Anne stood with Charlotte as her maid of honor. Their "honeymoon" was a one-night stay at the Stevens Hotel in Chicago in the company of Marlise, who was on her way back to Valpo to finish her senior year. The three shared a room and celebrated by sipping champagne, singing favorite songs in three-part harmony, and sailing paper airplanes out an open window into the sultry Chicago night.

The next day, the newlyweds rode the train to Cleveland, Ohio. Albert was returning to his draftsman's job with the National Advisory Committee on Aeronautics, the forerunner to NASA, a job that had brought him to Cleveland just six months earlier. His duties involved top-secret research on airplane engines, work that was vital to the Allied cause in World War II. Although Charlotte was traveling to a city she had never seen with a man she deeply loved but barely knew, she had a deep faith in God's power to provide for their needs and to guide them through whatever lay ahead.

The apartment they moved into was in Lakewood, the same Cleveland suburb where Charlotte's father, Reverend Fritz Zucker, had begun his ministry career thirty-five years earlier. Along with her faith, her luggage, and her new husband, Charlotte arrived in Lakewood with a list of her father's many church friends who were eager to welcome this new couple into their midst. Albert and Charlotte quickly became active in Lakewood's Pilgrim Lutheran Church. They both sang in the choir, Charlotte taught Sunday school, and Albert advised the Walther League youth and served on the church board.

The Zinks were an energetic, ambitious, hard-working couple. Charlotte once referred to their lifestyle as "tearing around like tadpoles." Albert wrote in a letter home that "things are piling up around me like dirt around a ditch digger." Not long after the end of World War II, Albert wanted to get out of research at the National Advisory Committee on Aeronautics and into construction, his true passion. In February 1946, he accepted a job with an engineering and construction firm in Cleveland, the H.K. Ferguson Company. Albert's first big opportunity came when he was placed in charge of all heating, ventilating, and air conditioning systems for a huge rayon plant in Tennessee. The successful completion of this job landed him a promotion to "Group Leader, Mechanical," for design and drafting work on construction projects in New York, Virginia, Illinois, and Texas. His success meant increased financial security, but it also meant that out-of-town travel would become a frequent necessity.

IN THE MIDST of their busy lives, Albert and Charlotte had a strong desire to have children. But by early 1945, it was not happening. They went to doctors for fertility tests. Albert went first for testing on his sperm count. A few days later, he returned to the doctor's office to learn the results. His embarrassment level, already high due to the reason for his visit and the fact that he was the only male in a waiting room filled with young, pregnant women, shot into the stratosphere when the doctor strode into the waiting room and exclaimed, "My boy, you have millions!"

A month later, Charlotte learned she was pregnant, and several months later, she wrote to her parents, "I certainly hope and pray that the lessons God has blessed me with will be passed on to my children through my efforts along with all the other gifts He's given me. We want our home to be a real light shining before men; with God's help I know we can."

Three months before this first baby was due, with financial help from Albert's parents, the Zinks purchased a house in the suburb of Rocky River, Ohio. They soon transferred their church membership from Lakewood's Pilgrim Lutheran Church to the new mission congregation in Rocky River, St. Thomas Lutheran Church. Charlotte commented in a letter to her parents that she looked forward to working in a new, young congregation and that "maybe later, you'll be hearing more about St. Thomas," words that would prove to be an immense understatement.

The baby who made Al and Charlotte Zink parents—Stephen Alan Zink— was born on December 6, 1945. Charlotte had already been preparing herself for this role that would become the center of her life for the next quarter century. In her second-year psychology class at Valparaiso University, she researched and wrote about how parents can train children for ultimate independence. While pregnant, she attended a course for expectant mothers, and upon completion, she received a certificate that proclaimed her a "Prepared Parent." In a letter to her parents, Mom said, "I guess I should hang it right over the baby's bed in case of complaints."

Albert provided essential support in the first weeks after his wife and son came home from the hospital. The doctor's rules for new mothers were strict: in bed for two weeks, no stairs at all for four weeks, and only one stair trip per day for six weeks. So, when Mom needed to get up or down stairs, Dad carried her. When diaper duty was due, he took over—changing Steve, carrying the dirty diapers to the basement, where he hand-washed them and hung them to dry.

Soon after Mom and Steve came home from the hospital, Dad's sister Anne, Mom's best friend from Valpo, and Anne's husband, Bob Springsteen, arrived with their year-old son Rob to help with the first few weeks of newborn care. Writing to her parents, Mom described Anne as "always so cheerful, calm, and nice about everything that she's perfect for the morale of the household." Anne was chosen to be Steve's godmother, and, a few weeks later, when Steve was baptized, Anne held him in her arms and made the promises of the baptismal covenant that Steve was too young to proclaim on his own.

Not long after Steve's arrival graced my parents' lives, Mom became pregnant again. Steve was fifteen months old when I arrived on the scene, sixty-seven weeks after his birth. I made Steve an older brother.

I AM A CHILD OF WINTER, born on March 20, the last day of winter in 1947, at Fairview Park Hospital in Cleveland, Ohio. The calendar declared the next day the beginning of spring, but Cleveland weather has notorious disregard for the almanac. On March 26, the day my parents were scheduled to bring me home, this headline blazed across the front page of the Cleveland *Plain Dealer*, the city's morning daily: "Blizzard Leaves Two Dead, 16 Hurt, City Groggy; Snow Is Year's Worst. Utilities Staggered by 65-mph Gusts." Power was lost, schools were closed, and inter-city bus travel was "abandoned" in the wake of this "vast whirlpool of wind," the newspaper reported. Staff spent the night at the hospital. Travel home was impossible. Mom had a candle-light breakfast in the hospital on our intended homecoming day.

It was customary in those days for maternity hospital stays to last a week or more. Shorter stays required a ride home in an ambulance. So it was that an ambulance delivered Mom, Dad, and me home along snow-covered streets, past shovelers, digging out their cars. We crossed an icy bridge and finally arrived in our drift-decorated driveway in Rocky River. Dad took Mom's elbow and helped her through the snow drifts, her snugly-wrapped baby bundle held close to her winter coat. Standing at the door holding Steve in her arms was Mom's younger sister, Irene, who looked after Steve while Mom was in the hospital.

A few weeks after my parents took me home, the water of Holy Baptism was sprinkled on my forehead, and I was declared a Christian. My parents played with some names before they settled on Thomas Christopher. I am grateful they discarded Dad's proposals—Xavier York Zink, to be otherwise known as "XYZ," and Xavier Raymond Zink, dreamed up so they could call me "X-Ray" for short. My baptism took place in the small, white clapboard building in Rocky River that was the home of St. Thomas Lutheran Church. In the Gospel story, Jesus had a disciple named Thomas who has been saddled for centuries with the nickname "doubting Thomas" because he required tangible proof of Jesus' resurrection. In my early years in Sunday school, I learned that "faith" was good but "doubt" was not. For years, my Biblical namesake was no hero to me.

Down the road from St. Thomas Lutheran was a large stone edifice with a massive bell tower, stained glass windows, and an attached school building. This was St. Christopher Catholic Church. In the little piece of the world where I grew up, Lutherans were "us" and the Catholics were "them." The Catholics crossed themselves in church, genuflected, and prayed to the Virgin Mary. Lutherans followed none of these practices.

One of the creeds common to both religions is the Apostles' Creed. The original wording of the creed, dating from the fourth century CE, includes the line, "I believe in the Holy Spirit, the holy catholic Church," with "catholic" here meaning "universal." The shock waves from the rift between Martin Luther and the Roman Catholic Church 400 years earlier lingered still in our little corner of the world. Our Lutheran church did not utter the word "catholic" in the worship service. The phrase "the holy *Christian* Church" was used instead. While my first name could have come from our Lutheran church, my parents' choice of the local Catholic church for my middle name was unthinkable.

It is far more likely that my parents chose my middle name, Christopher, as a gift. "Christopher" means "Christ-bearer." I learned this from my mother when I was about six years old. I took the news very literally: Was I to carry the body of the Messiah himself? Slender in build, short of stature, and small-boned, it overwhelmed me to think I must bear the Savior of the whole world on my narrow shoulders. My middle name also afforded me a nickname: Christy. In my birth announcement, Mom penned this parody of "'Twas the Night Before Christmas:"

> 'Twas the day before springtime and all thru the air
> A feeling of new life was definitely there.
> While Stephen was sleeping all snug in his bed,
> His daddy and mommy to the hospital sped.
> Not long before dawning, at six forty-four
> On Thursday, March twenty, there was one Zink boy more.
> Thomas Christopher's the title, he's "Christy" to friends;
> He's twenty-one inches between the two ends;
> Seven pounds and nine ounces was shown on the scale.
> Both he and his mother feel hearty and hale!

OF COURSE I don't remember my homecoming on the day after the blizzard, but I do wonder if that experience primed me to welcome snow in a very personal way that was deeply reassuring. As I grew older, I anticipated snow with the same eagerness that I felt on Christmas Eve or the first day of summer vacation. Falling snow took me home and gave me reason to hunker down, quiet my pace, and relish the feeling I think of as *gemütlichkeit*, a

German term my father used on occasion to express a deep sense of conviviality and well-being.

I loved to stomp on puddles coated with a layer of thin ice, to hear it crackling as it shattered, and to watch the murky water underneath seep up onto the ice and over the toes of my galoshes. Steve and I pushed ever-growing balls of snow around the backyard to help Dad build "Abe Lincoln," a snowman as tall as Dad was, sporting a top hat, a stubby stick nose, and a jutting chin. On frigid nights of twenty below zero Fahrenheit, I would venture outdoors to inhale deeply through my mouth just to find out how air that cold felt as it rushed down my windpipe. I stared in wonder at the tiny feather-like fingers of frost on our bedroom window that Mom said were the fingers of a guy called Jack Frost.

In high school, a snowstorm even guaranteed me a top grade on a term paper. Snow started falling on a Wednesday afternoon in December and continued into the early hours of Friday morning. When I went to bed Thursday night, the blizzard was howling outside, but I slept through the sounds of the wind, the muffled voices downstairs in the living room—and my alarm clock. I only woke up when I heard my mother say "Good morning" and felt her touch my shoulder. I looked at the clock and jerked up to a sitting position, crying, "I'm late for school!"

"Don't worry, you won't be going today," my mother said. "In fact, nobody's going anywhere today. And nobody could go anywhere during the night either and seven of them spent the night on our living room floor."

I looked out the window and saw that the storm had buried the two-lane state highway we lived on under three feet of wind-blown, drifted snow. Scattered in front of our house, trapped in the snow, were five cars, a pick-up truck, and an eighteen-wheel trailer truck. I followed the smells of coffee brewing and breakfast cooking downstairs to the living room where the drivers of those vehicles had spent the night.

Schools were closed for the whole next week, and I used my unexpected free time to finish writing a term paper due before Christmas that I had been procrastinating on the entire semester. My mother said the good grade I earned was just lucky; I preferred to think of it as a special gift of winter, the kind no other season can provide.

My father also loved the snow. "You have no idea," he wrote in a letter to my mother before they were married, "of the exquisite beauty into which the woods can be transformed by a wet, sticky snow that clings to anything and everything." One winter Saturday when I was about seven years old, a windless snow was falling. Dad led Steve, our younger sister Kelly, and me on a walk to a park we called "The Valley," a greenway straddling both sides of the Rocky River near our house. We walked the short distance to the park entrance, then along a road that wound downhill towards the river.

Near the bottom of the hill, Dad left the road and struck off through the new-fallen snow, leading us towards an immense open field. We trudged after him, knees lifted high, straining to keep up with his long strides. When he reached a grove of pine trees, his head brushing against branches dangling low with snow, he stopped. And he looked. In silence. The three of us children stopped as well, wondering what we were supposed to be looking at, or hearing.

The silence of that moment was nearly reverential, as if we were standing in church at the end of the service as our pastor gave the closing blessing. The stillness of the scene—the snow-heavy branches bending near us, the vast white patch of playing field, the shale cliffs above the river showing a zebra-like contrast of bright snow-stripes and dark rock—was broken by the sight of a rabbit, bounding quickly, quietly through the deepening snow.

Steve saw it first and broke the spell of the moment, yelling, "Hey! Lookit that rabbit!" His body tensed, ready to give chase. Dad quickly reached out his hand and placed it firmly on Steve's arm, stopping its rapid upward swing as he prepared to dash off in pursuit. "Shhh . . . just wait," Dad said in an audible whisper. "Let him run." Again, we kept silence.

A few moments later, Steve could contain himself no more, and off he ran after the rabbit, snow flying wildly in his wake. Soon, Steve's feet could no longer keep up with his body, and he fell face-first into the snow with a howl of delight. Kelly and I dashed off after him, falling freely, letting ourselves be swallowed by the snow. In the end, I sensed that Dad hadn't meant for us to be looking *for* anything. We were just supposed to *be*—feeling the snowflakes alight on our noses and cheeks, hearing the silence—so we could recall these rare moments of serenity.

THE ADDRESS OF OUR HOUSE in Rocky River was 19517 Riverview Avenue. Dad's extended family in Baltimore used a numerical shorthand to refer to family homes, and Dad followed suit. So our house was always referred to as "19517."

The house was like many of the houses in its Rocky River neighborhood—a tall three-story white box with a simple gable roof sloping fore and aft, a gravel driveway to the left of the house, and a narrow tree lawn, separating the sidewalk from the street. At the end of every driveway was a one-car garage. Every front yard on the street was the same: two tiny swatches of lawn perched on either side of a walkway that led from the sidewalk to the front porch. In the front yard, four barberry bushes next to the sidewalk marked the corners of our front lawn. Our house was on the second lot from the corner of Riverview Avenue and the side street Rockland Avenue.

What was unique about 19517 was that the standard, forty-foot house lot on our corner was vacant. We called this open space the "Side Yard," and in the twelve years our family lived at 19517, it served us well as a vegetable garden, baseball diamond, football gridiron, magnet for neighborhood children, scene of raucous games—like Red Rover, Kick the Can, and Pom-Pom-Pullaway—and practice ground for novice bicyclists. The gnarly trunk of an old quince tree served as home base for games of Hide-and-Go-Seek. It was here on this small patch of land I practiced pitching with my neighbor Tim, who was crouched behind a small home plate made from a hunk of plywood. I imagined myself as a pitcher for the Cleveland Indians striking out Mickey Mantle and finally defeating the loathsome New York Yankees. It was here I watched my dad punt a football in a perfect spiral as high as the clouds. And it was here that we had room to run and chase down fireflies after dark on summer evenings and to lie down and count the clouds or stare at the stars.

The front porch, five steps up from the front walkway, spanned the full width of the house. Centered in the front door was an elongated oval window, a window that has always made me think of Santa Claus. The house had no fireplace or chimney for the jolly old man. So I knew without a doubt that Santa had to enter our house on Christmas Eve by that front door. All the hopes, dreams, and magic of Christmas were, for me, wrapped up in that front door and its oval window.

In the center of the house, between the dining room and the living room, was the staircase to the upstairs. Ten steps led up to a landing, where the staircase took a 180-degree turn to three more steps that led to the second floor. A window at the landing brought daylight to the staircase. It was to this staircase I snuck away and hid to remove the eye patch an eye doctor ordered me to wear over my stronger eye to improve the sight in my weaker eye. I'll never know if the doctor's scheme was ill-conceived or my resistance sabotaged it, but I have worn glasses ever since the age of four. It was also from this set of stairs that the rhythmic "bump, thump, bump, ka-bump" sound came when one of our baby sisters lost her balance and rolled to the bottom. The wail of pain that immediately followed that final "thump" set our mother running to comfort and soothe.

When the laughter, loud voices, and singing of our parents' cocktail parties kept us awake at night, Steve would whisper, "Hey, Christy, let's go listen."

"Daddy'll get mad," I said.

"They won't hear us," Steve said. "C'mon."

We'd tiptoe to the top of the staircase and sit down next to each other. Sometimes we'd hear Dad crack a funny joke that made everyone laugh, and Steve and I had to cover our mouths with our hands to muffle our giggles.

"Boy," I whispered, "everybody's sure a lot louder and funnier tonight than they are in church on Sundays."

"That's 'cause it's a party, silly."

If we heard Dad's voice coming close to the bottom of the stairs, we'd hightail it across the landing and up the last three steps and back into bed.

At the top of the steps was a hallway with doorways to the three bedrooms and the home's only bathroom. My brother and I slept in the room at the top of the stairs, sharing a double bed, a tall dresser, and the early days and nights of our lives together. Bedtime often found us under the covers, on our sides facing each other, our buzzing lips the engine sounds as we drove our little metal cars and trucks around on the sheet. Steve said, "Let's say this truck is going to the hardware store to get Dad some more nuts and bolts."

"Okay, but keep it off my side of the bed. My red car is taking all of us to Wallace Lake for a swim."

STEVE WAS A PRESENCE in my life from the moment I was carried through the snow drifts to the side door and into the warmth of my new home. He was my big brother, and I looked up to him from my first awareness of others in the world. He was always there, as essential as breathing, eating, sleeping. Steve was my roommate, playmate, sparring partner, and protector. In my first three years, Steve, along with my parents, was my earliest entertainment. Before there was television in our house, before the sound of the radio wasn't gibberish to me, I had my brother.

When Dad played marches on the piano, Steve showed me how to march around the living room, knees high, arms waving, and beating on a tom-tom. He was my foil, the yang to my yin. Mom reminded me some years later that, at times, she would leave Steve and me playing on our own in the den. I would antagonize Steve—messing with the block tower he was building, for instance—and he'd swat me in frustration. I'd cry, and Mom would rescue me and scold Steve. But most of the time, Mom once told me, Steve and I played well together, like the best of friends.

When Dad was home after work, play was even more fun. Our father was a giant, standing six feet, six inches tall. I clearly remember the feelings of vertigo when he'd pick me up in his arms and hold me so I was looking back over his shoulder. I was awestruck by how far away the floor was and how close the tops of the door jambs had suddenly become. It was a strange new world up there in Dad's breathing zone. I could feel his whiskered cheek with my fingers and smell the residue of his most recent cigarette on his breath.

I loved playing "lap trap" with Dad. He'd be sitting in his favorite over-stuffed chair absorbed in the day's *Plain Dealer*. The way he crossed his legs with one ankle on the other knee formed a nifty toddler-sized opening between his legs. I would sneak over and crawl up into the hole and place my arms on his thighs, hoping that this time he really *was* absorbed in the paper. Without lowering the paper, he would push his thighs together, squeezing a squeal of delight from my body. "Lap trap" was a regular "Do it again, Daddy!" game on quiet evenings in the living room.

OUR FAMILY TREE is laden with the fruits of long-distance travel, including Mom's six-year adventure in India. Her mother, Agnes Zucker, traveled on her own by ship from New York to Madras, India, in 1912 to marry Fritz. Fritz's grandmother, Charlotte Kremmer, made a giant leap of faith that led to the ultimate in blind dates. In 1852, at the age of 31, grandmother Charlotte accepted a long-distance proposal from a Lutheran missionary serving in India, whom she had never met. She set sail from London bound for Madras, India, by way of the Cape of Good Hope. After 108 days at sea, on Christmas Day, the ship arrived in Madras, where Charlotte met the Reverend Carl Kremmer and married him ten days later in a union that lasted thirty-four years, until Carl's death.

Dad and Mom traveled by foot, bicycle, bus, train, or taxi, for the first six years of their marriage because they couldn't afford a car until 1948, when they bought the Green Hornet, a 1940 two-door Chevy that unleashed our parents' pent-up passion for exploring new places. One of Mom's favorite songs was "The Happy Wanderer," a German folk song; singing it allowed her to express her and Dad's love of traveling and discovering new places.

A month after they brought the Green Hornet home, my parents took Steve and me, and the family dog, a huge boxer named Lady, on what Mom called "the first real Zink family auto trip," an afternoon ride through the rural countryside west of Cleveland. Steve and I rode on the back seat; Lady rode on the floor between us. She was no fan of automobile travel and showed her distaste for the whole idea by vomiting her latest meal onto the carpeted floor.

A year later, our brave and adventurous parents packed Steve and me, two cots, a massive TripTik from the American Automobile Association, and a mountain of luggage into the Green Hornet to visit Mom's parents in Miami, Florida. Agnes and Fritz were "Opa" and "Oma"—the German terms for grandfather and grandmother—to Steve and me. On this two-week odyssey to see them, the Green Hornet covered 3,633 miles at an average speed of forty miles per hour and burned 198 gallons of gasoline. My father, the engineer, kept the travel log, did the calculations, and passed on to his children a penchant for recording trip mileage, calculating fuel efficiency, and reading road maps that continues to this day.

In 1951, Dad wrote to relatives about a difficult decision Mom and he had to make. His words show his fondness for his cars and for wordplay:

> We have finally decided to lay away an old, old friend.... She has been our constant companion for three eventful years now, and has caused us few anxious moments. Although she did not die, we think she has developed some sort of autoimmune disorder.... We all suffered a tug at our heart strings when she left us.... Now, just in case you haven't been able to decipher the double talk, we have retired the "Green Hornet" for a paltry $300,... a car whose personality has been woven into our family life for the past three years.

The family's new "car" was a two-tone, oversized brown bomb called a DeSoto Suburban. With its fold-down jump seats in the rear, it could seat nine. The Suburban was not only huge but funny: The back doors opened to the rear, exactly opposite of the front doors. On our way to church, Steve would pull open that back door so quickly, it nearly took off my nose. "Hey, watch out!" I'd holler, as he scrambled back onto one of the jump seats with me right behind him. Head room was tight in the back. When Dad hit a bump, we'd bounce up and down, our heads touching the ceiling. When Dad turned a corner, Steve and I leaned against each other, wailing in phony distress until Dad raised his voice from way up in the driver's seat: "Quiet down back there," he'd say, reminding us of Cardinal Rule Number One of Zink family travel: "Don't distract the driver!" At nearly nineteen feet from bumper to bumper, the Suburban was so long Dad had to hire a contractor to knock out the bottom half of the back wall of the garage at 19517 and add an extra eighteen inches.

Selling the two-door Green Hornet, buying the nine-passenger Suburban, and expanding the garage were the signs of change in the Zink family. Our numbers were growing.

Albert and Charlotte Zink pose with their
sons, Steve, three, and Tom, two, in 1949.

The Zink family home in Rocky River, Ohio—known simply
as "19517."

Steve and Tom in 1949, when Tom was known
as "Christy."

2 Growing

ONE EARLY SPRING DAY just after my third birthday, my mother went away to the hospital. Dad brought her home several days later with our baby sister, Carolyn, who we came to call Kelly. Two years later, our sister Amy was born, and when she was two and a half, baby Judi came along. With our family now grown to seven in number, Dad couldn't resist a pun, and coined a term— "Zinkseven"—that sounds just like "Zink's heaven." Our new siblings brought about a new phase for the Zink boys: both of us were now older brothers.

Steve and I were eager to help care for our baby sisters and were allowed to hold them in our laps after Mom or Dad had carefully placed them there. We loved to see their little faces smile and to make them laugh, but things didn't always go as we imagined.

One Saturday morning, Steve, Kelly and I hatched a plan to entertain baby Judi in her bassinet. In our upstairs bedroom, we took one of Steve's shirts and a pair of his pants and stuffed them with crumpled-up newspapers. We filled a brown paper bag with balled-up socks to make a head and gave it a smiling face with a black crayon, then tucked the open end of the bag into the shirt collar. With great care we carried our "dummy" downstairs, over to Judi's bassinet. With much enthusiasm, Steve and I said, "Look what we have, Judi," and lifted the dummy up so she could see it. Judi burst into tears with a shriek that brought Mom running from the kitchen. We got a scolding for frightening our sister, our benign intentions gone awry.

ONE OF DAD'S great joys was taking photos of his family, starting with Steve and me before our sisters were born. One of the earliest photos shows me standing next to Steve who is a full head taller, his arm draped over my shoulders. I felt reassured by his arm and his height; both seemed to let me know that he would watch out for me. Looking back, it was as if Steve cast a shadow I was content to seek. The Zink brothers—Steve the Shadow-caster, Christy the Shadow-seeker.

Dad's income increased as his job responsibilities grew, and not long after

Kelly was born, he was able to afford a brand new camera. Like our family cars, Dad's Argus C3 thirty-five millimeter camera played a unique role in our Zink history. Moments both sublime and mundane became historic by the simple click of the shutter. My sisters and I look back sometimes and wonder if we remember incidents on their own merit or because we have seen the photographs so many times.

Picture a family with five children lined up, tallest to shortest. Dad arranged us this way many times in our early years to capture us in time with his camera. Niagara Falls was the backdrop for his first stair-step photo. Our happy wanderer parents had loaded all five of us kids into the DeSoto Suburban for a weekend getaway 225 miles from Cleveland. This was September 1954. Judi, all of six weeks old, was wrapped in a blanket in Mom's arms. Next to Mom stood Steve, me, Kelly, and Amy, each of us a head shorter than the next. A line drawn from the top of Mom's head on the right to the top of Amy's head on the left formed a perfect forty-five-degree angle with the bottom edge of the photo.

With parents who loved to explore new places, repeat visits were rare. The road trip to Niagara Falls in 1954 was our first and last visit there. Only once did we see Pymatuning Lake on the border of Ohio and Pennsylvania, a lake so thick with fish that the ducks and geese walked on the fish to get to the stale bread tossed by visitors. One summer, Dad's work took him to Portsmouth in southern Ohio for three days, and the whole family went along. While Dad worked, Mom took the five of us on a history expedition to the nearby Serpent Mound. The sign said that this 1,350-foot-long, twisting grass-covered hill was a burial site of ancient indigenous cultures. It was curious, but a bit tedious, and I couldn't help wondering who did the mowing.

Our only repeat road trips were to visit relatives, most often to see our favorite cousins, the Springsteens, in Valparaiso, Indiana, where our Aunt Anne and Uncle Bob had met as students at Valpo. Following his wartime service with the United States Office of Strategic Services, the forerunner of the Central Intelligence Agency, Uncle Bob became the business manager for Valparaiso University. Anne was a stay-at-home mom as well as a writer and a poet. By the time we were Zinkseven, there were six Springsteens, and the birthdates of the four Springsteen children were interwoven with our five. On one visit, when Dad lined us kids up tallest to shortest to take one of his stair-step photos, every Zink was between two Springsteens, and every Springsteen between two Zinks.

To get ready for a weekend trip to visit the Springsteens, we packed the DeSoto Suburban before Dad came home from work on the city bus. After a quick supper, Dad made sure the thermostat was turned down, the stove turned off, and one light was left on in the living room. Before Dad pulled the car out of the driveway, he paused while Mom said a simple, short prayer for God's protection on our journey. Heading west on the Ohio Turnpike, we munched on sandwiches, carrot sticks, and cookies. From my place in the fold-down jump seat in the Suburban, I could smell the aroma of fresh coffee when Mom opened the thermos and poured a cupful for Dad. Then and ever after, she made a point of holding that cup in front of him so he could hold onto it without taking his eyes off the road. Cardinal Rule Number Two of Zink family road trips was a corollary to Rule Number One: "Driving is a full-time job."

As the evening light faded on one of our five-hour Springsteen trips, our eyes grew sleepy, and Mom began a song in her gentle soprano voice: "Now the day is over, night is drawing nigh, shadows of the evening, steal across the sky." Dad softly added a baritone harmony. The steady hum of tires on roadway, Mom's soft soprano with Dad's harmony, and the darkening sky began to blur as sleep slowly took over. When we rolled into the Springsteens' driveway in Valpo, Dad woke everyone so we could sing our customary arrival song to the tune of "Auld Lang Syne." "We're here because we're here because we're here because we're here. We're here because we're here because we're here because we're here." The refrain ceased when the Springsteens' door swung open, and we were welcomed in from the chilly night.

FROM THE VERY BEGINNING, it went without saying in our family that on Sunday mornings, you belonged in church, not just in the obligatory sense that it was proper and suitable but also in the sense of knowing that you were part of something bigger than yourself. St. Thomas church offered nursery care for babies and toddlers during the Sunday service. Children too old for the nursery sat with their parents with clear instructions to sit quietly and amuse themselves with a coloring book or another quiet distraction from home. Steve learned he had to whisper if he had something to say, and Mom even quoted to her parents the mantra Steve used to prepare himself for church: "Be ki-yet in a lie-berry, and be ki-yet in a shursh."

Mom recalled one Sunday that the pastor was exhorting the congregation to keep God in mind every day of the week, not just Sundays, through prayer, devotions, and Bible-reading. Although he was absorbed in his coloring and whispering, Steve was listening. At lunch after church, Steve, without warning, whapped his fist on the table just as he'd seen the pastor do on the pulpit and hollered, "Remember the Lord!" Mom and Dad were shocked but pleased by how much Steve remembered.

To help us "remember the Lord," our parents read to us from family devotion booklets every night at the supper table. Each daily page had a couple paragraphs about the day's Bible verse, followed by a prayer. One night, we heard a New Testament verse that said, "The day of the Lord will come as a thief in the night." I had trouble falling asleep that night. What if a thief did come into our house when we were all asleep? I wondered if Dad would wake up in time to scare him away. And if Dad was out of town on business, would Mom wake up in time? And what was the "day of the Lord," and how would I know that it had come?

I was also sorting out in my mind things I heard in church. Readings of the Lord's Prayer and its proclamation "For Thine is the kingdom, the power, and the glory forever and ever," made me wonder about the concept of "forever." What did that mean? How long did "forever" last? Visits to the 19517 neighborhood by the Popsicle Man in summer also raised questions. He sold popsicles, of course, and ice cream bars as well as creamsicles and fudgesicles. Were these like the "versicles" and "canticles" I heard about in church? My wonderings continued.

ONE THING I DID NOT wonder about was my mother's love of singing. She had a veritable hit parade of songs she sang to us when we were young. She often started singing as she climbed the stairs to wake us up. "Good morning, good morning, how do you do, my dears" was the first line of a song from a Cleveland radio program called "Charming Children." The song's message epitomized our mother's attitude: Keep a bright, positive outlook—to "make our sun inside"—even if the sun was hidden behind the clouds. Singing suited Mom well. Some of her favorite tunes were short, fun songs with sound effects. There was the "Cannibal King," who wore a brass nose-ring and kissed his girl with a big smacking "smooch" sound. The song, "Plant a Watermelon Upon my Grave," called for a sloppy "slurp" noise as the "juice ran through."

During these early Zinkseven years, we all learned some of Dad and Mom's favorite tunes—"Home on the Range," "Down in the Valley," "Only an Old Beer Bottle," and "Oh, My Darling Clementine" among them—while we sat around the kitchen table after supper. Dad always sang harmony with Mom so it was natural for us kids to follow suit and learn harmony parts as we grew up. To this homespun musical diet I added popular songs of the mid-1950s that poured out of the kitchen radio, like "Sixteen Tons," "The Ballad of Davy Crockett," and "How Much Is that Doggie in the Window?" These were some of the first tunes I logged into the personal jukebox of my mind, my own peculiar collection of songs I remembered because, for reasons I could not then explain, they held meaning for me.

Most of the earliest music stored in my jukebox was church music. Central to my experience of belonging to the church of my childhood in Rocky River was the music, and so it was not long before I pieced together that "versicles" and "canticles" were chants for church, not treats from the Popsicle Man. I learned how to follow the church organ and sing along with the hymns and chants, aided by hearing my father's baritone voice on one side of me and my mother's soprano on the other.

Learning to sing melodies and harmonies to the music of my childhood happened almost imperceptibly by familial osmosis. One year when I was about ten, I stood in the kitchen of Granny Zink's home in Baltimore, where a host of relatives had gathered after the Christmas Eve service. A generation earlier, many of these same people sat on the front porch of this house and filled the summer evenings with musical harmony. On this festive night, someone said, "Let's do the Hallelujah Chorus," a Christmastime piece I had heard often enough to recognize. Standing between an uncle singing baritone and an aunt singing alto, I was transported by the sound in that kitchen. The chills that fingered my spine as I listened to those exquisite harmonies told me I was in a special place. I listened for a part I could mimic, and as I added my voice to the ensemble, I felt in the deepest sense of the word that I was home.

ON THE NIGHT before Mother's Day in 1956, a violent windstorm slammed into the Cleveland area. By one o'clock in the morning, the power had gone out. The freight-train roar of the wind woke our parents, who roused the five of us from our beds and led us all down to the safety of the basement. There, we gathered at the bottom of the stairs, Dad's flashlight the only thing between us and total darkness. The wind outside howled and screamed. My brother and I stood next to Dad. Mom held twenty-one-month-old Judi in her arms, and Kelly and Amy stood close beside her. I remember looking up the basement stairs at the side door, trying to imagine what it would be like to be standing outside in that raging wind. It felt like God himself was having a major temper tantrum.

In the silence of our basement, Judi's whimpers of fear were calmed by Dad's reassuring words. "God is here to protect us," he told us. Mom said a quiet prayer: "Lord, give us faith that you will keep us safe." The wait seemed to last hours, but soon the noise outside subsided, and the howling ceased. By three in the morning, the tantrum had run its course. Our house was intact. Mom and Dad led us all back upstairs to our bedrooms. Steve and

I crawled into our double bed while Mom brought the girls to their room at the back of the house. She lifted Judi into her crib and tucked Kelly and Amy into their beds.

Something happened then that I shall never forget. Even though Mom must have been emotionally and physically drained by the events of the night, she sat down on the floor in the hallway between our room and our sisters' room, her back against one wall, her knees bent and her feet against the other wall. In her clear soprano voice, she began to sing—soft, soothing melodies. She sang us hymns she loved, like "Beautiful Savior," and "Our God, Our Help in Ages Past," which includes a very telling line for that night: "our shelter from the stormy blast." Before I fell asleep, I was soothed by the songs we knew from our weekend trips to Valpo, like "Now the Day is Over" and Brahms' lullaby, "*Guten Abend, Gute Nacht.*" I can't be sure, but Mom may well have dozed off herself, singing this last one.

We woke the next morning to bright sunshine, blue skies, and random destruction throughout our neighborhood. Dad grabbed the Argus C3 camera, called Steve, Kelly, and me, and we walked outside to survey the damage. Several large trees had toppled right across Riverview Avenue. Down by St. Christopher's Catholic Church at the end of our street, two parked cars were smashed nearly flat by another fallen tree. Roofing shingles lay scattered like potato chips spilled onto front lawns, in the street, and up in tree branches.

IN MY FATHER'S senior class yearbook at Johns Hopkins in 1941, along with a list of his activities was this: "He can dish it out." Dad had a ready wit and repartee that stood him in good stead with his classmates and colleagues, and, socially, he had a reputation for firing off zingers and concocting practical jokes that could be taken either in good fun or as insults. He enjoyed being the life of the party, drawing attention to himself, like the time his contribution to a cocktail party at the home of friends was a glass whiskey decanter filled not with bourbon but very strong iced tea.

Dad was a man who liked to stir the pot, to raise the ante, while Mom was busy trying to lower it. Their styles could not have been more different. She was a woman without guile, reminding us to consider other people's feelings. Her attitude towards life mirrored the words from Martin Luther's *Small Catechism* to "put the best construction on everything," which she had memorized as a young girl.

My father was a catalog of puns and putdowns, tricks and teases, sight gags and smells. The man enjoyed amusing his children with plays on words, and he thrived on bad puns. If there was a way to tease a double meaning out of a word or phrase, Dad would find it.

"Are you going to the movies?" he'd ask if he caught you scratching your butt.

"No. Why?"

"I see you're picking your seat!"

When we were kids, you could dial "GR1-5555," and a recorded voice would give you the correct time. When Dad was home with us kids, and he felt we were getting too rambunctious, he'd pick up the phone and threaten that he was reporting us to the police. Then he'd dial GR1-5555 and talk as though he were speaking to the police. "Hello, officer, I'd like to report some unruly children. Yes, can you come and pick them up? Right, 19517 Riverview." We knew it was a tease but also a clear signal to shape up.

Dad set what our mother considered a bad example for us by encouraging bodily function humor, like calling one of us over to "pull his finger" when he had to fart. When Steve let out an SBD (Silent But Deadly), Dad did an exaggerated sniff, and resorting to his favorite euphemism, asked, "Phew, who dropped that lily?" Dad could let loose prodigious belches, and Steve soon learned to emulate Dad's ability to belch at will. Both could belch while saying, "All right."

Dad once called Steve and me to show us an "amputated finger" he said he had found somewhere. He told Steve to slowly open the small rectangular jewelry box he was holding. Inside was a pale, sickly finger with a blood-like substance around the second knuckle, where it apparently had been severed from its owner. To our eyes, it looked real. And very gross.

"Ew, where did that come from?" we asked.

"I don't know. I found it somewhere. Ain't it lovely?" Dad enjoyed his moment of fun and tucked the finger away until the next time. The gag lost its thrill when Dad showed us that he had drilled a hole into the bottom of a jewelry box and through the soft white cotton lining inside. Then he dusted his own middle finger with baby powder, to give it a macabre look, applied a bit of red food coloring around the second knuckle, and inserted his own finger into the hole he'd created.

I learned early that humor, in my family, could be risky business with a man who was a veritable minefield of jokes and teases because, sometimes, we kids were the punch line. Our father worked full time as a mechanical engineer, a job that required long hours at the office, working at home on weekends, and frequent out-of-town travel to his company's construction sites. Dad's practical joking, jocularity, and ribald teasing offered him some release from the stress of the job. But even though he often reminded Steve and me, "Don't dish it out if you can't take it," he was not good at taking it himself from the likes of us.

One Saturday afternoon, when Steve and I were pre-teens, Dad fell asleep on the living room couch and began his sonorous, baritone snore. What fun, we thought, agreeing to tape record his snoring and play it back to Dad when he woke up. He did not so much as chuckle, failing to appreciate humor at his own expense.

Dad's idle joking eventually created in me a sense of wariness. One evening when I was six or seven, Dad took Steve and me to our swimming lesson at the YMCA. I detested these lessons. The water was too cold, I could not float to save my life, and my skinny body shivered for the duration. My one goal at the end of a lesson was to dry off, dress, and get warm as quickly as possible. Standing by my locker with my shirt off, I unwittingly became the butt of a joke I did not see coming. Two prominent moles on my chest amused my father, who nudged Steve to bring him in as his ally, and said, "Hey, lookit those bullet holes on Christy!"

My father and my brother shared a good laugh at my expense. I felt humiliated. Their teasing camaraderie left me out in the cold just when I was trying to warm up. I was outnumbered, and any attempt to defend myself was sure to be laughed off and ignored. To Dad, it was just another harmless tease, tossed off with no thought of its impact. But his words cut to the core of my sense about what it meant to be my father's son. It was my first remembered time of wondering if I'd be able to measure up. Two things were clear that day: Keep my shirt on around Dad, and stay alert for situations that seemed ripe for ridicule.

Mom tried to guide the five of us away from making cutting comments to each other, often quoting Thumper, the little rabbit in Disney's *Bambi* movie, who said, "If you can't say sumpin' nice, don't say nuttin' at all." One of Dad's favorite lines was, "Don't open your mouth 'til your brain's in gear."

It was about this time in my life that I began to develop an internal sensing device, not unlike a Geiger counter, to assess any situation for potential risk of embarrassment or humiliation. I thought of this device as my Ridiculometer, a sort of psychic guardian that might prevent me from becoming the butt of jokes; it set off a soft "beep, beep, beep" only I could hear.

One of the first times my Ridiculometer came into play was Halloween 1956, but my play-it-safe strategy backfired. Our town of Rocky River held a Halloween costume contest every year. When I was nine, my father came up with a unique idea for a winning costume for me: a skyscraper. His plan was to take two cardboard boxes—a larger one to rest on my shoulders by means of suspender straps hidden inside the box, and a taller, narrow box with eye holes in the upper stories so I could see where I was going. In Dad's basement workshop, I helped him paint the boxes. Dad used a fine-tipped brush to make the square outlines of rows upon rows of windows, all the way from the bottom floor at my knees up to the top floor about two feet above my head.

Dad's Halloween creation was most unusual. Everything about it was homemade and very different from what other kids would be wearing. I figured my buddies would be dressed up as cowboys or pirates or television heroes like Davy Crockett. My Ridiculometer kicked in, and I wondered if it might it be safer to go to the contest in something more conventional. I asked my brother if he would wear the skyscraper costume, and Steve was game to give it a go. This was the perfect solution: Dad's novel creation would not go to waste, and I'd be able to take part in the contest without the risk of being laughed at over such a weird costume. Dad adjusted the skyscraper so it fit Steve's taller frame. I wore a Robin Hood costume. Wouldn't you know, Steve took first place, and was a gracious winner, never rubbing it in that the prize could have been mine.

WITH LITTLE BROTHER longing in my eyes, I stood on the sidewalk holding my mother's hand, watching as Steve boarded the big yellow school bus for his first day of school. With his crisp new blue jeans and his plastic pencil case, his departure into a new world of adventure was a path I yearned to follow. The bus that picked him up in front of 19517 took him to his morning kindergarten class at West Shore Lutheran School. The school had been organized in 1945 by St. Thomas and three other Lutheran churches in nearby towns. Enrollment was small enough in the early years that each classroom held two grades. The first and second grades were located in the basement of St. Thomas church, within walking distance of 19517. The third through eighth grades met in an old three-room schoolhouse at the Lutheran church five miles away in the neighboring suburb of Westlake.

Steve loved going to school, and he brought school home to me. I soaked up everything he told me. He read the Dick, Jane, and Sally books to me and showed me the pictures that went with the words: "See Dick. See Dick run." He showed me the letters of the alphabet and taught me how to spell short, simple words. But my favorite thing was learning about numbers. When Steve learned that one plus one equals two, he took a piece of chalk and showed me how to write those numbers on the small, square chalk board Mom bought for us.

When Steve advanced to first grade and was at school all day, he seemed a man of the world to me. He'd ride off in that yellow school bus, carrying his lunch box with the hinged wire bracket in the lid that held the thermos in place. He brought school books home and explained things to me—the Shadow-caster coming home to the Shadow-seeker. I was full of anticipation, waiting to hear the sound of the side door flying open and Steve dashing in for his afternoon snack.

"What'd you learn today, Stevie?" I'd call as I ran from the living room to the kitchen.

"Subtraction!"

"Sustracking? What's that?"

"Not 'sustracking.' *Sub-TRAK-shunn*. It means take away. C'mere, and I'll show you. If you have three oranges"—Steve drew three clumsy circles on the little chalk board— "and you take away two of them, how many are left?"

"That's easy! One! Take away is easy, Stevie."

Then he'd show me on my fingers how to do four take away two. It didn't take long for me to get what "taking away" meant. It was the beginning of my fascination with calculations of numbers and dates that still provide me countless moments of idle amusement. I seem to have acquired through the years a propensity for remembering dates, partly from the thoughtful, loving way my mother observed our birthdays and partly from the need to memorize dates in social studies classes. All those dates would roll around in my head just waiting for my calculating mind to find a connection.

Calendrical calculations that highlight the symmetry of significant dates fascinate me. Kelly, the oldest of my three sisters, was born March 23, 1950, three years and three days after me. As the year 1970 approached, I noticed that it would be an auspicious year: In March, I would turn twenty-three on the twentieth, and Kelly would turn twenty on the twenty-third. I noted with much excitement the historic occurrence in my lifetime of a palindromic/reciprocal year. The numerals of the year 1961 read the same upside down and backwards as they do right side up and frontwards. It was the first such year since 1881. Another will not appear until 6009.

By the time I was old enough to get on the school bus with Steve, I was blessed with a tremendous advantage. I knew what to expect at school and had already learned some of the basics. Arithmetic, reading, and spelling all came easy to me. In second grade, my teacher, Mrs. Sagehorn, asked me to help other children with their arithmetic, and, to this day, I attribute my early school success to my brother. Because of the head start he gave me, I began to see myself as a good student and a boy who enjoyed school.

By second grade, other students looked up to me as someone who got As, could outrun all the other kids, and even helped the teacher by tutoring classmates. Second grade was a place in which I cast a few shadows of my own. At recess, I took charge of the boys. We imagined we were in a military unit, marching in a long column, two-by-two across the field to the gravel parking lot, then around the cluster of girls sitting and gabbing by the swings. I marched alone at the front of the column because I was the major. I was fair and generous; each day I appointed a different boy as my lieutenant to march just behind me and relay my orders to the rest: "Company...forward march!" "Company...halt!"

Our second grade class was a blend of kids from all four of the West Shore churches. My two best buddies—Terry Fibich and Tom Leopold—and I stuck together. We were the only ones who went to Sunday school at St. Thomas. We were the only ones whose parents knew each other. And we were the only boys in our class. Girls outnumbered us by three to one.

I was the oldest boy in our class, and my place as leader was seldom questioned. One day, a new boy named Warren started in the first grade. Other kids were saying that he was a pretty fast runner, but they told him he'd only be considered fast if he could beat Christy. And so it was that one day, Terry drew a line in the parking lot gravel with the handle of a baseball bat. We all agreed that Warren and I would dash across the parking lot to the hedge along the church property line, turn around, and race back to Terry's line.

Warren got a jump on me with a quick start, but I'd nearly caught him by the time he'd reached the hedges. I knew I had him because he was new, and I'd made this 180-degree turn in many other impromptu recess races. I skidded my Buster Brown shoes to a sudden stop, made the required touch on the hedge, and took off back towards Terry, Tom, and all the other kids. I could hear Warren's feet behind me as I sped across the gravel to yet another validation of my place in the pecking order of West Shore School's first and second grades.

The creeping self-doubt I would come to know so well later on snuck in one winter morning when we slept too long. The Zink family, always and invariably on time for everything, was running late. Our school bus rolled to a stop on Riverview Avenue as usual and waited for the Zink boys; we were normally standing there on the sidewalk on time ready to go, but this day was different. With a wave of her hand out the front door, Mom signaled the driver to keep going. Dad had to take us with him in the car on his way to work in downtown Cleveland. Normally riding in the car with Dad was a treat, but not so on this day since Steve and I had missed our bus.

Dad dropped me off first at St. Thomas church, where my second-grade class met. I said good-bye to him and Steve and watched them drive off to Steve's fourth-grade class at the schoolhouse in Westlake, unaware that I was about to enter a scene I would remember for the rest of my life. It was a cold, snow-crusted day. I was wearing my black galoshes, the kind you pull on over your shoes. Each boot had five hinged metal clasps. You worked them one at a time, tightening each one down snug. Small seven-year-old hands could turn this into a time-eating ordeal.

My glasses fogged up as I walked down the steps to the basement cloak-room in our church, steps I'd used countless time before. The door from the cloakroom to the classroom was already closed. I set my lunch box on the shelf, took off my mittens, and wiped my glasses. As I plopped myself down on the bench and reached down to begin unfastening the clasps on my galoshes, I heard our teacher, Mrs. Sagehorn, begin to play the piano in her stiff, by-the-book style. Voices of the other children singing our daily morning song stung my ears as I realized the school day had begun without me. My Ridiculometer was signaling to me, softly.

A cloud of doubt as foreboding as that morning's gray winter sky engulfed me. How could my teacher begin the day before I'd walked through the door? Had no one noticed I was missing? I felt invisible. Maybe they thought I was sick. If I opened that door, would everything stop? Would twenty-five pairs of eyes turn toward me? In the absence of answers to my questions, I decided entering was too risky. I couldn't face the potential for humiliation. I watched my hands as they started re-fastening the clasps on my galoshes. I put my mittens back on, grabbed my lunch box, and walked back up the steps, out the door, and home.

The next year my second-grade classmates and I moved up to third grade. We now rode the bus with all the older kids to the three-room schoolhouse in Westlake. It was a whole new world for Terry, Tom, and me. No more playing military and marching around the playground or taking on all comers in foot races. We had to make our way carefully among all the big kids. I became more timid than I'd been in second grade. The pecking order was changing, and we all had to make adjustments.

Our combined third- and fourth-grade class had a new teacher that year, an attractive young woman named Miss Mueller. Steve's fifth- and sixth-grade room was across the hall, and next to it were the seventh and eighth graders, taught by the school principal, Mr. Wolter, a tall, hard-nosed veteran of the trade, stern of visage, with a balding head, a hooked nose, and a severe temper to match his looks. He kept the school on a strict course of good-quality Lutheran education. We had religion class every day, a chapel service once a week, and Bible passages to memorize for homework almost every night.

One day in January, Miss Mueller called me up to her desk and told me that she had talked with my parents and that I was going to get to start doing schoolwork with the fourth graders. And because in our small parochial school two grades shared each classroom, I wouldn't have to change desks. The fourth-grade reading book did look rather appealing to me, and I was pretty sure I could handle the arithmetic problems I saw the older students working on every day. So I walked back to my seat, pulled out my third-grade books, handed them to Miss Mueller in exchange for the fourth-grade books, and stashed them in my desk. The Skip, as I have come to think of that day, was that simple.

I was still in the same classroom with my third-grade buddies, Terry and Tom, but something began to change. Ever so subtly, my self-assurance began to wilt like Miss Mueller's window-box flowers when she forgot to water them. I had to comport myself so as to fit in with my new peer group of older and mostly larger kids. After being the oldest in my class, I was now the youngest. I was in the middle of an invisible paradox: in one day, I advanced a year in school and retreated a year in age. I had to grow up quickly. I welcomed the challenge of being a fourth grader but tried to ignore my concerns about fitting in. This suddenly grown-up me decided it was time to lose the nickname I'd had since birth. One evening at the family supper table just before my ninth birthday, I announced that henceforth I was to be called "Tom." I allowed them all a grace period of several weeks to get acclimated to my wish; after that I refused to respond to "Christy."

OURS WAS AN UNREMARKABLE suburban neighborhood with houses equally spaced along straight tree-lined streets, aimed due north and south or east and west, as if plotted out based on a plumb line from the North Pole. Corners where the streets intersected were perfectly square. Automobiles, one per family, were parked in driveways like proud trophies of their owners' modest success in moving up from dependence on public transit. School buses motored by on weekday mornings and afternoons. Within this organized grid of streets and sidewalks, we learned not to play in the street and to look both ways before crossing.

The structured framework of our German Lutheran heritage and upbringing, with equally parallel and perpendicular lines, taught us the difference between right and wrong—sometimes the hard way. Such a lesson came the day a group of neighbor boys gathered in the Side Yard, and a couple of the older boys showed us the Paddle Machine. One boy stood with his legs wide enough apart so another boy could crawl under him. The rest of us lined up behind the first boy to form a jeans-clad tunnel of legs. Somehow, the first boy picked to crawl through the machine was Johnny Hottel, a long-legged boy with a small, trusting face. He got down on his hands and knees and crawled through the tunnel while the rest of us paddled his butt as it came by.

Johnny was the only one unlucky enough to go through the Paddle Machine because at just that moment, Mom peered out the kitchen window. When she saw our game, she was out the door in an instant to stop it. Steve and I were called inside to face our fate while the rest of the group dispersed. Ensuring the punishment fit the crime, Mom gave us each a good paddling of our own, teaching us that Zink children don't gang up on others; into this she wove the implicit lesson found in the Golden Rule: "Do unto others as you would have them do unto you."

A few lessons also came via the Olson family boys, who lived next door. Jimmy and Dicky were both older than Steve, and were the only kids in the neighborhood who somehow managed to have illegal fireworks on the Fourth of July, much to the dismay of our parents who were trying to follow the Biblical admonition to "train up a child in the way that he should go." Mom and Dad were concerned about the influence these neighbor boys might have on Steve and me—perhaps with good reason.

On a late July afternoon, my brother and I were playing catch in the Side Yard. "Throw me some grounders, Steve," I said. "I wanna practice my fielding."

"What do you want—hard or easy?" Steve said.

Before I could answer, Dicky Olson ambled towards us from his house.

"Hey, Dicky, you wanna play some catch?" I called to him.

"Sure," he said, "but I gotta get my glove outta the garage." He walked back and disappeared into his family's one-car garage. When he came out a minute later he hollered, "Hey, you guys, you should come and see this!"

Steve and I looked at each other and hesitated. Steve then dropped his glove and said, "C'mon, Tom!" and dashed off towards the Olson's garage. I followed him to where Dicky was standing at the structure's side door; the front door was closed and the air inside stank from years of automobile fluids seeping into the dirt. Yard and garden tools hung from nails on exposed studs. Decaying leaves blown in by past autumn winds littered the floor. A couple of old paint cans with lids missing added to the odor. The only light came from a single, dusty window in the side wall.

Dicky had a book of matches in his pocket, no doubt obtained on the sly with his older brother to set off forbidden fireworks.

"Hey, fellas, whaddya think would happen if I tossed a match in there?" Dicky said, nodding at one of the open paint cans.

"You'd better not!" Steve and I said in unison, our voices a mix of urgency and eager curiosity.

We knew full well our protest would matter little to Dicky: he would toss the match, and even though we knew it was wrong, we were secretly dying to see what would happen. Dicky flicked a lit match toward the paint can. Fire instantly leapt out of the can, a blaze of red, yellow, and orange fury. A pillar of thick, black smoke churned above it and quickly filled the garage.

"Hurry!" Dicky screamed. "Get the hell outta here!"

We ran to the side door, gasping for breath, slamming into each other, shoulders crashing into the door jambs, trying to escape the foul stench. Being the smallest, slowest, and last to reach the door, I tripped on Steve's heels and fell out onto the grass just outside the door.

Dicky's mother came running out of their house, yelling, "What the hell's going on out there? Dicky? Dicky! Are you all right?"

"Yeah, Ma, we're okay. It was an accident. I lit a match 'cause we couldn't get the light on, and Steve bumped me, and the match fell in the paint can."

"No I didn't!" Steve protested. "Dicky tossed…"

Dicky cut him off. "Yeah, so it's good we got out of there so fast," he blurted.

As the last remnants of paint in the can were consumed, the fire dwindled, and Dicky's mom pulled open the main garage door to let the rest of the black smoke escape.

Steve and I retreated back to our game of catch. "That was scary," Steve said.

"Yeah," I said as I picked up my glove, "and what if the whole garage burned down? You think we'll get in trouble when Daddy gets home?"

Steve tossed me an easy grounder. "Why should we?" he said. "Dicky threw the match."

"Yeah, but I betcha Mom saw all that smoke." I threw the ball back and crouched down, ready for the next ground ball from Steve.

"I know. But maybe she didn't see the smoke and didn't hear Mrs. Olson, and we can act like nothing happened."

Neither Mom nor Dad ever did hear a word about the flaming paint can from Steve or me or from Mrs. Olson. We were in the clear. But our scheme to get our hands on outlawed comic books did not end so well.

Popular comics, like *Superman*, *Archie*, and *Donald Duck*, were frowned upon by our parents. Horror story comic books, like *Tales from the Crypt*, *Tomb of Terror*, and *The Vault of Horror*, were completely off-limits to Steve and me. Our comic book diet was limited to the *Classics Illustrated* series, which presented famous works of literature in comic-book form. Ivanhoe, Robin Hood, King Arthur, and the Knights of the Round Table were our heroes. But right next door, Dicky had a great comic book collection. Steve and I knew the forbidden fruit was just beyond our reach and were curious to see it for ourselves.

All three of us were sitting and talking in Dicky's backyard one day when Dicky said, "You guys wanna have a campout in our backyard Friday night?"

"Yeah, sure," Steve said, "but we don't have a tent."

"We don't need a tent. We can use my dad's big tarp and tie it onto the fence like a big lean-to. You boys bring some cards, and we can play War and Crazy Eights and stuff. I can bring some of my comic books, too."

Steve and I shot each other a quick look. An anxious anticipation coursed through me. "Really?" I said to Dicky. "Comic books?"

"*Deff*-in-it-lee!" said Dicky, emphasizing each syllable.

Steve and I said good-bye and walked back to our house. "We're not supposed to read those comic books, Steve," I said. "Do you think we'll get caught?"

"I hope not," he said. "I mean, we'll be outside in Dicky's backyard under his big tarp, so no one would see us, right?"

We got Dad and Mom's permission to camp out with Dicky. On Friday afternoon, we gathered some blankets, our pillows, two flashlights, a deck of cards, and some snacks, careful not to show too much excitement about our comic book caper.

"If Mom or Dad asks what we're going to do," Steve told me, "just tell 'em we're going to tell ghost stories, eat our potato chips, and play Crazy Eights and War."

"Yeah, but what about Dicky's comics?"

"Just keep quiet about that, and it'll be fine."

We set up the tarp so there was enough space for all three of us to squeeze in under it.

Steve and I brought all our gear, and Dicky, of course, brought the Holy Grail, the comic books. When darkness fell, the secret stash was revealed. With one hand on our flashlights, the other turning pages, Steve and I lavished in the luxury of looking through the wave of comic books before us.

Then we heard footsteps.

"Someone's coming," Steve said. I felt the anxiety I heard in his voice.

Dicky knew that Steve and I weren't usually allowed to read comics. As our co-conspirator, he held up his part of the deal. He ordered us to quickly push the comics up against the fence and sprawl ourselves out against them to ensure they'd stay hidden. Footsteps crackled on the Olson's gravel driveway on their way towards our lean-to. They came closer. It was Dad, flashlight in hand, simply coming over to check on us and see if everything was alright. We couldn't tell if he suspected anything.

Dad looked in and saw the three of us, lying on our sides, one elbow on the ground and heads resting on our hands, comic books—we hoped—out of sight. We looked up at Dad with our most nonchalant and innocent-looking faces.

"Oh, yes, Daddy, we're doing fine." Guilt and fear gnawed at Steve and me.

"Well, sleep well, fellahs," Dad said, turning back to our house.

The next morning, after returning home, Steve and I learned our deception had failed. Dad gave us a scolding so harsh that I could feel the tears burning my eyes—tears of shame and regret at our false assumption that we might actually get away with something that was fun, adventurous, and expressly forbidden. Dad sent us up to our room until supper time.

"It's not fair," I said to Steve as we sat together on our bed. "How come *Dicky* gets to have those comics, and *we* are stuck in our room?"

"Oh, be quiet," Steve said. "There's nothing we can do about it."

From that day on, it was clear that innocent mischief by the Zink brothers was certain to be discovered and punished. With five children mucking about in the house, discipline became more of a challenge for our parents, but they continued to run a pretty tight ship. We did as we were told without whining, dawdling, or complaining. There was no room on this craft to hide in the hold and skip out on a chore like Jonah in the Bible, who stowed away to avoid God's command to go to Nineveh. As long as you were part of this family, you pulled your own weight. Mom used mostly words to set us straight when we wavered. Thumper's tiresome line to keep quiet unless you could say something nice was a frequent directive. It's little wonder that I was fast becoming a quiet, soft-spoken boy.

ON MY EIGHTH BIRTHDAY, my parents gave me a gleaming new, red-and-white Schwinn bicycle with big balloon tires, a battery-powered horn inside a compartment under the crossbar, and a headlight on the front fender. Dad held on and kept me upright on my first tentative attempts in the Side Yard. I also learned by watching Steve's misfortunes—like the time he began to wobble on his bike and then toppled into the pricker bushes.

One memorable spring day, Dad decided it was time for me to try riding on the side street, Rockland Avenue. He held my bike, and I climbed aboard and started pedaling. Dad ran alongside me, keeping a firm grip on the bar under my seat. I was excited to be riding on a real street and relieved that my father was holding on to me. Then came that magical moment when I glanced back and realized Dad was no longer keeping me upright. Standing thirty feet behind me, a big smile on his face, he was clapping and shouting,

"Way to go!"

As Steve and I got more comfortable on our bikes, our world expanded into the quiet streets of our Rocky River neighborhood. We could ride on our own to the library a block away, down to Johnny Hottel's house or to my school buddy Tom's house a couple blocks away. Another favorite destination was the unsightly, undeveloped tract of land we called the Sand Pit, an exotic place of mystery and excitement. Were there really bums—men with fearsome, unshaven faces and ragged clothes waiting to jump us—that bigger kids in the neighborhood had warned us about? The possibility was tantalizing.

One day Johnny, Tom, and a couple other boys came over on their bikes. "Mommy," Steve hollered into the house from the side door, "Tom and I are going to the Sand Pit with the other guys." I followed Steve and the other boys as we rode down Riverview to Bidwell Avenue, the short, dead-end street that led to the Sand Pit. We pedaled hard over the rocky dirt and scrubby underbrush toward the first large hill. I stood up on my pedals, sweating to reach the top, then let out a "Whoopee!" on the way down. We all skidded to a dusty stop at the bottom, nearly crashing into each other. "Hey, watch out for the bums, you guys," Steve teased. He knew the big kids' warnings were nonsense, but I still wondered.

OUR SIDE YARD on Riverview Avenue was a magnet to kids in our neighborhood, the place where we learned to get along with others by following— and changing—the rules of games like Hide-and-Go-Seek, Red Rover, and Mother May I? We used the "No takes!" rule in our touch football games: if the other team's kick-off was not to our liking, we could just holler, "No takes!" and they had to kick it over.

Baseball was a staple in the Side Yard. Steve and I and a changing cast of neighbor boys filled many long summer hours, running bases and playing games of catch and Five Hundred, in which you scored points by catching batted balls; when you reached 500, you got to be the batter. One spring Saturday morning, neighborhood kids began to show up ready for a game.

"There's no game here until the yard is mowed, the grass raked, and all these twigs picked up," Dad barked at all of us.

We eagerly pitched in, taking turns pushing the old reel mower back and forth, and wielding rakes with too-long handles, knowing that when the jobs were done, the game could begin.

Dad played catcher for both teams—"permanent catcher," we called it— to keep wayward pitches from flying into Mom's flower beds. Dad's willingness to not only let us play but also join our game—once his conditions were met—showed how much he wanted to pass on his love of the game to Steve and me.

My family had a long-held attachment to baseball. In 1947, not long after I was born, my father managed to convince my mother to attend a Major League baseball game to celebrate their fifth wedding anniversary. The home-town Cleveland Indians played the Boston Red Sox on that June night. Even though the home team lost, 3-2, Mom and Dad were both enthralled with the drama and non-partisan spirit of the crowd. In the weeks that followed, Dad listened to Indians' games on the radio as often as he could.

The following year, the Indians were in contention for the American League pennant. By September 1948, the whole city was abuzz with Indians' pennant fever. And in the Zink kitchen at 19517, even my mother tuned into the games on the radio. The Indians' defeat of the Boston Braves in the World Series made them baseball champions for the first time in twenty-eight years. Six years later, in 1954, the Indians went on a roll, winning more games than any team in history and finishing well ahead of the rest of the American League teams.

Baseball fever slipped in the side door of our house that summer of 1954 and altered my outlook on the world forever. Steve was eight and I was seven when Dad brought the game to life on our kitchen table. After supper, we helped Mom clear and wash the dishes. Mom took our three younger sisters upstairs to bed, so it was just Steve and me in the kitchen with Dad, ready for the magic carpet trip to our imaginary world of kitchen-table baseball.

Dad brought out a large piece of cardboard and set it on the table. Using his considerable drafting design skills, Dad had transformed the cardboard into a colorful, geometrically accurate replica of a baseball diamond—the vivid green of the outfield grass, the infield a rusty brown, and a bright white home plate. The three bases and the foul lines were also rendered with Dad's draftsman's eye for detail and proportion, and Dad had even drawn a home-run fence, arcing across the edge of the outfield, and dugouts along the first- and third-base lines. To represent the players, Dad had raided our seldom-used Bingo game. On the blank side of the round Bingo markers, he had written, in the same neat draftsman uppercase lettering that he used to write Mom's letters in their courting years, a code to represent all nine players on each team by their positions: "P" for the pitcher, "C" for the catcher, "1B" for the first baseman, "CF" for the center fielder, and so on. All this, because Dad was eager for Steve and me to catch the allure of baseball.

With the miniature baseball diamond on our kitchen table, Dad took the Zenith radio from its spot on the kitchen counter, placed it at one end of the table, and turned the dial to 1300, WERE-AM, the radio home of the Indians. The sound of play-by-play announcer Jimmy Dudley's trademark greeting—"Hello, baseball fans everywhere!"—told us we were on the edge of another adventure. As Dudley announced the batting line-up for each team, Dad wrote down the names on a piece of paper.

If the Indians' catcher hit a single, we placed the "C" marker on first base. Later in the game, when Al Rosen, the Indians third-baseman, hit a home run for the Indians, we moved his "3B" marker around all the bases and back to home plate.

"That home run by Rosen gives the Indians one run, Steve," Dad said. "So now you write a '1' on the scoreboard there. Who's up next, Christy?"

"It's says 'Wertz' on your list, Daddy," I said.

"That's Vic Wertz, the first baseman," Dad explained. "Christy, take that Bingo marker that says '1B' and put it next to home plate there."

"Which side?"

"Well, is he a left-handed batter or right-handed?" Dad said.

Steve piped up. "Left?"

"You're right," said Dad. "Put him on the left side of the plate because that's where he stands when he bats."

"Daddy," I said, "when do I get to write the runs on the scoreboard?"

"Wait 'til the next inning when the Yankees are batting, Christy," Dad replied.

Sitting at our kitchen table miles away from the stadium, Steve and I were beginning to see the action in our mind's eye. Playing out on the display screen of our imaginations were all the double plays, high-pop fouls, and home runs landing in the left-field seats.

The Indians' record-breaking 1954 season ended in total collapse. They lost the World Series in four straight games to the New York Giants. But it didn't matter. I had caught the bug. I started using my allowance to buy Topps bubble gum baseball cards. I studied the baseball box scores every morning in the *Plain Dealer*. I memorized players' batting averages and pitchers' won-lost records. With my father's help, I entered the esoteric world of baseball score-keeping, a simple, logical method of keeping track of every single play in a baseball game. Baseball produced a vast quantity of numbers that proved welcome fodder for my predilection for numerical calculations. I became a walking compendium of baseball trivia.

IN 1955, OUR PARENTS decided that Steve and I were ready for the big time, and they took us to see an Indians game at the mammoth Cleveland Municipal

Stadium, located near the shores of Lake Erie. No more imagining the scene. No more pushing Bingo markers around a cardboard field. No more wondering how a Bob Feller fastball sounded as it slammed with certitude into the mitt of his catcher, Jim Hegan. This was the real thing. No thrill for an eight-year-old could match that magical first glimpse of the immensity of the stadium, the vast green expanse of outfield grass, the rich brown dirt of the infield, the clean white foul lines, all illuminated by the banks of lights on the stadium roof.

The grandstand was a heady mix—the aroma of roasting hot dogs, the smell of cigar smoke, the call of the vendors: "Beer here!" A stellar moment for me came when four men sitting in the row in front of us wondered aloud who the Indians' top batter was. What a thrill to have my father proudly offer them my statistical acumen; I promptly told them his name—Al Smith—then showed off a little by adding how many home runs and runs batted in he had.

Baseball continued to define my world in the late 1950s. My baseball card collection grew. My birthday gift one year was a subscription to *Sport* magazine. My ability and eagerness to observe, understand, record, and recall the intricacies of baseball statistics increased, even as the Indians' success waned. While I had my baseball cards, my favorite team, and my love of statistics, I dearly wanted to play the game. Little League beckoned, but they didn't take just anyone back then; you had to be selected after tryouts.

One Saturday morning in spring, a few months after The Skip moved me one grade ahead in school, I tried out for Little League. Afterwards, I came home and told my friends I was sure I would make the cut, but I was mistaken. My best efforts were not good enough; the shrinking self-confidence that began with my leap into fourth grade continued outside of the classroom as well. I began to take on a state of mind much like Eeyore, the old, gray stuffed donkey in A.A. Milne's Winnie-the-Pooh tales. Sad-faced and melancholy, Eeyore often struggled to find the bright side.

My mother, sensing my disappointment and desperation to play, signed my brother and me up for a summer parks program, called Minor Little League, which excluded no one. If you were registered, you were on a team, but playing time depended on skill. When I did play, I was sent out to right field to watch and wait for a ball to come my way. On one of my few turns at bat, I managed to hit the ball through the infield and get myself to second base for my first—and only—double, a two-base hit. This was new. I'd never been on second base before. I was in uncharted territory, an alien visitor, watching a baseball game from a strange, unfamiliar vantage point. I had arrived. I dreamed of getting that far again, but summer and Minor Little League soon ended and there were no more doubles.

Steve, nine, and Tom, eight, stand in front of their West Shore Lutheran school bus.

The Zinkseven in 1957. Left to right: Dad, Mom, Steve, Tom, Kelly, Amy, and Judi.

3 Trying

ON SUNDAY AFTERNOONS in the summer of 1957, the Zinkseven vacated the house and piled into our 1953 Chevrolet station wagon, the successor to the DeSoto Suburban, so prospective buyers could come through. Our parents had put 19517 up for sale because they wanted a home with more room, inside and out. They found what they sought in the neighboring suburb of Westlake. Moving day occurred on the first day of a new school year in September 1957.

Westlake is the suburb that borders Rocky River to the west. The house sat at the east edge of a five-acre property that was one hundred feet wide and half a mile long. On a city plot map, its footprint resembled a bowling alley. We were practically living in the country; our bowling alley lot was a hodgepodge of dense underbrush, wildflowers, thistle bushes, and countless small oak, maple, and elm trees. We had lost our Side Yard, but now we had the Back Acres; Dad referred to them as the Back Achers, probably thinking of the extensive lawn behind the house with easily ten times more grass to mow than the Side Yard.

Mom's first letter to relatives after the move gave some clues to the reason she and Dad decided to leave 19517 for the more rural suburb. She reveled in being able to look out her bedroom window and see "the sky, the clouds, and all the expanse of open fields in the back" instead of the wall of the Olson's house next door in Rocky River. A large area just beyond the vast back lawn became the garden, where each of us children eventually had our own plots to care for as we raised our own tomatoes, corn, carrots, and radishes.

A two-story, ranch-style house, 3250 had a gable roof that sloped to the front and the rear with a broad dormer across the front. Under the dormer was the large middle bedroom that our sisters shared. The room Steve and I moved into on that first day of school was at the end of the upstairs hallway. Steve and I ran upstairs to inspect our new digs.

"I call the far bed," Steve said, tossing his school books onto the bed near the window. The room's one window faced north so there was never direct sunlight in the room. "This isn't like our old room, Tom," Steve said as he sat down on the bed.

"Yeah, but it's gonna be cool," I said. "Look at how the ceiling slopes way down to the short wall over there. It's like being in a huge tent at a Scout campout."

"We'll be hitting our heads on the ceiling when we get outta bed," Steve said.

"Well, *you* will, for sure."

We started unpacking our boxes of clothes. Steve grabbed a hanger, draped a shirt over it, and said to me, "I'm using this side of the closet. The ceiling on that side's too low for me."

A set of three built-in cabinets along one wall were spaced far enough apart so that our new twin beds could roll between them. A long bookshelf above the beds connected the tops of the three-foot high cabinets. We unpacked more boxes. Steve placed his completed fighter jet models on his shelf, along with the novel he was reading, a Boy Scout badge book, a couple Scout neckerchief slides, and a mechanical drawing set from his last birthday. I stacked my old issues of *Sport* magazine on my shelf, along with the chemistry set I got for my birthday, a redwood souvenir box from our family trip to New Orleans, the Rolls Royce model I had made, and the program from a Cleveland Indians' baseball game.

In the first few weeks in this new room, before I fell asleep at night, I was mesmerized, watching the headlights of passing southbound cars out on Columbia Road paste shifting window-shaped trapezoids onto our sloping ceiling; the shifting shapes slid north as the cars moved south. These ghost-like images were a reminder that Columbia Road was much busier than Riverview Avenue.

Not long after our move, another family bought a house on Columbia Road about a half mile away. These were the Fangmeiers, and their son Tim joined Steve's seventh-grade class at West Shore Lutheran School. Both Steve and Tim were tall and lanky guys and soon became best friends. After school and on weekends, Tim often came over to our house to play catch, shoot baskets, explore the Back Acres, or play touch football. The three of us spent a lot of time together, riding our bikes to a nearby city park or to the Westgate Mall.

While the backyard was expansive and private, our new home was on Columbia Road, a state highway that created a barrier to any sense of neighborhood. Directly across the street from our new house, a sign the size of a small billboard, declared, "URBAN DISTRICT, Reduce Speed, 35 mph." I surmised that the public safety authorities had deemed that the speed of Columbia Road traffic warranted this blatant reminder to slow down.

Because our new location was more rural, we had to drive everywhere.

We lost the convenience of being able to walk to church, the library, the hardware store, the grocery store, and the Beach Cliff Theater, where Steve, Kelly, and I used to walk to Saturday matinees on our own.

Westlake's network of roads resembled the familiar square street grid of Rocky River. The main roads intersected at right angles, and it wasn't long before Mom pointed out that since you had to slow down any time you made a turn, the quickest route was the one with the fewest turns. The grid pattern meant that to drive from our house on Columbia Road to St. Thomas church on Detroit Road, a single turn at the intersection of Columbia and Detroit was the quickest route. And thus evolved Cardinal Rule Number Three of Zink family travel: making fewer turns equals more efficient trips.

I found myself paying attention to traffic safety stories in the newspaper, especially those reporting how many people died as the result of traffic crashes on long holiday weekends. The speed limit on the turnpikes we traveled to Valpo to visit our Springsteen cousins was seventy miles per hour. It was easy to see how long-distance holiday travel at speeds like that could result in so many fatalities. So, I was skeptical when I saw an article that said most traffic fatalities occurred within five miles of home.

This information was relevant to me as long-distance family road trips became an annual occurrence for the Zinkseven after we moved to 3250. Judi was four years old, and Steve almost thirteen when we loaded the family station wagon for an October 1958 journey to visit Opa and Oma Zucker, who had recently retired and moved to New Orleans, Louisiana. The following summer, our destination was Great Smoky Mountains National Park on the border between Tennessee and North Carolina, and, in 1960, we headed to Baltimore, Maryland, to visit Granny Zink; our grandfather John J. Zink had died in 1952.

Steve was fourteen the year we visited Granny, and I was thirteen. On the final day of our visit, Granny asked Steve and me to walk to the store to buy her a couple loaves of bread, and she asked us to please take Chippy, her feisty Boston terrier. We made our way through her backyard to the next street and continued down the hill when a full-grown Weimaraner spotted Chippy and recognized prey. It bolted across the street towards Chippy, and just as the large, gray hunting dog was about to pounce on the much smaller terrier, Steve grabbed Chippy up into his arms. The Weimaraner leaped at Chippy, but its teeth found Steve's left forearm instead.

After the owner of the Weimaraner called off his dog and apologized, Steve and I turned around and hurried back to Granny's house. The bread could wait. Granny wrapped a kitchen towel around Steve's arm to stop the bleeding, and Dad drove Steve to the hospital, where he got a tetanus shot, several stitches, and a large bandage over the wound. Steve's heroics made me recognize his new level of maturity, which I could only wonder at and envy.

DAD COMPLETED the family income tax forms every year. When it came to listing "Spouse's Occupation," Mom insisted that Dad represent her work with the term "Homemaker," a life calling in which she took great pride. Instead of a customary "Hello" when she answered the phone, Mom invariably said, "the Zink home," to convey the importance she placed on ensuring our house was a home, and an organized one at that.

As we five children got older, Mom found ways for us to help with her many homemaker responsibilities. She developed a chore chart that was posted on the refrigerator every Sunday night: five children, five rotating chores, one week each. Steve and I took our turns with vacuuming, bathroom cleaning, and washing dishes, and agreed to help our younger sisters if one of them needed a hand. Mom instituted other efficiencies as well.

She devised a systematic breakfast schedule that meant one less morning decision for her to make. Each day of the week had its designated menu for breakfast. It became entrenched in our very beings that when we woke up on Wednesdays, the smell of pancakes would fill the house. Eggs—fried, scrambled, or soft-boiled—were the order of the day on Mondays and Fridays. On Sunday mornings in the mad rush to get ready for church, we gobbled down store-bought baked goods—muffins, doughnuts, or coffee cake. My favorite mornings were Tuesdays, Thursdays, and Saturdays, for those were the cold cereal days when we could have our choice of cereals for breakfast.

While Mom worked on the home front, Dad worked in his company's downtown office and served as the family's financial provider—a fact of which he was quite proud. Once in a while he'd come home on payday, and with a touch of humor and high drama, he'd count out the twenty dollar bills and set them in front of Mom on the kitchen table. Payday was always on a Friday, and when Dad got home, we felt a relaxed sense of the weekend about to begin.

On Saturday afternoons in the summer, after we'd all helped Dad and Mom with mowing the lawn and our house-cleaning chores, Dad liked to relax in the sunshine on his chaise lounge out on the backyard patio. As he worked on his tan and listened to the Indians' game on the radio, he sipped from a bottle of Pabst Blue Ribbon beer in a habit with which we were all familiar. By the fifth inning of the game, he'd call to Steve or me, "Hey, will one of you open me another beer and bring it out here?" Steve and I knew better than to than to try and sneak a sip on our way from the refrigerator out to the patio because Dad's enjoyment of alcohol did not translate into a permissive attitude about drinking. He had clear boundaries: if you weren't of legal drinking age, you weren't allowed to drink.

Even though Mom seldom drank, Dad's alcohol consumption was as unalarming and unremarkable to us as having cereal for breakfast on Thursday mornings or Bible devotions every night after supper. Weekdays after work, when he wasn't away on a business trip, dad would lean back in his favorite living room chair with a martini, a cigarette, and the day's *Plain Dealer*. After assisting those of us who needed homework help, he'd have a nightcap while he watched his favorite western shows on television. Alcohol was also the social lubricant Dad and Mom both used when they went out every few months to a Saturday party with the "couples club" of church friends. Alcohol use among the grown-ups in our lives—church friends, relatives, Dad's co-workers—was an accepted fact of Lutheran life. Among the church crowd, they joked that "whenever you find four Missouri Synod Lutherans together, you're sure to find a fifth."

On special occasions, Dad occasionally took the family out to dinner at a restaurant where he knew the manager and was a familiar face. We could never tell beforehand whether this would be one of "those nights," when Dad would drink so much that he started talking louder, flirting with the waitresses, and generally drawing unwanted attention to our table. Dad's demand of good manners on our part was the only thing that kept my siblings and me from crawling under the table in embarrassment. On these occasions Mom would quietly but firmly tell Dad that she was going to drive home.

Dad's proclivity for taking up the space in a room was exacerbated when he got drinking. He'd burst into group conversations with glib, pithy comments that instantly changed the tone of the ongoing dialogue. Once during a visit with the Springsteens, as we all relaxed in the living room, I recounted a recent surprise I had had at school and said, "It just hit me that..."

Dad interrupted with, "Where'd it hit you?"

Because his question evoked laughter and follow-up jokes from others—"Weren't you wearing your helmet when it hit you?"—it redirected attention away from my story and over to him.

Interruptions were common around the family supper table, a sign of a busy, healthy, chatty family. None of us liked having our own stories sideswiped by someone else, so Mom decided we needed a nonverbal signal to prevent interruptions. We were to cross our fingers quietly to remind us of a thought we had while someone else was talking, then we could say it when there was a break in the conversation. When a thought struck Dad, he managed, in his inimitable way, to cross his fingers in a gesture so visible and obvious that he may as well have just blurted it out.

Every year in his job with the H. K. Ferguson Company, Dad's prospects and status improved. Dad was in charge of the design and engineering of the endless minute details in the construction of large industrial buildings. His dedication, thoroughness, and attention to his employer's bottom line carried him gradually up the ladder of success. Among his co-workers, keeping up and fitting in also required drinking "with the boys," and if his drinking escalated in these years, it did not register on our naïve, child-like radar.

Dad became the chief mechanical engineer for projects with Allis-Chalmers, Proctor and Gamble, Morton Salt, and Corning Glass Works, among many others. His company did the design and engineering work for the United States Atomic Energy Commission and the National Reactor Testing Station in Idaho, which was testing the feasibility of powering submarines with nuclear reactors.

As Dad became accustomed to frequent out-of-town travel, often on short notice, we became accustomed to his absence at home. For some trips, Mom drove him to the airport early in the morning, and he returned home by cab late the same night. Other trips extended over several days, some much longer. In 1957, just before our move to 3250, Dad was away for several weeks in Idaho to fill in for a field manager who was ill. I remember thinking how cool it was when my father received a plaque that certified him as one of the early members of United Airlines' 100,000-Mile Club.

A NEW PASTOR came to St. Thomas Lutheran Church not long after we moved to 3250. In his thirty years as a Lutheran minister, the Reverend Paul Streufert had built a reputation as an inspiring preacher, congregation-builder, and leader within the Lutheran Church Missouri Synod. He came to St. Thomas from a church in New Orleans, where he and his wife, Pauline, were friends with our Opa and Oma Zucker. To those closest to him, Reverend Streufert was known simply as Pete. We soon began to think of the Streuferts as our adoptive grandparents. Dad took to referring to them as Uncle Pete and Aunt Polly, and they were occasional dinner guests at our home. They were an engaging couple, at ease with children and always interested in our activities.

Our family's Sunday morning routine seldom varied. We got up, got dressed, ate our baked-goods breakfast, did our best to pile into the car without bumping or teasing, and rode the five miles to St. Thomas church, sometimes amiably rehashing last night's television shows or Monopoly game; other times we rode in a carful of profound if-you-can't-say-sumpin'-nice silence. When we reached the church, the car doors swung open, bodies, arms, and legs rolled out, and moved towards the church doors, looking for friends to gab and gossip with as we drifted towards our Sunday school classrooms.

Our Sunday school lessons were stories from the Bible—stories about God and Jesus, and miracles and promises, and city walls falling down, and water turned to wine, and a shepherd boy killing a giant, and angels floating in the sky near Bethlehem. There were stories about people who had faith and people who didn't. Stories about publicans and lepers, prophets and wise men, and a woman at a well. And we listened as we were able and learned what we could and after an hour, we got a short break to run around outside and be kids for a few moments before we returned to church, where we knew to be on our "ipsy-pipsy Yankee Doodle best" behavior that Dad insisted on.

By sheer force of repetition, we learned the elements of the worship service. Most of it was the same every week: recite the Lord's Prayer, chant the Gloria Patri, say the Apostles' Creed, in which we'd state that we "believe in the holy Christian Church" to be absolutely clear that we were not Catholics. When it was a Communion service the first week of every month, we kids sat quietly and watched the grown-ups and teenagers who had already been confirmed file up to the altar rail, eat a wafer, and drink the wine from tiny, clear plastic cups. People would then return to their pews, bow their heads, and pray silently, a slight hint of alcohol on their breath. After Pastor Streufert blessed us, and we sang the closing hymn, church was over for the week. But our family's religious practices continued at home.

On Sundays, our main meal of the day was called dinner because we ate at the dining room table using the fancy new silverware Dad got Mom for their anniversary. The rest of the week we ate supper at the kitchen table. All these meals were book-ended with a grace. Before we could touch our food, we prayed, "Come Lord Jesus, be our guest and let these gifts to us be blest." And no one left the table after the meal until "Oh, give thanks unto the Lord for He is good and His mercy endureth forever" had been said.

Between dessert and this closing grace, we had devotions. One of us read the page for the day from a daily devotional booklet: a Bible verse, a short lesson, and a prayer. We talked about what the lesson might mean in our everyday lives. Then we launched into what Mom dubbed "special prayers." Anyone with a special request to God could voice it. They sounded like: "Dear God, please help me to know my memory work for school," or "God, please bring Daddy home safely from his trip." Only after these final offerings and thanksgivings were we excused to wash dishes, finish homework, or play outside.

Mom and Dad taught us how to cultivate the soil in our backyard garden plots, drop the seeds and cover them, weed and water the plants, and watch them grow. In the same way, their insistence on Sunday school lessons, Communion services, the singing of hymns, and family devotions sowed our seeds of faith. We were learning the art of believing things we could not see. Our parents' faith gave our lives grounding.

THE LUTHERAN CHURCH and school were our world, and when we were old enough, we were enrolled in West Shore Lutheran School. Our parents were frugal, and Mom kept close track of the family budget, but they never regarded the private school tuition as a luxury. They were committed to seeing their children educated in a Lutheran setting with a focus on growing faith. When each of us graduated from eighth grade, it went without saying that we would attend the Lutheran high school.

Our family's circle of friends was almost exclusively Lutheran. We were growing up within the traditional doctrinal confines of the Lutheran Church Missouri Synod, which dated back to the Synod's founding in 1847. Early church leaders were determined to preserve and protect the German Lutheran heritage they had brought with them from Germany. In *Flame of Faith, Lamp of Learning*, Dr. Richard Baepler summarized the early Lutheran Church Missouri Synod as the "tight matrix of congregation-school-family, a triad that actively reinforced the beliefs and roles of all members of the community." A century later, we Zink children grew up within this zone of exclusivity.

We were learning to live by the book. Or better, by the books: The Holy Bible (King James version); Luther's *Small Catechism* (1943 translation); the Lutheran Hymnal (1941 edition); school textbooks; step-by-step instructions on proper assembly of model airplanes; the Boy Scouts' *Handbook for Boys*. All these and more defined, described, and delimited our everyday activities. There were choice points along the way, but we were restricted by our structured lives to select only paths that seemed to be already laid out, to take the route with the fewest turns. Living by the books gave our lives predictability and reassurance, yet somewhere along the way, our childlike spontaneity got lost in the open spaces between the grid lines. We very likely would have been unsettled and ill-at-ease were we to be handed a map without roads or structure.

It went without saying that when Steve entered the eighth grade—and when I did a year later—we would attend the Saturday morning confirmation classes at St. Thomas church to prepare with our classmates for the solemn ritual of Lutheran confirmation. Pastor Streufert's instructions to the young confirmands included a very thorough grounding in the Lutheran faith as professed by the Missouri Synod. Luther's *Small Catechism* formed the basis of the course. We had to memorize and be ready to recite Luther's simple explanation of the meaning of all the major elements of Lutheranism—the Ten Commandments, the creeds, the Lord's Prayer, and the sacraments.

Steve dutifully noted in his diary some of the tasks required over the nine months of classes: recite Psalm One, King James Version, from memory; during Advent, the church season leading up to Christmas, recite from memory four stanzas of "O Come, O Come Emmanuel"; study and discuss the Ten Commandments using Luther's *Small Catechism*; recite all the articles in the Apostles' Creed and the Nicene Creed from memory; study sin and know the difference between original sin and actual sin.

The confirmation process concluded with two significant events. The first was the "questioning service," a Sunday morning observance in which the pastor asked the students a long series of questions about the Christian faith. Successful participation in this exercise demonstrated a readiness for confirmation.

The second big event was the confirmation ritual itself, the significance of which was not lost on Steve. His Sunday, May 17, 1959, diary entry read, "Today is a big day. I was confirmed at the altar and then took Holy Communion with the rest of the class. We had a picture taken also." In that class picture, two small details stand out: Steve is the only one of the eight boys wearing a bow tie, just as Dad often did. Steve is also the only one of the eleven confirmands who is wearing what could best be described as a smirk, that half-smile worn by someone who thinks he's gotten away with some minor mischief.

Pastor Streufert chose for each of the confirmands a special Bible verse intended to be significant in their lives. The verse he chose for Steve was from the Old Testament book of Joshua. Forty years of wandering in the wilderness were about to end for the people of Israel. Joshua was the man God had chosen to lead them into the Promised Land. Steve's confirmation verse was God's promise to Joshua at this critical point in his life: "Be strong and of a good courage; be not afraid, neither be thou dismayed; for the Lord thy God is with thee whithersoever thou goest."

The confirmation rite of passage in our church meant not only that you could take communion with the grown-ups but that you were also old enough to join the youth group, known as the Walther League, the same Missouri Synod organization that our Aunt Marlise belonged to when she was "ordered" to attend Valpo by the Kretzmann brothers. Steve became a Walther League member in the fall of 1959, and I followed him a year later.

A FEW WEEKS after Steve's confirmation service, West Shore Lutheran School held its eighth-grade graduation ceremony. Along with their class of eighteen, Steve and his best friends, Wayne Peters and Tim Fangmeier, received their diplomas. In September 1959, Steve, Wayne, and Tim began their freshman year at Lutheran High School West.

During that summer, Steve and I were fairly constant companions. One day, a book of quizzes we found at the library helped us pass the hours on a rainy afternoon.

"Okay, Tom, what's the capital of Alabama?"

"Is it Mobile?"

"Wrong. Another 'M' city."

"Then it's gotta be Montgomery."

"Yup." We went back and forth through the state and foreign capitals; Steve asking, me answering.

"Okay, my turn. Let me see that book," I said.

"Here. Ask me some history questions."

"Okay. Who was the second president of the United States?"

"Easy, Thomas Jefferson."

"Nope, he was third."

"So, who was it?"

"John Adams."

We passed the summer playing baseball on the back lawn with Tim Fangmeier and our neighbor Tom Livingstone, playing ping-pong in the basement, working together on jigsaw puzzles and crossword puzzles, and we often amused each other by reading the jokes and riddles on the "Think and Grin" page in *Boys' Life*, the monthly Scouting magazine. Special times for both of us were when Dad took us to a movie, bowling, or miniature golf. And we didn't mind the grunting and sweating it took to help Dad saw, split, and stack firewood for the living room fireplace.

Steve's passion tended towards building plastic models of cars and fighter jets or mechanical contraptions with his Erector Set—a child's construction kit with metal parts of varying lengths and widths that could be assembled using nuts and bolts. One winter, Steve spent hours building a tower crane, complete with a little electric trolley that moved back and forth along the crane's long horizontal jib.

I was an avid fan of team sports, and Dad supported my interest. He often played catch with Steve and me, or hit grounders to help us practice our baseball fielding skills. In the fall, he enjoyed throwing the football to us as we took turns running pass patterns across our massive back lawn. But Dad's most significant gift to me was to design and build a basketball backboard that would fit on the sloping roof above our garage at 3250. Steve helped nail the frame together and tighten the bolts. The rim of the basket was exactly the right height, ten feet above the paved driveway that served well as a small basketball court. Every chance I got—in rain, wind, or sunshine—I was outside practicing my lay-ups, free throws, and hook shots.

One Saturday afternoon in the early fall of 1960, with basketball season coming soon, I headed outside and grabbed the basketball from the rack in the garage.

"Steve, c'mon out and shoot some baskets with me," I called to him.

"I wanna try and finish my go-kart," he said as he came outside carrying one of Dad's wrenches and a screwdriver.

While I practiced my dribbling and shooting, Steve was around the side of the house tinkering with his project. He had built a small wooden contraption resting on a two-wheeled axle that he had somehow attached to the back of our self-propelled reel lawn mower, so it followed the mower like a trailer. How my brother came up with these devices was beyond me.

After a time, he called me to come and help him.

"Okay, but will you play basketball with me after?"

"I guess" was his response.

"What do you want me to do?"

"You're gonna be my test pilot," he said. "C'mere, sit back there on that trailer and hold onto the mower handle."

"Is this safe?"

"If you hold on and steer it right, yeah. Okay, I'll pull the rope and start the mower."

"Wait a second!" I hollered. "How fast is it gonna go?"

"You've mowed the lawn with this mower before. It's not that fast."

"Okay, go ahead." Steve yanked on the pull cord, put the mower in gear, and off I went across the back lawn with Steve chasing after me. Over the roar of the engine, I barely heard him screaming, "I'm not sure how to stop it!"

In a few seconds he had caught up to me. Moving briskly alongside the mower, he managed to disconnect the spark plug cable. The engine coughed once, then died. I exhaled, relieved I had not crashed Steve's creation. He declared the first test run a success. I did not volunteer for the second.

"Now can we play basketball?" I asked.

"Sure. Fine," said Steve. He stowed the mower and his seat contraption in the garage.

"Who gets the ball first?" he said as he came out onto the driveway.

"Whoever hits two shots first, like always," I said.

I usually won this pre-game test. For Steve, practicing basketball shots usually took a back seat to tinkering with his Erector Set or finishing up the plastic Revell model he was building. Steve's first shot clanged on the rim. I took the ball, dribbled a couple times, and shot. The ball caromed off the backboard and through the basket. Steve tried again and missed. I took a two-handed shot and swished it right through the net.

"Okay, it's your ball," Steve said.

Although we were only fifteen months apart, Steve's growth spurt gave him a distinct height advantage over me. When we stood next to each other, the top of my head could fit neatly under his chin, just as it had in photographs my father had taken ten years earlier.

I dribbled to my right to try and get around him and go to the basket. He got in my way, but I shot the ball anyway. He reached up a gangly arm and brushed the ball away. "Hey, no fair!" I yelled.

"What?"

"You didn't even jump!"

"There's no rule like that. Why jump if I don't have to?"

"Well, anyway, you fouled me on the arm so it's still my ball."

"Baloney. All I touched was the ball. It's my ball now."

"Oh, fine!"

Steve grabbed the ball, carried it to the far side of the driveway and started dribbling.

"That's not how you dribble," I said.

"That's not how you dribble!" he replied, mocking. "Who do you think *you* are, Bob Cousy or somebody?"

"I dribble better than you do any day!"

"So? Big whip."

He bounced the ball a few more times then threw a shot at the basket. It bounced twice on the rim but didn't fall through. I reached up to take the rebound of his missed shot. Steve closed in on me. I saw his long arm reach over me and bat the ball off onto the side lawn.

"My ball. You touched it last," I called.

"Fine!"

We played for a while longer. Steve soon got bored and just walked off into the garage and down into the basement. I stayed outside, practicing my dribbling and shooting. Our ability to play a friendly game of basketball on this day had worn itself out.

My passion for team sports could not be dampened by Steve's indifference. I followed closely the fates of teams I identified with—the Cleveland Indians, the Cleveland Browns pro football team, the Ohio State University basketball team that won a national championship. It was nearly impossible to detach my self-esteem from the rise and fall of my favorite teams. I was learning to see the world through zero-sum glasses. You either won, or you lost. There was no middle ground. Mine was an either-or, all-or-nothing world. To truly inhabit it, I wanted to play on a team and to wear the school's team uniform, a clear sign that I had standing among my peers.

In my first year at Lutheran West, I tried out and was selected for the freshman basketball team. In practice one day, our coach had us practice lay-ups. If you missed one, you had to run three laps around the gym. My hours of practice on the basketball hoop at home paid off: I was the only player that day who didn't have to run laps. Unfortunately, the skills I had practiced at home against imaginary opponents and my older brother did not equip me well for game situations. The frequent mistakes I made due to my frantic nerves consigned me to the role of bench-warmer, alongside my friend Rich. We were known as "reserves" and only got to play during "garbage time," the last two minutes of a game when the outcome was no longer in doubt.

DAD HAD NOT EXPERIENCED the fun times and the trying times of growing up with a brother, but he did his best to promote peace and harmony between Steve and me. Sometimes we found common ground making music together. We took weekly piano lessons for several years and sometimes, just for fun, we'd sit together on the piano bench to play some simple duets. We could crank out the C, A minor, F, and G chord progressions, and the high-end melody of "Heart and Soul" with ease. Individually, Steve played trumpet, and I took up the drums. At Lutheran West, Steve played in the school band, and I played a variety of percussion instruments in the orchestra—the snare drum, kettle drums (tympani), bells, and chimes.

One afternoon, Dad came home with a second-hand trumpet for me, and Steve helped me learn the fingerings so I could play a simple scale. Once I had that mastered, Dad orchestrated the next step. He opened the Lutheran Hymnal to the joyous Easter hymn he wanted us to learn, "Jesus Christ is Risen Today." After several weeks of practice during the church season of Lent one year, Steve played the melody, and I managed the alto harmony well enough for Dad to make a tape recording of our Easter duet. I recall those precious moments still today whenever I hear that hymn on an Easter morning.

In 1959, a pair of singing brothers named Don and Phil Everly had a hit song called "Take a Message to Mary," a lovelorn young man's letter to his fiancé written in his prison cell. Steve and I heard the song on the radio and asked Dad to help us learn the two-part harmony. We both wanted to sing the melody. After some wrangling, I agreed to sing the harmony part; Steve took the lead. Unlike the more famous brothers, we sang the song without any instrumental accompaniment.

WITH ONE CAR, two drivers, and seven family members all involved in outside activities, our parents increasingly relied on Steve and me to ride our bicycles. They made sure we were clear about the rules for safe cycling, with some of the basics being to ride on the right with traffic, be sure to signal before a turn, and turn on your bike light at dusk. Steve and I often rode our bikes to and from school, and we rode to Monday evening Boy Scout meetings at the Methodist church, often returning home after sunset. The trickiest part of those evening rides was the last half mile along Columbia Road, a stretch of road with no sidewalks. With bike lights turned on, we would ride along the right edge of the pavement as we had been taught. Headlights from behind told us a car was approaching, our signal to dip off the road and down onto the gravel shoulder. The approaching car's headlights illuminated our path onto the shoulder, our narrow ribbon of safety. When the car passed, we were back onto the pavement, our lights showing the way down the last little slope to the 3250 mailbox, to the driveway, and home.

In February 1960, our bicycles became vehicles of commerce for Steve and me when we started our first jobs. We became paper boys for Cleveland's morning daily, the *Plain Dealer*, a name chosen by the paper's first editor in 1842 because it "fits the principles of the country, which are democracy and modesty." Mom heard that two routes were available nearby and made the arrangements for us to take them on. And so it was that Steve started his route on the state highway we lived on, Columbia Road, and I took over the route on Rose Road, a quiet nearby side road. Rose Road ran east and west, perpendicular to Columbia and intersected it a few hundred yards from our house.

The daily papers were dropped off at the edge of the road next to the mailbox, bundled with a brown paper wrapper and stiff baling wire—one bundle for Steve's route, one for mine. The Sunday comics and ad flyers came on Thursdays, so on that day, we got twice as many bundles. Six mornings a week we each loaded our papers into the wire baskets attached over our rear bicycle wheels and rode off in opposite directions to bring the news to our customers' mailboxes or front doors. Sunday morning's bulky paper required the help of our parents and the family car. For young teenaged boys always in need of more sleep, it was challenging at first to wake up in the dark and be functional enough to get the job done by the mandatory delivery deadline of seven in the morning.

Eventually, a morning routine evolved that had us waking up at five thirty and delivering the papers by six fifteen. Then, we'd head back to bed for another hour's sleep before we had to get ready for school. Most days, our deliveries were done before sun-up; while our bikes were equipped with head-lights, the hard-shell bicycle helmets so common today were not introduced until fifteen years later.

On Sunday mornings, the combination of comics, ad sections, leisure, real estate, and news sections produced a heavy, bulky two-inch-thick whack of newsprint, far too much for boys on bicycles to tote around. So, on Sundays, our deliveries were done from the back of the family station wagon with the tailgate wide open. Steve and I piled the eighty-some papers on the floor behind the back seat. Mom and Dad took turns driving us around both routes as Steve and I rode on the tailgate, our feet dangling close to the road.

Sunday morning traffic on Columbia Road was rare. One Sunday, we were both up at the road retrieving bundles. Steve stopped and took a long look both ways at an empty Columbia Road: no vehicles as far as you could see in either direction. He looked over at me and said, "Hey," and nodded his head toward the road. Whistling in idle nonchalance, we walked to the center stripe and lay down on our backs, hands clasped behind our heads, feet crossed at the ankles, feigning naps. Whenever we did pull this little prank, we developed precise timing to jump up and haul our papers back to the garage before we heard the sound of a car in the distance or Dad yelling at us to get out of the road. It was one of the few bits of mischief we managed to pull off.

Being paper boys taught us the meaning of work. I can still remember the feeling I'd have as I raised the garage door over my head and looked out at the mailbox in the dark, seeing our newspaper bundles. Many mornings, I felt a strong urge to pull that door back down, lock it, and go back to bed. But I knew that there were people out there in the morning darkness who would soon be waking up for a morning routine of their own that included coffee and a copy of the *Plain Dealer*; it was my job to get it to them. So I'd let go of the garage door handle, utter the deep sigh of a teenaged victim of unjust sleep deprivation, bring in the bundles, load the papers into my bicycle baskets, and head off to do my job. Steve and I learned to be undeterred by menacing dogs, snowdrifts, mailboxes frozen shut by overnight ice storms, and the temptation to remain in the cozy warmth of our beds when the alarm rang. Grabbing a whiff of that freshly percolated coffee as I dropped the paper inside a customer's kitchen storm door made it all a tad more tolerable.

STEVE AND I HAD ENJOYED Cub Scouts in our younger days in Rocky River when Mom had been our den mother. With pride, we wore our dark blue Cub uniforms with the badges sewn on the front, attended the annual Scouting banquets, and worked on our merit badges. One of my proudest achievements was earning the Cub merit badge for automobiles by learning to identify all the mid-1950s makes and models with their wrap-around windshields, flaring tail fins, and fancy grilles. When we moved to Westlake, Steve joined the Boy Scout troop right away. A year later when I turned eleven, I too became a member of Troop 191. I was anxious about what Steve had told me about how the older Scouts "welcomed" newcomers like me.

The hazing ritual that introduced new boys to the Scouts at the time was known as "pantsing." It was meant to be quick and humiliating. A posse of older Scouts would surround the new kid, pull him to the ground, pin down his flailing arms and legs, and drag his pants down around his ankles. Then they'd walk away and leave him. When I first joined Steve's troop, there was one other new boy. I recall one warm spring evening, just at sunset outside the church before the meeting began. The Scouts gathered around this other new boy and "pantsed" him. With my Ridiculometer in overdrive, I watched, standing alone and off to one side against a wall, making myself as small and silent as I could. The older Scouts never noticed me. I joined the troop, relieved I'd avoided their "welcome."

Steve and I went together on weekend campouts with the troop, learning how to pitch a tent, tie square knots, bowlines and double half-hitches, and build a campfire guaranteed to start with a single match. I soon began to notice, though, that Scouting held much greater appeal for Steve than for me. The "pantsing" ritual put me off, and so did my patrol leader, a short, slightly overweight dad with a tired-sounding monotone voice and a face that, even smiling, seemed disinterested.

A week at summer camp did little to sustain my interest. Steve and I shared a walled tent at a Scout reservation east of Cleveland in the summer of 1959. At the swimming beach, I endured the ignoble fate of being the only one in my group not skilled enough to go beyond the beginner's rope. One afternoon, a downpour drenched the camp. All of us sought the shelter of our tents. Tiny rivulets of water flowing down the hill behind our tents gathered into a torrent, seeped under our tent wall and rolled down the center, making islands of our two cots. Steve and I snatched our gear off the ground, and sat cross-legged on our cots, wondering if this could get any worse. It did.

The camp's mid-week Parents' Night was not a good idea for marginally homesick campers like me. Mom drove out to camp for the evening. When the campfire program was over, and it came time for Mom to leave, I was desperate to go home with her. I pleaded once or twice, saw it was fruitless to continue begging, and stayed to complete the week. On the final day of camp, my effort to earn my Second Class rank fell short because I was unable to build a fire hot enough to fully cook my foil-wrapped baked potato, as required in the Scout handbook. The pantsing ritual, my bored patrol leader, and the half-baked potato sealed the deal. A short while later, I decided to quit the Scouts.

Steve thrived in the Boy Scouts, though. He worked hard to earn the badges and advance his rank up to Second Class: compass- and map-reading, basic first aid skills, and safe use of a knife, saw, and ax. He got along well with his peers and the Scout leaders. In the summer of 1960, Steve's Troop 191 embarked on an adventure that widened the gap between the two of us.

For a whole year, the Scouts and their leaders prepared for a trip to the Philmont Scout Ranch near Cimarron, New Mexico. Steve would be the first Zink child to travel such a long distance without the family. In advance of the adventure, the troop's major project was to retrofit an old GMC school bus into a home on wheels for two dozen Scouts and their adult leaders. Dubbed The Welded Wanderer and destined to carry the troop the 1,650 miles to Philmont and back, the bus had "Simmer on to Cimarron" painted on its side. In July 1960, The Welded Wanderer took away my fourteen-year-old brother and, three weeks later, brought back someone different.

Steve's one letter home was a daily log that summarized the troop's hikes, service projects, campsite locations, and their dehydrated meals. His thoughtful, caring side showed in his closing words: "Love and kisses, Steve." We celebrated Judi's sixth birthday while Steve was away, and clearly, he remembered this too, as his postscript said, "Don't tell Judi, but I bought her a birthday present."

One requirement of moving to the Scout rank of First Class was to complete fifty miles of hiking at Philmont. Steve's previous problems with asthma were a cause for concern, but by the end of two weeks at the ranch, Steve—along with his fellow Scouts—had surpassed the fifty-mile goal. In August 1960, Steve brought home with him a small oval plaque to commemorate his success. A raised image in the center of the plaque showed two well-worn hiking boots. Above the boots, all in uppercase letters, were the words, "I made it!" Near the bottom, just above the small Philmont logo, Steve hand printed his name.

The Scout's return trip to Westlake was timed to coincide with a festive Welcome Home event the parents were planning. Mom wanted our family to join the welcoming committee so she had us help her make a large banner that said, "Welcome Back, Troop 191." A photographer from the local newspaper was on hand for the gala return and snapped a photo of my mother holding one end of the banner and me, her slender, thirteen-year-old Scout-drop-out son, holding the other end. I was glad to see my brother return safely, but I still remember how small I felt compared to Steve, home from his big adventure to New Mexico, his face tanned and his hair blond-streaked from the New Mexico sun. Dad took us all out to dinner that night, and Steve regaled us with tales of Philmont.

My envy was palpable that night, but I didn't know its name. I only knew that my brother and I were growing apart, our temperaments, interests, and skills pulling us in different directions. Our divergence was unremarkable and probably all but inevitable for two brothers traipsing through the front door of adolescence. The space between us was opening bit by bit, day by day, growing so subtly that we neither noticed the changes nor had much time to miss the childhood companionship we were leaving behind.

STILL, IN THE QUIET PRIVACY of the room we continued to share, our brother bond remained strong. We invented secret little games to lighten an evening of school work. We sat at opposite ends of a large rectangular wooden table, each of us with a desk lamp, a desk pad, and an empty peanut butter jar to hold our pens, pencils, and slide rules. Our school books stood in the middle of the table, held up by bookends Dad had made for us. Every so often, without warning, one of us would disrupt the silence with a faux belch from deep in our throats. We exchanged silent stares across the divider of books. Chair legs scratched the floor as we backed away from our desks. We both stood, our faces wrinkled up in feigned anger, and did heavy, slow, Frankenstein walks towards the other. We began grappling, growling, and giggling until we fell together onto one of the beds, smothered in laughter. In a few moments, by unspoken mutual consent, we got up and went back to our homework as if nothing had happened.

After lights out, especially on wieners-and-beans-supper nights, we played our game of Undercover Farts. One of us would let fly with a noisome emission of digestive gases under the covers. Not to be outdone, the other would answer with a lily of his own. But the real fun came from lifting up the covers, ducking our heads under, and inhaling deeply the delicate aromas only two teenage boys on a post-bean supper night could produce. We giggled so hard our stomachs hurt, our eyes watered, and more lilies came forth.

If the volume of our silliness rose too high, we would hear Dad holler from the bottom of the steps, "You boys pipe down up there, or I'm coming up!" Our laughs faded to giggles, and then began the whispered quips—riddles and one-liners about bodily functions we'd heard and told many times before, but still tickled our funny bones. Jokes about elephant snot or giants with diarrhea. The five thirty alarm for our paper routes always came too quickly.

Steve often took full advantage of the first-born's innate prerogative to tease and poke fun at his younger brother, as if the brotherly camaraderie of our bedroom fun were a mirage. Each incident on its own was inane and trivial, but, taken together, they had a compounding effect because I felt I had no recourse to justice from my parents. One time, Steve came walking through the living room while I was practicing for my next piano lesson. Right in the middle of my Mozart Minuet, he plunked both hands on the high notes on the keyboard, moved behind me and then pounded out a couple bass notes then scampered up the stairs.

"Hey," I hollered to anyone who might have been listening, "Stop bugging me!"

His face then appeared from behind the wall on the stairwell. In a scratchy, artificially low voice, he spewed his current favorite insult, "Hey, you pimplety navel hair!" His silly insult had absolutely no conceivable meaning except that he'd snuck in another small win.

When I'd be sitting on the couch reading the baseball box scores, the newspaper held up in front of me, Steve liked to tiptoe over and flick a finger at the newsprint to make a crisp "Snap!" that made me jump.

"Hey, cut it out, you booger!"

"Make me!"

"I don't make monkeys; I sell 'em."

"Takes one to know one."

Steve's petty insults got my goat far more often than any comments I fired at him got his. Our quarrels were always verbal; we never came to blows. But his darts hit home. I envied his easygoing, carefree manner, and my envy compounded all the petty grievances that were building inside me. I fell into a quiet resignation, warmed by the grudges I harbored. When I tried to even the score by mocking or harassing him, my words were either turned back against me or fell useless to the floor. It was all unfair. Unable to get the upper hand, I lived with a pervading sense that I was perpetually in second place, the one who could never win.

At least once a week in church I dutifully recited the Lord's Prayer, saying the words, "And forgive us our trespasses as we forgive those who trespass against us." But they were mere words. Forgiving Steve was not happening unless he relented, and I expected that to happen about as much as I expected to see the Cleveland Indians win the World Series in my lifetime.

IN AUGUST 1961, our annual family road trip took us to New Jersey to visit Mom's older sister Dorothy Ziegler and her family. The days were filled with side trips to places like the Corning Glass Works in southern New York, New York City, the Empire State Building, and the shrine of my dreams, the Baseball Hall of Fame in Cooperstown, New York.

Even more memorable than Cooperstown, though, was the place I recall most clearly: Letchworth State Park in western New York, home of the five-hundred-foot-deep Genesee River Gorge, known as the "Grand Canyon of the East." The sight from above, of the three separate rambunctious cascades roaring through the gorge, made us gasp in awe—except for Steve. His fifteen and a half years, rolled-up sleeves, I'm-cooler-than-you attitude, and experience of a whoop-de-doo trip all the way to the Scout ranch in New Mexico apparently made him too worldly to be affected by a mere gorge, and that entitled him to mock our excitement. His attitude irked me no end, but this was nothing new.

It was during the early weeks of the new school year when Steve was a junior and I was a sophomore that an unexpected opportunity arose to air my grievances about my big brother. My English teacher told the class to write an essay about a pet peeve. While my classmates planned to write about funny, mundane pet peeves, I was serious about making the most of this chance to even the score: My pet peeve was Steve.

What galled me the most about Steve was the way he rolled up his sleeves—to just the right point on his forearm, where he thought it made him look cool. Even short-sleeved shirts had to have a double roll-up. I would rather have eaten a bowl of Elmer's glue than to have been accused of imitating my big brother, so I kept my cuffs buttoned and found other routes to adolescent acceptance.

I made the Honor Roll in my first year of high school and played on the freshman basketball team. Of necessity as brothers, Steve and I were together a lot but mostly indifferent to each other's skills and interests. Like begrudging fellow travelers on our way through adolescence, our parallel paths seldom intertwined. But both of us were members of the St. Thomas Church Walther League, and, in a rare alignment of interests, the group chose Steve as president and me as treasurer at the annual officer elections in May 1961.

BY THAT FALL, we were all accustomed to Dad being away overnight on business trips, and this season was no different. Dad learned that his company had landed a major construction contract in Rio de Janeiro, Brazil and that his expertise was needed on the project. With less than a week to get ready, he began a crash course in Portuguese, trying to master a few basic phrases like *obrigado* and *por favor*. While we knew we would miss hearing his voice in the house and the rustle of newsprint as he scanned the day's paper, we also knew our lives would carry on in his absence.

Before he left, Dad said to Steve and me, "You boys want to go see 'The Guns of Navarone' on Friday night?" Did we? Of course we did. These movie nights with just Dad and the boys happened maybe once or twice a year, so it was an offer not to be refused. Dad would buy our tickets and take us to a restaurant at which he knew Steve and I could order our favorite fare: deep-fried shrimp, French fries, and coleslaw.

For this outing, the movie was a World War II battle film, featuring two of Dad's favorite actors, Gregory Peck and Anthony Quinn. In the car, instead of sitting in the rear while Steve rode up front with Dad, I squeezed into the middle between them, my feet propped up on the transmission hump in the floor. As we drove, we talked about things I've long since forgotten, but I will always remember how that night embodied the lifelong bond the three of us shared.

Dad was scheduled to leave for Rio de Janeiro on Wednesday, October 4, and expected to be away at least a month. There was something different about this trip in that he was traveling further than he'd ever been away from us—five thousand miles away, to a completely different continent. We checked our world atlas and could not believe that Rio de Janeiro was as far to the east as Greenland, and it was two time zones *ahead* of Cleveland.

To keep track of the days Dad was away, Steve made a chart on a piece of cardboard. Across the top, Steve wrote "Rio de Janeiro." Below that, he glued a photo of Dad from his company's monthly magazine when he was chosen Builder of the Month. The bottom half of Steve's chart was the tracking table with three columns—the first marked "Gone," the middle marked "Days," and the third, "Weeks." Each day following October 4, Steve made a single tally mark, clustering them in fives with a diagonal mark to indicate every fifth day.

On October 5, 1961, with one tally mark on Steve's chart, Dad called home from New York City. Telephone service to Brazil was either very rudimentary or extremely expensive in those days, so he said another good-bye and told us this would be his last call for the duration of his trip. Just as Mom's short prayer at the beginning of our family road trips reminded us of God's protection, we always took for granted Dad's safety on his frequent business trips. His absence this time, though, left a new level of uneasiness among us at home, although we didn't talk about it.

With Dad gone and our family equilibrium a little off-center, we seem to have had more than the usual spats and hurt feelings. I kept a diary that year, rarely recording anything but facts. On the day when Steve's chart had eleven tally marks, I wrote this: "We had trouble getting along in the family," a telling indication that we were feeling Dad's absence more than we were letting on.

Five thousand miles away in Rio, Dad was not faring much better. On letterhead from the luxury Copacabana Palace Hotel right on the beach where the company had put him up, he began a letter to Mom with "My dear Nostalgia." His words sounded depressed, due in part to the case of Brazilian diarrhea he had contracted, but with a hint of his sardonic wit:

> This must be the dirtiest, craziest, most beautiful town in the world and I'm very rapidly getting sick of it. That's no alliteration, I'm fed up with it—already.... It seems that we have been gone for nearly a month rather than a week. Every day I'm away from you and everybody I hold near to my heart is multiplied by the miles that separate us to arrive at a figure showing how much I miss you.... And so it goes! If the blasted Brazilian Diarrhea doesn't get me, the ulcers of frustration will. But here in Rio you got two strikes against you—1) the language problem, and 2) the filth problem. I promise you we're going to button up this job as quickly as possible, delays or no delays.

The weather was unseasonably warm on the day that Steve's fourteenth tally marked the conclusion of Dad's second week away. The thermometer topped out at seventy-nine degrees. The peak of the autumn colors in the trees in our backyard had passed, and the leaves were beginning to fall. Soon we would be hauling out the rake and gathering up the leaves to toss onto the compost heap to use in next spring's garden. We ate supper outside for probably the last time in the year, and a friend of Amy's came for a sleepover that night.

The next day, a Thursday, promised more of the same warm fall weather. The day got off to an unfortunate start. Steve and I were usually up at five thirty to deliver our papers, but on this particular day, we both slept through the alarm and woke up in a panic at around six fifteen. Ohio was still on daylight savings time, and it would be dark for another hour.

We threw on some clothes, clattered downstairs, and tied on our shoes. I unlocked the garage door, and as I was lifting it up, Steve ducked under and walked out to the road to bring in his bundle of daily papers and a bundle of Sunday comics. He returned to the garage to get his bike and said to me, "There's another bundle out there." I hustled out to bring it in to the garage. We counted out our papers, got on our bikes, and rode off in opposite directions, Steve heading north along Columbia Road and me heading south towards Rose Road.

As we rode off, the only difference between this day and so many hundreds of others since we had started as paperboys twenty months earlier was that the eastern sky had started to lighten in anticipation of the sunrise. At that time of year, we were used to darkness. Waking up late that morning made things feel a little different as I rode away, knowing there wouldn't be time after I'd finished the papers to crawl back into bed for my usual hour of sleep.

The last customer on my route was the Moldovan family. Two concrete steps led up to their small front stoop. Clutching my last paper of that morning's route, I took the stairs in a single leap and dropped the folded paper inside the screen door. As I let it close and turned to leave, an ambulance drove past. It seemed to be in no hurry, although the maraschino cherry of a single red light on its roof was flashing. No siren was sounding. One word flashed through my mind: Steve.

Racing thoughts and questions seized me: Something's happened to Steve. Why an ambulance with a silent siren? Why did I instantly think that the ambulance had anything to do with my brother? Standing on the Moldovan's top step, I did a quick geographic calculation, thinking of Cardinal Rule Number Three in Zink family travel: fewer turns mean more efficient trips. If the ambulance intended to take the fastest route from the Westlake public safety building to Steve, it would not be traveling on Rose Road. I convinced myself that there was no way this ambulance had anything to do with my brother. And yet, accompanying this well-reasoned conclusion was an uneasy sense that on this morning, logic might well fail me, that there was a reason beyond my understanding that the ambulance passed by at the moment I finished my paper route.

Feeling on edge, I walked back to my bike and began pedaling home.

Steve and his sisters, Kelly, Judi, and Amy, on the day of his eighth-grade graduation in June 1959.

Tom and Steve at a Boy Scout "camporee" in Westlake, Ohio, in 1959.

WHEN I GOT HOME, I rolled my bicycle into its space in the rack in the garage, and noticed that Steve's bike was not there. I rationalized that sometimes he takes longer to finish his route than I do. Inside the house, my mother was setting breakfast cereals out and preparing to wake my three sisters and Amy's sleepover friend. I took a quick shower, got dressed, and went to the kitchen for breakfast. I said nothing about the ambulance, clinging to my airtight logic that Steve was fine. I fought with my gut instinct that he wasn't. Maybe he had a flat tire or just stopped to visit Tim Fangmeier, who lived on his paper route.

While I ate my Cheerios, Mom pointed out that Steve had not returned from his paper route yet. I mentioned the ambulance. She said that I had better ride up Columbia Road and find out what was going on. My insides resisted, but my outsides relented. I had no choice: Dad was in Rio, and Mom had to be home with the girls who were just waking up. It was up to me to go. I wanted to start this whole morning over again, to call out "No takes!" like we did when the kick-off in a Side Yard touch football game was not to our liking. I searched for explanations for Steve's absence. Maybe somebody's dog bit him, or he broke his leg.

I started riding north on Columbia Road, following the route that Steve would have taken to deliver his papers. About a quarter mile along, just past Maple Ridge Cemetery, I caught sight of a police car blocking the road, its lights flashing. An officer was detouring traffic onto a side street. Just beyond that, several police officers were talking near a car parked on the east side of the road. Onlookers stood nearby, watching. There was no ambulance.

When I reached the scene, I tried to take in what I was seeing. Across the road from where I stood, straddling my bicycle, I saw Steve's bicycle upside down, leaning against a large tree in Mrs. Brown's front yard. The front wheel and handle bars had broken off and lay nearby. The two wire baskets that spanned his rear wheel were upside down with a scattering of undelivered *Plain Dealers* on the ground. In the driveway, I saw both of his brown, lace-up shoes and one of his socks.

With the police presence and the bystanders, I felt as if I were an intruder in an investigation I could neither fathom nor explain. I knew this was my brother's broken bike, so I knew the situation was serious. And yet, I had this creepy feeling that I did not belong there, that I was not welcome and, most of all, that I should certainly not ask questions. I ignored my fear, put down my kickstand, left my bike on the opposite side of the road, and started walking towards one of the officers. His body language as he approached told me I'd better have a good excuse for being there.

We met in the middle of Columbia Road. I said, "That's my brother's bike. How is he?" His answer was short and blunt: "Well, son, your brother's dead." I had no words, no thoughts, no feelings. Standing near the yellow center line, I felt swallowed by his five words. I left part of myself in that place, lost in the moment. All around me, swirling madly, time in all other dimensions moved on. But for me, there were no seconds or minutes or hours. Time stopped in my soul, frozen on the cold wind of the police officer's words.

The officer then softened a bit. He told me to get into his cruiser, and he would take me home. His police radio crackled as he called to the ambulance. It had reached the hospital, and a voice over the radio said simply, "DOA." I had learned from television shows that "DOA" meant "Dead On Arrival." Sitting in the back seat, I twisted to the rear and looked through the window to the spot where my life stopped and time raced on. Part of me stayed on that spot, a stunned statue standing alone in the middle of the road.

The officer drove back towards our house. He knocked on the side door that led to the kitchen. My mother opened the door, still wearing her house-coat over her pajamas. The policeman told her the news and then turned to go back to his car. I did not hear what he said to her, nor do I recall the reaction of my mother, this forty-one-year-old woman who had lost a playmate to malaria as a child in India and a teenaged older sister. The news had come home. Suddenly the Zinkseven family arithmetic had changed. Seven take away one equaled six.

My anger simmered, as I struggled to hold in check the disbelief and fear. I went right upstairs to a bedroom that was no longer "ours." As I walked by the door to the room my three sisters shared, the words "Steve is dead" passed across my lips like a handful of daggers flung with abandon at a target I hoped they'd miss. Our brother was dead, Dad was in Rio, and I was suddenly plunged into a role that was as new and foreign to me as the sounds of those Portuguese words Dad struggled to learn before he left two weeks earlier.

I felt called to serve as the man of the house, but I had no clue what that meant I needed to do. I just knew one thing: I could not cry or fall apart. Almost before I experienced them, I sealed my emotions deep within and accepted the unthinkable. I moved through the day, zombie-like, saying little, remembering less, feeling nothing. Mom must have begun making calls soon after the officer came by with the tragic news. I expect that she first called Dad's company to get him home as soon as possible. Next on her list would have been Pastor Streufert. Anne Springsteen—Steve's godmother—may well have been the third call.

Pastor Streufert was the first to arrive at our house, bringing prayers, comfort, and help in delivering the news. It was Pastor Streufert who sent the telegram message to relatives in other states: "Stephen Zink called to his eternal rest this morning at six forty-five. Struck by car on paper route in Westlake. Funeral arrangements not yet made. Will notify you later. Pray for us that we may have strength. We trust in the goodness of our Lord."

A reporter from the *Cleveland Press* came to cover the story for the afternoon paper. Mom handed him Steve's most recent school picture but told him in no uncertain terms to take no photographs in the house. The article appeared above the fold on the front page that afternoon under the headline, "Westlake Boy, 15, Is Killed by Car While on Bicycle." The opening sentence summed it up: "A 15-year-old Westlake youth was run down and killed instantly this morning while delivering papers on his bike near his home." The only photos that appeared were Steve's school picture and three taken at the scene: one of Steve's damaged bicycle, one of the damaged car, and one of the police measuring the skid marks.

The call from the H.K. Ferguson Company reached Dad in Rio at about eleven in the morning, Rio time. The message from the company's president simply said: "One of your sons was killed in an accident. Return home on next plane!" Dad would write later that day, "The words that came over the phone were dull stunning hammer blows against my brain." While he waited for his ride to the airport, "I rested my head on my desk, prayed for strength from above, and cried a bit." He described what happened next in a letter he would write to me twenty-three years later:

> At 11:40 a.m. a company Jeep and a crazy Brazilian driver left the [company's] office to make the Pan-Am noon flight to New York's Idlewild Airport [now JFK]. Instead of following the paved roads to the airport, and mingling in with noon traffic in Rio, we drove as the crow flies—across public parks, through parking lots, wrong way on one-way streets, construction sites, and arrived ten minutes late! But the plane was still there, waiting for me! I ran through "Check in," grabbed my pre-arranged ticket to Cleveland, sailed up the boarding ramp and collapsed into the first empty seat I saw. After we were

airborne the stewardess brought me a large Bourbon on the rocks, remarking that perhaps it would help me relax! But it was impossible to relax when faced with 13 hours in the air thinking about which one of my sons was killed, how did it happen, was it Tom? Where did it happen, why do I think it was Steve? No answers! Then I began comparing personalities, habits, strengths, weaknesses, etc., and I concluded that there was no reason in the world for God to take either one of my sons out of our family without my prior approval. From New York to Cleveland, as I sat in the co-pilot's seat in the company plane, I cried angry tears against God for letting such a thing happen to our "wonderful family"!

Dad was met at the Cleveland airport late that night by Pastor Streufert. Without even so much as a "Hello," Dad asked, "Which one?" He had to know which son was gone, which was still alive. When he arrived home at 3250 just after midnight, he knew I was the son he would find sleeping, not Steve. He came up to my room. I felt the mattress move as he sat down on the edge of my bed. I woke up. I had not allowed myself to feel anything until that moment. He wrapped his long arms around me, and we both began to cry.

Earlier that first evening, Mom told me a phone call had come from Terry Fibich, my buddy from grade school. Since the time of my Skip five years earlier, Terry and I saw a lot less of each other. He was one year behind me at Lutheran West, but we still saw each other at church on Sundays. To escape the rustle of muffled conversations in the living room among the many friends who had come to express condolences and bring food, I went to the quiet of my parents' downstairs bedroom to call him back. I dialed Terry's number. His mom answered. She expressed her sympathy about Steve, asked how I was doing, then called for her son.

When Terry got to the phone, he said, "Hi. How are you doing? You okay?"

"Well, y'know. That's hard to say. I guess you know the news by now, hunh?"

"Yeah, I heard in school today. The news spread like wildfire before first period. When I didn't see you before school, I thought maybe you were sick. Boy, I wish now that you were out sick and not 'cause of this."

"Yeah, well, I guess I'm not sick."

"So what happened? Do you know what happened to him?"

"I'm not completely sure. Nobody seems to know. Best we can tell, he was riding his bike, doing his papers, and got hit by a car. I guess he was dead just about right away."

"Man, I can't believe it!"

I was silent, my empty voice spilling over into the telephone line.

"But y'know," Terry continued, "it may actually be better that he died because if it had been less severe, he may have lived but be completely paralyzed and maybe a whaddya call it, a quadriplegic. That could have been even worse than his dying. Maybe it's better this way. At least you know he's not suffering."

"Yeah, maybe you're right."

As harsh as they might seem, Terry's words were a modicum of comfort to me. Here was someone in my world willing to talk about the accident. I can't recall anyone in our living room that evening who seemed able to mention Steve to me, to talk about what had happened, or to ask me what I had seen and heard that morning on Columbia Road.

Before I went to bed that night, I opened the little black day book I was using as a diary that year and wrote: "Steve is dead. God, I guess, decided our family needed a faith strengthener—something to bring us closer together. A whole lot of people came today. I stayed home from school. Dad is coming right home—tonight. Many relatives are coming."

BY THE NEXT MORNING, the weather had turned. An autumn chill rolled in overnight with clouds and wind, bringing rain mixed with a few snow flurries. The wind tugged more leaves from the trees, swirling them up into tiny eddies in the driveway. My *Plain Dealer* supervisor had told us they would take care of my route until I was ready to start back. It might seem that going back to school the day after my brother died would be the last thing a fourteen-year-old needed to do, but this fourteen-year-old needed to return to some semblance of normalcy and routine.

Dad gave me a ride. The first person I saw when I walked into the building was Mr. Greve, a social studies and religion teacher whose no-nonsense, results-oriented approach also made him a successful basketball coach. He was manning the school store in the main lobby that day. When he saw me, he said, "Tom, you did not have to come to school today." I uttered a muted assent, my usual response to an authority figure's voice, but inside I knew Mr. Greve could not possibly have understood how much I needed to be in school that day. I needed to begin building my life—the After Steve chapters. Staying home would have felt like hiding.

That afternoon, the house was a bustle of activity—church friends bringing even more food, relatives arriving, people sitting around the living room, so unsure of how to talk about what had happened that any other topic was a welcome diversion. Our Ford station wagon was parked in the garage with one tire flat and a spare in need of repair. Dad and I were puzzling out what to do about it when Roy Hagedorn, a good friend from church, showed up. Roy offered to take both the flat and the spare to his friend's auto shop and get them fixed. He left with the tires, and Dad pulled down the overhead garage door from the inside.

In the darkened garage that late autumn afternoon, he put his arm around my shoulders and pulled me towards him. As I leaned my head on his chest and felt the shake of his sobs, I knew it was okay once again for me to cry, just as I had when he came home the night before. Tears of grief for our family's sudden loss. Tears of relief for the love and support pouring out to us from all directions. And tears for the boy we knew and loved as son and brother who was now gone.

Our shared loss brought me closer to Dad than I had been in years. It felt strange and new with Steve missing from the trio. So many times I'd looked forward to Steve and me helping Dad split and stack firewood or Dad taking us to the movies or to an Indians game. Just me and Steve tagging along with our tall, confident Daddy. I longed to hold onto my father and the bond that drew us together, but I felt somehow compelled to take Steve's place in my father's eyes, to somehow *be* Steve while still trying not to lose myself. It was during that brief time we were alone together in the garage that he told me that he and Mom had visited the morgue earlier in the day. He spared me the details, simply telling me that Steve "really took a beating" when he was hit.

SUNDAY MORNING was church, the twenty-first Sunday after Trinity. The service bulletin listed the sermon title as "A Glimpse into Our Resurrection" and noted that the anthem "Willing Gifts for Christ, Our King" would be sung by the Cherub Choir during the collection. Among the bulletin announcements was this:

> ASLEEP IN JESUS. Stephen Alan, son of Albert and Charlotte (nee Zucker) Zink, was called to his eternal home on Thursday morning, October 19, at the age of 15 years and 10 months. Christian burial will be given from our church tomorrow morning at 10 o'clock. Condolences may be extended the family at the Jenkins Funeral Home on Dover Center Road this afternoon from 3 to 5 o'clock. May our gracious Lord comfort the family with His loving promise, "I will not leave you comfortless."

We drove to the funeral home that afternoon. I recall so little of those two hours that I wonder if I was ever really there at all. Displayed on an easel was a poster Mom had assembled of photos of Steve. The closed white casket rested on a stand against the back wall. Friends and relatives gathered in small clusters, chatting quietly. I sensed I was not the only one who expended a great deal of energy trying to hold emotions in check. But when I saw Wayne Peters walk in with his family, my feelings surfaced. The quivering of my lips and the catch of my breath signaled to me that I was not alone in my grief.

Wayne and Steve had been friends since they played together in the St. Thomas church nursery fifteen years earlier. They were classmates from kindergarten at West Shore Lutheran School right through to their junior year at Lutheran High School West. I knew Wayne's family would come to Steve's wake. What shook me was seeing them walk in. The simple fact of their presence was a grace for me at that moment. Wayne came over to me with tears in his eyes, and we hugged. Words were superfluous. The agony of grief is to bear it alone. But in that moment I cherished my good friend's companionship.

MONDAY MORNING dawned bright and sunny without a cloud to mar the blue sky. Steve's funeral was to start at ten o'clock. By nine o'clock our living room at 3250 was packed with my family and all of our out-of-town relatives. Just before we all left for the drive to the church, Dad read this brief meditation he had written:

> Before we all leave for the funeral service and burial of our dear son, brother, nephew and grandson—let us all stand just a little taller today and from now on, knowing that each of us has had a part in this boy's brief passage through life, and though we have had a little part or a big part, we can smile through our tears knowing that each influential act or work in his behalf—be it a mere, "Hello Steve," or a fatherly discourse on the pitfalls of teenage life—has added, little by little to the ultimate angelic stature which he has now achieved.
>
> May God give us all strength, courage and especially the insight to draw our spiritual motivation from the fact that we walked and talked with one of God's elect.

My family was driven to St. Thomas church in a funeral home limousine. When we arrived at the church, we were directed to a separate room to wait until the service was about to start. The church filled quickly. Students and teachers from the high school were permitted to leave school to attend. The high school choir was there to sing the funeral anthem, J.S. Bach's "Art Thou with Me." Many members of the St. Thomas congregation came as well. Dad remembered later having "a secret feeling of pride" about the number of people who crowded into our church that Monday morning. Those who came were a silent witness to the many lives Steve had touched.

Two other people came whom none of us would have recognized had we known they were there. They entered quietly, were barely noticed, and left immediately after. They were the man who drove the car that struck Steve and his wife.

Every seat was taken when we processed in to the reserved pews in the front: my parents and sisters, Granny Zink and Opa and Oma Zucker, several aunts and uncles, and five of my cousins. I recall feeling shielded and protected in the company of these adult relatives who had traveled many miles to stand with us on this day. Most striking about this family procession down the center aisle was my mother's dress. A dramatic departure from the typical color of grief, the dress had a white background with brightly colored flowers.

My cousin, Marlise Anne Reidenbach, remembered that the service was "the funeral of a young boy, a tragic, sudden death, and Charlotte's dress spoke volumes about her faith. She was so quiet, yet without a single word or a single tear, she led us, she taught us what this ceremony was really about. It was just so remarkable to me that her dress was *so* lovely, a dress of joy and celebration." To Mom, this was Steve's "graduation" day, his homecoming, his triumphant return to his God in heaven. It was a dress worn by the same woman who, as a young girl in India, when informed of her little friend's death in mid-December said cheerfully, "Well, then, she will celebrate Christmas with Jesus in heaven!"

Midway through the service, Pastor Streufert stepped into the pulpit. He began his sermon by reminding us all of Steve's confirmation verse from the Book of Joshua. (See page 225.) The verse concludes with the words, "The Lord thy God is with thee withersoever thou goest." He declared that God kept that promise and offered words of comfort that Steve's death was not a sign that God had abandoned us but rather that God was very much present in the events of the past five days. But there were also words I found difficult to square with some of what I'd learned growing up in a religious family.

The pastor told us that God could have ordered his holy angels to stop the car on Columbia Road. Instead, he depicted God telling the angels, "Keep your hands off that car. I want that boy—now!" This clearly did not mesh with the comforting words I knew well from Psalms that assured me that God "shall give his angels charge over thee to keep thee in all thy ways." Wait a second, I thought. *All* thy ways? What about riding your bicycle on Columbia Road? Where were these keep-thee-in-all-thy-ways angels Thursday morning when that car came along?

The pastor also described Steve as one who "recognized his weaknesses and recognized his sin." I was a kid who was used to accepting the words of my elders, but this made no sense to me. Was he talking about the same Steve I knew? I took it all in and kept to myself the questions the pastor's sermon ignited. I wondered: Where was the God I had worshipped all my life? I had no one with whom to voice my questions.

The sermon that morning did give me a vivid image about how to live my life that has remained with me ever since. Describing how God has a plan for each individual, the pastor imagined God having given every person a banknote for each day. "And each day, God turns over the bank-note of time. How big is your stack? God knows when your last number is coming." God doesn't reveal it to us because God wants us to know "just like Steve, it can be tomorrow." And because we don't know when our stack will be gone, the pastor said, "God wants us to plan as though we'll live forever, but wants us to live as though we have to go tomorrow."

The combination of Steve's sudden death and the pastor's picture of my stack of "banknotes of time" gave me, at the age of fourteen, a keen sense of my own mortality. The pervasive adolescent myth of invincibility—that tragic losses such as ours only happen to other people—was effectively dispelled. The keen attention to safety and aversion to risk I had learned by this point in my life became even more deeply ingrained.

At the end of the sermon, the congregation stood to sing the hymn that expressed the essence of the pastor's message: "What God Ordains is Always Good." After the closing hymn, the six pall bearers—some of Steve's best friends, including Tim Fangmeier and Wayne Peters—came forward and assembled around the casket. They lifted it off its cart and carried it down the aisle, through the church doors and to the waiting hearse. We all followed them out of the church for the ride to the cemetery.

My parents, sisters, and I rode in the limousine that followed the hearse to Elmhurst Park Cemetery. I didn't know it at the time, but about ten years earlier, Dad and Mom had purchased four burial plots in this cemetery. I only learned some years later that they and many other German Lutherans may have taken advantage of a reduced-rate offer on burial plots that seemed too good to pass up.

Along the way to the cemetery, I remember sharing Dad's "secret feeling of pride" that Steve's funeral procession was so long that it stopped traffic at successive intersections. I was beginning to quietly internalize the harsh truth of my new reality as my parents' brother-less son. During those five days between Steve's death and his funeral, no one said to me, "Well, Tom, you've got a big responsibility now as the oldest child!" Although that idea had already begun creeping into my thoughts, I kept it to myself, assuming I would figure it out on my own. I waited for someone to ask me about what I'd seen and heard Thursday morning on Columbia Road—for the chance to ask questions and to talk. But no one asked.

At the cemetery, the pallbearers carried Steve's casket from the hearse to the grave site. Two lines of uniformed Boy Scouts from Steve's Troop 191 formed an honor guard standing at attention and saluting as the casket passed by. At the grave site, a canopy had been set up, under which our parents and grandparents could sit down out of the warm autumn sunshine while Pastor Streufert said the prayers and blessings. Granny Zink always carried a little white handkerchief in her purse. When a family visit in Baltimore was over, and our car was backing out of her driveway, she would wave the handkerchief in farewell. Sitting under the cemetery canopy, she held that handkerchief in her hand. As Steve's casket was being lowered into the ground, I caught a glimpse of Granny's handkerchief waving good-bye.

Other details are lost in the blur of things forgotten, except for the final moment at the cemetery. After Pastor Streufert pronounced the benediction, I remember hearing the sound of "Taps" played on a bugle as a special tribute to Steve's role as trumpeter in the school band. The bugler was standing behind some nearby trees, and I couldn't see him. It was as if the plaintive notes were emanating from the pine trees, the blue sky, and the sunshine on that warm October morning to bless these final moments with Steve: "Day is done, gone the sun, / From the lake, from the hills, from the sky, / All is well, safely rest, / God is nigh."

The assembled members of our extended family had traveled many miles to bring us their love, support, companionship, and to share our grief. It was time for them to return home. Our good friends from church, Roy and Barbara Hagedorn, hosted a farewell luncheon for them all. We said our good-byes to Granny Zink, Oma and Opa Zucker, the Springsteens, and our aunts and uncles, and wished them safe travels on their journeys home. After they had all departed, Dad drove Mom, my sisters, and me back home to 3250.

SIGNS OF OUR LOSS were everywhere at home. In my room was Steve's empty bed. In the garage was an empty place in the bike rack. At our round kitchen table, the seventh chair was soon moved to the basement. Going through

Steve's dresser a few weeks later, Dad found an old pair of socks in the back of his drawer, still pungent with what Dad called "the familiar odor of Liederkranz cheese." Dad said years later that it was the only time he ever cried over smelly socks.

Yet for all that was missing, Steve's presence remained. An eight-by-ten enlargement of his high school yearbook picture, mounted in a plain frame, was placed on the mantel above the fireplace. On a living room bookcase was the last model Steve made: a thirty-two-inch replica of the USS Constitution, "Old Ironsides," a three-masted frigate launched in 1797 that won major victories for the United States Navy in the War of 1812. The model kit contained more than 1,200 pieces ranging in size from the two halves of the hull down to the tiny eyebolts. The eyebolts anchored the yards of rigging Steve had cut from a spool of black thread. When Steve had finished it, Dad told him how proud he was of his patience and diligence.

A few weeks after his death, a large cubical package arrived in the mail addressed to Steve—a prize in an essay contest Steve had entered, in which he described the Battle of the Bulge as the most important battle of World War II. We opened the box to find Steve had won a six-volume set of Winston Churchill's *History of the Second World War.* Dad placed the books on the bookcase next to the "Old Ironsides" model.

Five days after the funeral, all six of us rode out to the cemetery. The grave marker—"Stephen Alan Zink, 1945–1961"—was already in place, surrounded by the colorful explosion of flowers from Monday's funeral. Mom placed a new bouquet of fall mums into the metal vase next to the marker while Judi carefully poured water into it. Mom said a short prayer, thanking God for Steve's life with us and asking God to keep us strong in faith and to be present with us as we learned to live without our son and brother. Dad mentioned that, following this experience, we might feel a tendency to let our lingering fear immobilize us and keep us from ever wanting to venture outside again. I remember a clear sense among us all that this was not how we wanted to live our lives.

Donations in Steve's memory poured in to the church. After some discussion with Pastor Streufert, Dad and Mom agreed on a memorial gift of a fifteen-foot-tall cross to be suspended high above the altar from the peak of the A-frame ceiling of the church. The cross, designed by Dad and constructed under his watchful eye, was an important healing project for him. The thick redwood crossbeams echoed the sturdy look of the laminated beams that supported the church roof. Narrow brass bars were inlaid into the center line of the two perpendicular cross-pieces to highlight the strong linear feature of the cross. This silent, yet majestic testimony to Steve's life was dedicated at the Sunday morning service on December 31, 1961.

My aunt Anne Springsteen had a very special connection with Steve. She was one of the first to arrive at 3250 on the day he died and was ever a calm, reassuring presence, despite her own grief. It was the combination of that grief and her deep faith in God that inspired Anne in the year following Steve's death to compose a free-verse poem that conveyed with eloquence and passion Steve's life as a child of God. "The Trumpeter, In memoriam, S.A.Z." was published in December 1962 in *The Cresset*, Valparaiso University's journal of commentary on literature, the arts, and public affairs. (See page 230.)

My parents made a practice of designing a Christmas card every December to send to relatives and friends, accompanied by a letter about the Zink family's year. Dad hand-lettered our 1961 communication, which he and Mom composed together. Written less than two months after their first-born died, it is a testimony to their faith, humility, and gratitude:

> Blessings: Through the years our friendship has been stronger and deeper because we share a faith and love in the Christ of the cradle and the Cross. It was this faith and love in the Child of Bethlehem that moved you to share our burdens when our beloved first-born was called home. We will long remember all the endearing evidences of your Christian love and sympathy—the gift in memory of Steve; meeting every need of ourselves and our guests; the overwhelming helpfulness at every turn. For all this we are deeply and humbly grateful. We pray the peaceful light of Christmastide will brighten your hearts and home and show you the Way through all your tomorrows. Love, Al and Charlotte

Mom and Dad planned for us all to visit Steve's gravesite on December 6, his sixteenth birthday. Mom bought some flowers during the day. The plan was to drive out to the cemetery as soon as Dad came home from work. It was a Wednesday night. I had a geometry project to finish and tests in my Latin and health classes the next day. If I went along to the cemetery, I told them, I'd never get the homework done. They were disappointed but allowed me to stay home while all three of my sisters went. If Mom's saying about "fast becoming what you are going to be" was true, the choice I made that night to stay home and finish homework, passing up a chance to visit Steve's grave, spoke volumes about what might lie ahead.

Stephen Alan Zink's grave marker in Elmhurst
Park Cemetery in Avon, Ohio. (photo credit:
Mike Kemper.)

In Memory

*"Be thou faithful unto death and
I will give thee a crown of life."*

Stephen Alan Zink, a student of the Junior Class, was born on December 6, 1945, in Cleveland, Ohio. He was received into the Savior's arms in Holy Baptism in January, 1946. Steve attended West Shore Lutheran School from which he was graduated in June, 1959. He then enrolled at Lutheran West.

Steve died suddenly in an automobile accident while delivering his papers on the morning of October 19, 1961. With his many gifts, Steve walked humbly before God and man and endeared himself to all.

Steve's parents, brother, and sisters live to praise God for his goodness to Steve, who now lives in heaven to praise the same God for the same goodness.

This page in memory of Steve appeared in the Lutheran High School West yearbook in spring 1962. The photo was taken in fall 1961, when Steve was fifteen years old and in the junior class.

5 Closing Down

THE EVENTS OF October 19, 1961, would soon define two kinds of people in my life: "before" people who had known Steve and knew me as his younger brother, and "after" people who did not know Steve. A girl named Carol, the daughter of a Lutheran pastor who had just moved to the Cleveland area, started at Lutheran West the day after the funeral, when I next returned to school. The empty locker assigned to her had been Steve's just a week earlier. She was the first of the "after" people, with whom I left Steve out of any conversation. I rarely, if ever, talked about Steve even with friends who did know him. We all knew what had happened, and nothing we might say to each other could change that.

I was a schoolboy at an age when fitting in with my peers was paramount. Before losing Steve, I sometimes felt different because I was short, skinny, and wore glasses, but I knew there were other kids like me. If I got teased for getting good grades, I could rest assured that I had friends who did as well. But when the difference was that my older brother had been killed suddenly in a car crash, there was a stunning uniqueness about it I could not escape. To minimize this unwelcome fact, I simply tried my best to freeze my personal story and act like the same guy I had always been. I didn't talk about Steve. No one asked about him, and life went on, seemingly pretty much as before.

When school was over that first day after the funeral, I walked to the edge of the school parking lot to wait for my mother and my sisters to pick me up in the car. It was not customary for Mom to pick me up; normally Steve and I rode the city bus home, but this was an unusual day. The big family station wagon pulled up, my three sisters in the back seat. I opened the passenger side front door, got in, and sat down. Judi was seven years old and had not yet grasped that our brother was gone for good. She piped up from the back seat with a very natural, innocent question, "Hey, where's Steve?" Always and forever in her world, she had two older brothers. Now there was just me.

I had no patience for her innocence. Any empathy was buried under my rage. I turned quickly in the front seat to glare at all three of them and, in a rare outburst of anger, yelled at Judi, "You *know* he's not coming!" A heavy, awkward silence fell over us for the rest of the fifteen-minute drive home.

Mom managed to say something to the effect that we were going to have to get used to not seeing Steve after school anymore.

My parents were strong models of forgiveness and grace. Two days after the family's cemetery visit on Steve's birthday, a Mr. Johnson came to visit them. I recognized his name; he was the driver of the car that had struck and killed Steve. His wife came with him, just as she had accompanied him to Steve's funeral. My parents said almost nothing ahead of time to my sisters and me about this meeting, so I had no idea at the time whether my parents or the Johnsons had initiated it. Many years later, I learned from Mom's younger sister, Irene Benson, that the Johnsons had asked to meet with Mom and Dad and that my parents had turned down the Johnsons' offer to pay for the funeral expenses. The simple fact that these two couples met and talked about the incident that had changed their lives in such a tragic and irreversible way bore witness to me of the Johnsons' courage and to my own parents' understanding of the healing power of forgiveness.

In the first weeks after Steve's funeral, it began to dawn on me that his place as the oldest child was vacant. I had big shoes to fill. I was now the oldest. Steve's death pitched me headlong into a role that fit me about as well as his size twelve Converse All-Star shoes or his size thirty-two-long blue jeans. Unlike the events in London in 1936, when King Edward VIII abdicated the throne and the British royal cloak fell on his younger brother, Prince Albert, who became King George VI, for me, there was no ceremony or recognition of my new status. There was just a silent, subtle turning into something I never wanted to be. Unprepared and ill-equipped, I nevertheless knew I needed to just get on with it and fill the void.

Like the Skip in elementary school, losing Steve in high school added another dimension of responsibility that I had to navigate, but this one came without a set of texts or any kind of chart. There was no book to live by now. I acted as if everything was fine, and I knew what I was doing. When you've got denial riding shotgun, honesty takes a back seat.

I slowly began to make myself over into an ersatz—or replacement—oldest child. My new identity cloak took over quickly. One week after the funeral, my mother wrote in a letter to relatives that "Tom has been so steady and calm through all of this—I think his witness of faith is going to be the strongest of all. In his gentle, pleasant way, he seems to have grown already to a more mature level." Her words are clear external evidence of my own sense of growing up fast. Yet I struggled to fit myself into the "oldest child" identity cloak that Steve had worn with such affable ease.

To appear steady, calm, and mature was nothing more than my attempt to fall in line with the received wisdom of the mature Christians in my life.

I tried to remain the familiar me, the obedient kid about whom my parents never had to worry. I was a good Lutheran boy, and the clear message I heard from the funeral sermon, the condolence cards, and our relatives' comforting words was that this all was God's will. A couple months after the funeral, my grandmother Oma Zucker wrote in a letter that "the absence of Stephen is still uppermost in our minds, and we have to grip our feelings firmly to not think only of ourselves and the loss for the present—but to God's promises. We must just submit to God's superior wisdom." It was not ours to ask "Why?" It was not ours to get angry at God. It was ours to accept the words we sang in the funeral hymn, "What God Ordains is Always Good."

The implicit message, as I understood it from all sides, was that I was to view my experience of sibling death from the mature perspective of the young man I was fast becoming, not from the perspective of the child I no longer was. Steve's death made me immune to surprises. The worst imaginable thing had happened; from here on, what could possibly shock me?

MY DREAMS of a bright future as a basketball star rested on making the junior varsity team that was made up of sophomores as well as any freshmen who showed outstanding skill. The coach was Mr. Greve, the teacher who had greeted me at school with such genuine concern the day after Steve died. He worked us hard in the pre-season practices. My legs ached, and my lungs burned from the wind-sprints. But I was sure I would make it, just as I'd been sure after my Little League tryouts five years before. Then, two freshmen— much taller, stronger, and more athletic than Rich or me—joined the practices and were selected for the team. The school had only twelve uniforms. Rich and I were cut.

Mr. Greve invited Rich and I to become equipment managers—in other words, uniform-washers, ball boys, and scorekeepers. It felt like a humiliating descent from playing to managing. But the lure of tracking player statistics, calculating scoring averages, and riding the team bus to away games—all so I could be immersed in the magnetic energy of competitive team sports—convinced me to take the job. I became a vociferous fan from my place behind the scorer's table, tracking each player's attempted shots, successful shots, and rebounds.

Under Mr. Greve's no-nonsense tutelage, the junior varsity team won sixteen of its eighteen games that year and was thus the most successful sports team with which I had ever been associated. In the reflected glow of such a spectacular season, I tried with mixed success to ignore the Eeyore whispers in my mind—"Yes, Zink, but remember that 16–2 wasn't because of you; *you* were just an equipment manager."

Although I never wore a team uniform after my freshman year, I still looked up to those who did, and I kept working on my game. I spent most of my free time at home in the driveway, shooting baskets. Even in the middle of a February thaw, when a warm day melted the snow on our driveway, I was outside dribbling and shooting the wet ball, retrieving errant shots from the snow piles. Being on our court was a tonic for me. It allowed me to be alone, to be active outdoors, and to improve athletic skills that I valued.

MY FAMILY'S NEW NORMAL without Steve was interrupted by a generous offer from Dad's company. His expertise was needed on a job in Paris, and Mom was invited to go with him for several weeks. At first, she could muster little interest in the prospect of travel but later agreed to go, thinking that some time away from home and routines might give her perspective. They left for Paris on February 22, 1962, and my sisters and I were farmed out to the homes of church friends, each of us to a different family. I moved in with the family of Terry Fibich, my grade school buddy who had called me the day Steve died. The Fibiches were good to me, but their house wasn't home. I missed my parents and my sisters, my bed, my paper route, and our dog Heidi. Terry and I began to get on each other's nerves. I was depressed and homesick.

Delays kept Mom and Dad in Paris longer than expected. Beset with worry, I made silly mistakes. A letter I wrote to my parents was returned by the post office the next day. I'd forgotten to add the essential word "France" to the address. One morning I came down to breakfast, unaware that I had buttoned my shirt incorrectly until Terry's dad pointed out the crooked front of my shirt. Diary entries tell the anxious tale: "I wanna go back home. I think I'm getting kinda homesick." "I wish Mom and Dad would let us know when they're coming back—at what exact time." "I was tense all day, hoping and praying they'd come home tonight." Mom did come home, three weeks after she left. Dad returned six days later.

I COULD HANDLE most schoolwork with relative ease. Figuring out on my own how to ask a girl out on a date was a different story. Steve had had several dates with a girl in his class, but I no longer had him to turn to for advice. I was a rookie at relationships. My first date was a gift; a girl in my class invited me to the annual girls-ask-boys Sadie Hawkins Day dance. This seemed to me a sure-fire way to fit in, but from then on, my timidity and self-doubt dueled with my longing for other dates.

A wobbly little vicious circle soon developed: I'd reason that calling that week's girl of my dreams on the telephone when I was at home in the evening would be less threatening to my fragile ego than asking her face-to-face in school. I would pick up the phone—my heart pounding—dial the first three numbers, then put the phone down. I'll just wait, I reasoned, until I see her at school, where I'd feel more nonchalant and relaxed (read "cool"). The next day in school, when I saw the object of my intentions—heart racing again—I'd realize that if I walked right up and asked her, she might very well look at me like I'd just asked her to gargle with a mouthful of carpet tacks and walk away. I'd postpone again and retreat to my phone call strategy as being the safer way to go. It took the better part of a year, but I did eventually manage to interrupt the cycle and experience the surprise and relief of asking a girl out and hearing her say, "Okay."

My parents never let me get too lost in the swamp of normal, everyday teenaged stress, though. They gave me space to figure out that my angst *du jour* would soon pass but were ready with support when I needed help. When I was sick in bed with the flu, Mom got up early and delivered my papers. When I was confused by an algebra assignment, Dad sat down with me and gave me a hand. With deadlines looming on three school assignments one evening, Mom stepped in and typed up the book report I had to hand in the next day.

Toward the end of my junior year, I decided to run for student council treasurer. To do so, I had to recruit another student as my campaign manager. My pessimism about my prospects for being elected grew as several friends turned me down. On the evening before the deadline to sign up, my mother listened patiently as I whined hopelessly about my desperate situation. When I calmed down, a new name popped into mind. A senior, the top student in his class, agreed to be my campaign manager. He gave his nomination speech to the school assembly the next day, dressed in a lab coat, extolling his candidate as the "element" the student council needed as its treasurer. Posters soon went up around school with my name spelled "Zinc." I never found out if it was an oversight or done with the chemical pun intended, but it didn't matter: I won the election by a slim margin. With student council treasurer now on my resume, I felt closer to being part of the "in" crowd.

DAD LOVED TO PLAY GOLF and used our large backyard to practice his short iron shots. The summer after Steve died, he bought me a second-hand set of golf clubs and took me along to play nine holes at a nearby par-three course. His encouragement and tutoring inspired me. We went together to the driving range to work on our tee shots. One of my fondest memories of the following summers was getting up before sunrise with Dad on many Saturday mornings, playing eighteen holes of golf, and arriving back home by ten in the morning, about the time my three sisters were just waking up. He found time to take me to an occasional movie, play ping pong in the basement, and show me how to change a tire on the car.

But my father was still the guy whose 1941 college yearbook picture was accompanied by a line, "Al can dish it out," that neatly summed up his love of ribbing his classmates. It was the way his male world operated in his college days and still did in his professional field. But the friendly fire of good-natured joshing requires a two-way street. With my dad I was on a one-way street, but there were rare—and memorable—exceptions.

On Thanksgiving Day in 1963, I was invited to play the tympani for a choir anthem at a Lutheran church in Cleveland. The whole family came to the service. On the drive home afterwards, the streets were nearly empty. Dad repeatedly pumped the brakes until someone said, "Hey, stop it!" Dad replied, "We should be *thankful* for the brakes." Then he steered right and left and right and left, not endangering us, but having fun. Mom said, "Al, you're setting a bad example," to which he replied, "*Thank* the Lord for good steering!" Bored and sitting behind Dad with my tympani sticks in hand, I absent-mindedly began tapping out a rhythm on the back of his seat. "Hey, cut that out. You're distracting the driver!" he said. I dropped my ingrained deference to Dad, and blurted out, "We should be *thankful* for rhythm and tympani sticks!"

I learned to live with Dad's style of humor and what seemed to be his insistence on perfection. I often felt like I was coming up short, despite my best efforts. One day, when Dad came home from work, I showed him the ninety-six marked on my algebra test, thinking he would be pleased. "You mean you didn't get a hundred?" he remarked, a putdown that he may have intended to be humorous but which I took as a critique. My best had not been good enough. I felt crushed and resolved to work harder.

While Dad's remarks could sting, I dared not fire back. He had a temper that could flare from zero to sixty in a matter of seconds and just as quickly simmer down. I was not one to stir the pot or rock the boat. So I kept my own anger and fear inside, where they grew into a deep well of resentments, which became a wall between us. It took me years to learn how to let his thoughtless comments fall harmlessly at my feet.

One evening at home my "steady and calm" veneer split open. In response to a scolding from Dad, I stomped up the steps, down the hall to my room, and slammed the door behind me. When Dad heard my door slam, he marched right up after me and strode down the hall to my room, his six-foot-six frame filling my doorway. He yelled at me for slamming my door. He was trying to extinguish my anger by expressing his own. The moment of irony was lost on us both. I retreated, apologized, and slunk off to finish my homework. He returned downstairs to his favorite living room chair, his nightcap, and his television program. Beneath our rough-on-the-surface behavior, abrading like two sheets of sandpaper rubbed together, lay two hearts so blanketed with grief from the death of Steve that neither of us could say the words that loomed like unholy ghosts in our family. Three simple words, never heard, though desperate to be spoken: "I miss Steve."

ON RARE OCCASIONS, something unexpected would appear and lead me back to remembering Steve. I injured my ankle playing basketball at home on my fifteenth birthday. The next day with my foot in a cast, I stayed home from school, and in the middle of the boring day, something on a living room bookshelf caught my eye: the reel-to-reel tape recording of Steve's funeral. I set it up on Dad's tape recorder and gave it a listen. Memories and a few tears trickled into my consciousness but little more. I put the tape back on the shelf and forgot about it.

About a year later, in February 1963, I felt an intuitive impulse to start transcribing Pastor Streufert's sermon at the funeral. Had I been asked at the time to explain my intention, words would have failed me. I suppose I may have felt that completing this project would please my parents, affirm their perception of me as the mature and responsible ersatz oldest and help me to hold on to some essence of Steve, whose memory I felt slipping away.

The work of writing the sermon out by hand, and then typing it, reminded me that the most telling part of Pastor Streufert's sermon was his portrayal of God's answer to the question on everyone's mind: Why? The message seemed clear: The Almighty ruler of the universe was not answerable to humans. God did have a plan. Just because we didn't understand it did not mean there was no plan. Although I struggled with this, I settled uneasily into a resigned acceptance of something I could not comprehend.

I kept typing, determined to complete the very practical transcription task, not aware how much it was causing my perspective to shift. Sometime after I finished, I went back to my 1961 diary. The words I had written on the day Steve died—"God, I guess, decided our family needed a faith strengthener—something to bring us closer together"—now seemed like my feeble attempt to make sense of what had happened, to latch on to some explanation that could justify such an unspeakable tragedy. I crossed out those words and over top of them, I wrote, "His ways are unsearchable," acknowledging for the time being my acquiescence that the answer to "Why?" was inscrutable.

I kept my doubts safely tucked inside in deference to the early Sunday school lesson that cast a negative light on my namesake, "doubting Thomas." The faith I had come to know left little space for questioning. Within our highly churched family structure, I seldom tried to talk my way out of going to church, the Sunday youth Bible class, or our church youth group. Church was a familiar place in the changed landscape of my life. The hymns, the prayers, my friends, and the building itself with Steve's memorial cross, front and center, kept me grounded.

In the summer of 1963, this entry appeared in my diary:

> I believe I've figured out why I can't seem to get a job. Steve always would do something before I did, sorta lead the way. I seldom did something he hadn't done. Now that he's gone, I still depend on someone to lead me, but no one's there to do it. I can't seem to lead myself. This seems to go for asking for dates, inviting someone over to our house, going somewhere, most everything. And at home in the summer, oh, how I really miss him. Sometimes not so much like during the school year. But now, I wish he were here.

I wrote this about twenty months after Steve died. I had just finished my junior year of high school. Almost all my diary jottings were about facts and events, like sports scores, homework demands, Dad's trips, weather, but seldom about feelings and never about missing Steve, so this entry was significant. I was aware that Steve had been my leader. Steve always stood ahead of me, casting a shadow that I was content to stand within. I ping-ponged back and forth between my desire to continue seeking safety in the shadow and the clear knowledge it was now up to me to lead.

Growing up fast brought some changes in my hobbies and lifestyle. First, I gave up my paper route. I was busy being an honor roll student, student council treasurer, school newspaper co-editor, basketball team manager, and Walther League officer. It was time for me to stop being known as a paper boy. I missed neither the meager weekly earnings nor the pre-dawn alarm bell.

By the age of sixteen, I had chewed my way through unnumbered pounds of Topps bubble gum sticks to obtain my treasure trove of baseball cards. My attachment to them was visceral. I had spent hours poring over the statistics printed on the back of each card, memorizing highlights of my favorite players' stellar seasons. In the first couple summers after Steve was gone, I created an elaborate fantasy baseball league with teams built from my collection of cards. Using a board game called All-Star Baseball, I staged my own mini-baseball season and kept detailed statistics, learning to calculate batting averages in my head. My baseball cards were my companions in my now brother-less bedroom. But in the summer before my senior year, I packed them up and gave them away—at no cost—to the boy who lived next door. I was no longer a child; I was putting away childish things. At the time, I felt no particular sense of loss. Today it is a far different story. I rue the day I sacrificed the lot of them in the service of my limited concept of maturity.

"THE WORLD STANDS ASIDE to let anyone pass who knows where he is going." This quote by David Starr Jordan, an early twentieth-century American scientist, university president, and peace activist, was chosen by the high school yearbook editors to accompany my senior picture in the yearbook. When I first read this quote, flattering as it was, I took it as a misprint. They had the wrong guy. If the yearbook committee truly thought these words described me at the age of seventeen, then I had surely put one over on them. My reaction to the quote showed the internal disconnect between the ersatz oldest image I'd been able to sell to the world and the shadow-seeker I still was at heart.

Lutheran West graduation ceremonies took place in the school gymnasium. Each year, the top students gave short speeches. My good friend Dave Manke and I were chosen to speak, and we processed together as the school band played the austere cadences of Elgar's "Pomp and Circumstance." This was a serious occasion. Our facial expressions reflected the gravitas of the moment. Standing in the front row of the audience right on the aisle was Mr. Kunze, the chairman of the Lutheran West school board and a family friend I knew well from church. As I strode past him, trying to look as solemn and grown up as I could, he leaned out towards me and said in a stage whisper, "Smile!" Easy for you to say, I thought. I didn't smile in that moment. I had a speech to give to the crowd.

As I walked up the steps to the stage and took my seat next to Dave, I thought about how Steve's death meant it was up to me to be the first in our family to experience this rite of passage. One year prior, Steve would have been more relaxed than I was, free of the responsibility I had to address the crowd. My ersatz oldest child identity cloak weighed heavily on me as I anticipated standing to speak. Mr. Kunze would not have needed to tell Steve to smile.

The ceremony proceeded. I pulled myself out of my daydream, walked to the podium, and delivered my speech. When we were all official graduates, Dave and I stood with the assembled crowd to sing the Alma Mater, and, with our classmates, we walked out of the gym and on into the rest of our lives.

MY NEXT STEP IN LIFE was almost a foregone conclusion. Given my family's history at Valparaiso University, it was no surprise that the college where I wound up three months later was Valpo. It was the only school I applied to, and I ran out of space on the line where you list relatives who had attended. Besides my mother, two aunts, and two uncles, there were three first cousins and one second cousin. Ten other students of the eighty-three in my high school graduating class chose Valpo as well. Valpo was the place that best fit within the tightly-woven grid lines of my Lutheran upbringing.

The university president, Otto Paul "O.P." Kretzmann, was one of those Kretzmann brothers who twenty-five years earlier had signed the warrant on the back of a dinner menu that my Aunt Marlise *must* attend Valparaiso "or else." O.P. had been a friend of the Zink family for half a century, and, at a reception for new students, he warmly welcomed me to campus. He said he was delighted that I had chosen Valpo. Closer to the truth was that Valpo had chosen me.

On Labor Day weekend 1964, my family made the familiar turnpike trip to Valpo to give me the royal send-off to college. On the morning my parents and sisters were set to head back to Cleveland, an interesting thing happened. My whole family was gathered with the Springsteens near the car for farewell hugs and good wishes. I hugged my sisters and gave my mother a hug and a kiss, then turned to my father. He looked at me and said something I have never forgotten nor quite understood: "I'm gonna kiss you good-bye this one last time," he said, "because the next time I see you, you'll be a man."

Dad's sister Anne and her husband, Bob, both worked for the university at the time I enrolled. In my first two years on campus, I had a standing invitation to their house for Sunday night supper, the one meal a week not served in the dormitory cafeteria. It was the next best thing to being home for supper. Valpo kept me within the safe, familiar circle of the Lutheran Church Missouri Synod, but I was about to find out how much wider and more flexible that circle could be than the one I had known in my parents' household and at St. Thomas church.

As the circles of my world were widening, the number of "after" people in my life grew. Still trying to shape myself into the ersatz oldest, I kept my Steve story hidden. The only "before" people at Valpo who knew about Steve were my high school classmates and the Springsteens. Or so I thought. On a cloudy fall morning at the end of a theology class, I learned otherwise.

The professor, the Reverend Ed Schroeder, was an enthusiastic, dedicated Lutheran theologian, civil rights activist, and a friend of the Springsteens and my grandmother Zink. Granny had asked me to bring greetings to him. When I spoke with him after class, he recalled some wonderful times with Granny. He remembered meeting my parents once when our family visited Valpo. When he understood my relationship to Granny and made the connection that my dad traveled all over the globe to destinations that included South America, he said, "Then you must be the one whose older brother got killed in that weird accident." I said, "Yes, that's me." Although I was keeping my silence about Steve, this incident made clear to me that Steve was still being spoken about by people outside of my family. It was a relief to know that an "after" person like the Reverend Schroeder could know the story and respond with empathy without me initiating the conversation or eliciting the response.

I remember that morning with Reverend Schroeder because it was so rare to talk about Steve with anyone. Likewise, I also found a sense of companionship when the words of certain popular songs spoke parts of my story to me. I'd learn the words and commit the song to my musical jukebox. To listen to Paul Simon sing, "I Am a Rock," a song about emotional detachment that begins on a winter's day and ends with the simple assertion that "a rock feels no pain," reassured me that I was not alone in keeping my grief and pain to myself.

ONE FRIDAY EVENING during those first three months between my dad's farewell declaration and the late November Thanksgiving break, I overheard Jim and a couple other high school buddies talking in the dorm about going for a ride with Jim's older brother, Pete, a Valpo senior. Pete had a car and the identification card that proved he was twenty-one, Indiana's legal drinking age. We all piled into his car, and Pete drove to a package store in town, where he bought a couple six-packs of beer. I was nothing more than a seventeen-year-old literally along for the ride, anxious to fit in and try something new. My dad's severe restrictions at home had successfully kept me and alcohol at a distance. Pete drove back to campus and parked at the far edge of a parking lot in a quiet corner of the old campus, well away from the street lights.

Pete was our driver; he didn't drink. The rest of us did, and as we opened our beer cans, the snap of the pulled pop tops and hiss of carbonated fizz created the sound track of my tentative foray into manhood. I came to name these nights after the soft but firm order Pete gave when headlights of an oncoming car bathed our position: "Cans down," Pete whispered, as if people in a passing car could overhear him. We all stopped drinking, lowered our cans out of sight, and pasted nonchalance onto our faces. I came to know the buzz of having a beer with my buddies, but I went along more for the camaraderie than for the alcohol.

Even given the new freedom that came with my first time living away from home, Cans Down nights were rare exceptions. I kept to the well-manicured habits I'd brought with me from home. I made it to all my classes—even the ones that started at seven thirty in the morning—completed assignments on time, and attended daily morning chapel several times a week. Mine was the mildly mundane life of living up to external expectations.

I wrote frequent detailed letters home, just as my mother had to her parents. One letter was dated Tuesday, October 20, 1964, the day after the third anniversary of Steve's death: "Last night and Sunday night in bed, I pondered and mulled over the events of three years ago, how it doesn't seem it could have been that long ago, and the meaning it held for each of us." It was significant that even in a letter to my family, I did not mention Steve's name or feel I could be more specific in my reference to his death.

Two weeks later, a letter from my father arrived. His words reflected sentiments similar to my mother's right after Steve's death when she described me as steady, calm, and mature. Dad wrote:

> It occurs to me that your adjustments to varying life situations over the years have been a fine example of the progressive and panoramic maturing of a man. I am deeply proud of the fact that you have consistently put the deeper and more meaningful things in life before the shallower and more frivolous attractions.

Given his farewell remarks at the Springsteens two months earlier about "becoming a man," he may have been declaring in this letter that he thought I was already there. In his letters, Dad usually expressed himself in more flowery and complimentary language than he used in person. It filled me with a quiet pride to know his positive perceptions of me. But his glowing words told me that, like Mom, he could only see and respond to my ersatz oldest identity mask because he was unable to see beyond it to the shadow-seeker I still was.

Dad's letter didn't spell it out, but I figured that Cans Down nights would be considered one of the "shallower and more frivolous attractions," which meant he could not have been aware of my growing familiarity with the after-effects of alcohol. The occasional keg parties hosted by the fraternity I joined in my second year produced a couple nasty hangovers that quickly acquainted me with my limits. On the occasions when I did drink, I avoided more limit-testing. When I came home for holiday breaks, I felt like I had a dual identity. I had sampled the forbidden fruit of alcohol outside my father's awareness. But the fact that he saw me as an example of "the progressive and panoramic maturing of a man" was of little consequence. Dad's strict rules still held sway at home: If you were underage, forget it.

I was home for Christmas vacation in December 1967, a few months before I turned twenty-one. One evening our whole family was invited over by the Depperts, church friends who lived a few houses away. My dad, Mr. Deppert, and I were in their basement recreation room. Mr. Deppert stood behind the small bar at one end of the room and said, "Tom, would you like a beer?" Before I could utter a word in reply, my father piped up from across the room, "No, he can't. He's not twenty-one yet!" Dad's clear line about alcohol had not budged an inch, nor had his inimitable scolding tone. The rituals of enjoying a beer had been well portrayed by my father over the course of my life as almost a coveted adult sacrament. Apparently, even though he acknowledged how much I had matured, I was still not mature enough in his eyes to handle a beer. Had I known then what I learned years later about Dad's own teenaged adventure with alcohol—when he and his buddy Bobby Coles helped themselves to the family's wine decanters on a Sunday afternoon and then Dad fell asleep in the bathtub—I might have tried appealing to his sense of fairness. Instead, I accepted Mr. Deppert's offer of a Coke.

Three months later, back at Valpo, the Springsteens invited me over for dinner to celebrate my twenty-first birthday. With high anticipation of a special evening with this family that had been so generous with me in my time at Valpo, I arrived at their house and rapped loudly on the door to announce myself. To my complete surprise, standing inside to welcome me was my father. He had gone out of his way to arrange a business trip to Chicago so he could drive the two hours to Valpo and join us for our dinner celebration. His presence made the day even more special, and I fully trusted in the safety of his presence. I set my trusty old Ridiculometer to silent mode. Big mistake.

Dad took the Springsteen family and me out for a nice dinner at a restaurant. We all sat down at the table—Dad, at one end, and me, the birthday boy, at the other. The waitress came to take drink orders, and in a voice loud enough for everyone else in the restaurant to hear, Dad announced that I was now "legal" and could order any alcoholic drink I wanted. In his view, I had crossed that sacrosanct line. In mine, I was indeed twenty-one—far too old for such loud, ceremonial pronouncements—and so I felt like I was seven years old again, in the YMCA locker room being teased about my "bullet-hole" moles. I ordered a Coke.

Although Dad's rules and scoldings could scrape me raw at times, there were—literally—moments of harmony for my father and me. I bought my first guitar not long before I left home for Valpo and began teaching myself to play the songs of the most popular artists of the 1960s folk music revival—

Pete Seeger; Simon and Garfunkel; Gordon Lightfoot; John Denver; Bob Dylan; Tom Paxton; Peter, Paul, and Mary. I discovered I had a natural ear for melody, harmony, and chords.

When I was home at 3250 on summer vacation, Dad and I sometimes sat on the backyard patio in the evening, he with his harmonica, me with my guitar. His exhales and inhales lifted the high, lonesome strains of "Home on the Range," "Oh, Susanna," or "On Top of Old Smoky" into the night air. I strummed my guitar, following his rhythm. In church, Dad and I could both sing either the bass line or the tenor line of most hymns. When I stood next to him on Sunday mornings, we could listen to each other and, without a word or a nudge, intuitively settle into the part the other was not singing, in harmony with each other and with the rest of the congregation.

BY THE END OF MY SECOND YEAR at Valpo, I faced the deadline for declaring a major with no clear sense of a career goal. I had a vague interest in teaching, but knew I didn't want to be hemmed in by poorly-informed choices made before I was ready. By an alphabetical process of elimination—paging through the university catalog from art to zoology—I finally settled on a history major. With four required courses already completed, I was well on my way to meeting the requirements. With that decision finally made, I was again struck by the irony of my high school yearbook quote—"The world stands aside to let anyone pass who knows where he is going." I couldn't have articulated it then, but I wonder now how much the loss of Steve, my leader, hampered my ability to make choices that would have any long-term implications. I found a very clear and reassuring way to express my own uncertainty when I learned to play Tom Paxton's song, "I Can't Help but Wonder Where I'm Bound," a tune that would serve as a theme in my life for years to come.

I may have been adrift about my career direction at that time, but one thing that was crystal clear was my continuing passion for team sports. It never occurred to me that my love of sports and games could actually be a career direction—much too lightweight and un-intellectual for someone like me who had a reputation for academic excellence to uphold. My teenaged growth spurt had added about eight inches and forty pounds to my slender frame since the time I had failed to make the high school junior varsity basketball team. I was now respected as an athlete and played intramural sports on the fraternity teams—basketball, flag football, and softball.

I became a sports reporter and then sports editor for *The Torch*, the same student newspaper my mother had written for twenty-five years earlier. And I exuded vicarious pride in the success of Valpo's varsity basketball team, especially the year it ascended to the ranks of the top ten small college teams in the country. But the athletic experience that had the most impact on my life began innocently enough when I let myself be talked into playing for the Valparaiso Volleyball Club.

Volleyball lived outside the mainstream of the college sports world in 1967, when I began my senior year. I knew only the rudiments of the game and had minimal playing experience. But when a fraternity buddy named Bill Dehoff invited me, with a hint of urgency in his voice, to join the team, I agreed to give it a try as a favor to a good friend. He was nearly desperate to fill out a ten-man roster, so I was assured a place on the team.

As a so-called club sport, the volleyball team got free weekly use of a small practice gym, hand-me-down school uniforms, and no university funding. I faced a steep learning curve. The basic skills of the game—bumping, setting, and spiking—were different enough from the more familiar skills of basketball that it took me a couple months to feel comfortable using them in practice. I worked hard to improve, motivated by this chance to play on a school team and wear the school uniform.

When the tournament season began, we paid our own way to places like Muncie, Indiana; Milwaukee, Wisconsin; and Chicago, Illinois. A tournament at Ohio State University in Columbus, Ohio, gave me an unforgettable athletic thrill. Wearing the team uniform of Valparaiso University, I played volleyball at St. John's Arena, on the same floor where my heroes on Ohio State University's 1960 national champion basketball team played their home games.

When we headed off to tournaments, we did it for the experience. Most of us were new to the game, and we had no illusions about winning. Our goal was simply to improve each time. This attitude allowed me to loosen my neurotic fixation on final scores and my self-imposed sports "loser" label so I could appreciate the opportunity to learn by playing against better teams. At a tournament in Milwaukee, we won one game of the eight we played but learned far more than anyone could have taught us by watching teams with top-notch players who would go on to become All-Americans and United States Olympians. Little did I suspect then how my increasing skill and passion for volleyball would impact my life in the next few years.

I SPENT MOST OF THE SUMMER before my final year at Valpo in California on a quixotic working holiday adventure with a fraternity brother. Our idealistic goal was to earn enough money to make it through the summer on our own. The only work we could find, however, was farm labor, which meant boarding the farm buses well before sunrise with the black, Chicano, and Filipino migrant workers. On the few days we were able to roust each other out of bed in time, we worked alongside the migrant workers in the hot fields and orchards of the San Joaquin Valley.

We heard a lot of Spanish and very little English. We picked boysenberries and apricots, earning about five dollars a day, barely enough to pay for our room at the YMCA, a morning vending machine coffee, and supper at an all-you-can-eat buffet. With my money running out, I made a collect call home. Beyond my money worries, I was anxious about asking Dad for help, knowing that his tendency to make thoughtless fun at my expense could easily deflate our whole California Dreamin' scheme. I was in for a surprise.

"Hello, Dad. It's Tom."

"Hey, how are you...*where* are you? Things going okay?"

"Well, we're in Stockton, staying at the Y for now, and, no, things aren't so good. The only work we've found is farm labor, and I'm running out of money. But we don't want to give up yet."

"No, don't do that. Too early to quit this thing."

Dad readily agreed to wire fifty dollars to me in Stockton. I thanked him, and he reassured me things would work out okay. The last thing he said was, "And, hey, keep the faith, baby." These final words were an echo of a hip phrase from the late 1960s, but I heard them not as a cliché but as a sincere show of support, even solidarity, with me for taking the risk to venture somewhere new and unknown.

Our experiment lasted less than two months. I had seen a side of life heretofore foreign to me. As a kid in Rocky River, diversity meant playing with the neighbor boys who went to Catholic school. In high school, the only black person I knew drove one of the school buses. When I left the white, middle-class German Lutheran enclave of my youth to attend Valpo, I was fairly oblivious to the issues of racial discrimination, bigotry, and civil rights. My first three years at Valpo had exposed my sheltered naiveté to the light. I once wrote home that I could "feel my outlooks and insights on life widening all the time." The summer experience in California not only made me aware of my own concern and empathy for others who lacked the privilege and benefits I took for granted, it also inadvertently prepared me for a new academic and social challenge.

WHEN O.P. KRETZMANN became president of Valpo in 1940, he challenged the university to respond to the pressing social issues of the times, in particular civil rights and racism in the Lutheran church. In 1959, he recruited to Valpo a man who would be instrumental in its social mission—and who would also irreversibly alter my outlook on the world. Reverend Karl Lutze came to campus to join the staff of the Lutheran Human Relations Association, a pioneering civil rights organization at Valpo, and to teach in the Theology Department. In his early ministry, Pastor Lutze had ministered to several black Lutheran churches in Oklahoma. Segregation in Missouri Synod churches was a harsh fact of life, especially in the 1950s South, and the fact that Pastor Lutze was white made his an unconventional ministry.

In an article in *The Cresset*, the university's journal of commentary on literature, the arts, and public affairs, James W. Albers attributed Lutze's success to his "congenial personality, his energy, his method of dealing with challenging situations, and his deep compassion for people." Lutze's wife, Esther, played an active role in his ministry with her engaging friendliness, her ready laugh, and her loving care for others. Soon after arriving at their first congregation in Muskogee, Oklahoma, the Lutzes learned the custom that wives of white pastors in black churches only took Holy Communion in white churches. Esther ignored the tradition, kneeling at the Communion table along with the black members of her husband's church.

As luck would have it, I met Karl and Esther Lutze long before I became a Valpo student. The Lutze family moved to Valparaiso in 1959 and bought a house right next door to the Springsteens. On our family visits with the Springsteens, I became friends with Karl and Esther and their oldest son, Peter, who was my age. It was a fortunate coincidence that I had an impromptu visit with Karl shortly after returning to campus from my California adventure. I had walked over to the Springsteens for a visit, and as I passed the Lutze's house, I happened to see Karl outside working in his garden. He asked about my summer and was eager to hear about our California Dreamin' weeks out west. Then he told me about a new course he was teaching called "The Church and the Race Issue" and encouraged me to take it.

On course registration day, I saw Esther at Karl's campus office. She took me aside and said, "Tom, you need take Karl's course. It will change your life." The timing seemed improbable yet elegant: a course on racism in the church right after my California summer among the migrant workers. I signed up. Esther soon became my cherished friend and guardian angel. She told me she would look over Karl's shoulder when he was grading class essays to make sure he marked mine with an "A."

ONE OF THE MAJOR ASSIGNMENTS in Pastor Lutze's class was to visit a black church and write a report about the experience. Pastor Lutze helped make arrangements for a classmate named Gary and me to visit a Lutheran church in Chicago. We drove the two hours from Valpo that Sunday morning and talked about what we thought it would be like. This was new for both of us. We found the church and were a little nervous as we made our way to the front door. Gary nudged me and nodded into the sanctuary as we walked in. We were the only white people in sight. Our initial anxiety was blown away by the warm welcome we received. We were treated as honored guests and encouraged to stand up and introduce ourselves to the whole congregation at the beginning of the service.

After church, we went home with the pastor and his family for Sunday dinner. We told them about Pastor Lutze's course. We listened as he and his family members shared some of the challenges and blessings at their church. I found myself drawing comparisons with Sunday dinners at the Zink home. Like most of my friends' moms whom I knew from our church, my mother exuded an upbeat sweetness in her manner. This was the tone she modeled at our Sunday dinners: pleasant, positive conversation, and good manners. All this was true of our dinner with the pastor's family with one exception: The pastor's wife spoke with firm conviction and evident bitterness about the many injustices endured by the members of their church. While I do not recall specifics, I will never forget how stunned I was. For the first time I saw clearly the gaping divide between the lives of white church folks and the lives of black church folks.

I brought my new sensibilities about religion and race home with me on my Christmas break. To complete another assignment in Pastor Lutze's course, I requested an appointment time with Pastor Streufert to discuss some of what I was learning about race relations within the Lutheran church. The meeting was cordial enough, though I must have seemed to him a St. Thomas product who had gone off to Valpo and been radicalized. Pastor Streufert was content with the status quo, and I left feeling more disillusioned than angry or frustrated. I was changing, but my home church was not. I was beginning to see that it was next to impossible to bring home the sometimes stirring new things I was learning when I was away. The church of my youth represented to me all that was unchangeable, closed-minded, and owned by older generations not mine.

THE FOURTH YEAR OF COLLEGE in the United States meant decision time. Like so many others I was now facing the question, "What next?" Do I play the job market, take whatever I can get? Should I sign up for a master of arts in teaching program? What about the third option I'd begun to consider in the past year of volunteering in the Peace Corps? Created by President Kennedy in March 1961, the Peace Corps was a United States government program through which American volunteers were sent overseas to share their skills, promote peace and friendship, and improve cross-cultural understanding in developing countries.

The Peace Corps offered a concrete and positive way for idealistic young Americans to respond to the challenge Kennedy had made in his January 1961 inaugural address: "Ask not what your country can do for you; ask what you can do for your country." The appeal of his visionary legacy may have been heightened in the aftermath of his assassination in late 1963, which was still very much on the public's mind. The attraction of altruism plus adventure drew thousands into the Peace Corps: the number of overseas volunteers reached a peak of fifteen thousand in June 1966. My interest was piqued when two fraternity friends of mine, both a year ahead of me, joined the Peace Corps and were assigned to Latin American countries. Their occasional letters mailed to the fraternity house made this option become very much alive for me.

The idea of serving my country in the Peace Corps fit well with my ancestral heritage and my grandfather Opa Zucker's missionary experiences—and his father and grandfather before him. These men had set an example of service beyond the borders of their homelands. My own parents' years of service in the community and the church were much closer to home but no less of an influence on my attitudes. I submitted the Peace Corps application. In the succeeding months, I took the Peace Corps' Language Prognosis Test, underwent a thoroughly invasive physical exam at a military medical station in Chicago, and was subjected to a full-field FBI investigation, in which strange men in suits roamed around campus asking some of my friends pointed questions, such as whether I was a racist or a closeted Communist.

It was at about this time that I noticed one of the Peace Corps' promotional posters in the Student Union. It was a simple photo of a glass of water and started with the proverbial question: "Is the glass half empty or half full?" Then came the Peace Corps challenge: "If you think it's half empty, maybe the Peace Corps is not for you. If you think it's half full, you've got the first thing we look for in Peace Corps people. Optimism. If you want to know more about what it takes to pass muster in the Peace Corps, write us." I was beginning to get excited about this new opportunity. I was able to set aside my long-standing Eeyore sensibilities and to re-imagine myself as one of those optimists the Peace Corps wanted. Not long after, someone in the Peace Corps office read my application and decided that I did indeed pass muster.

The letter informing me that I had been selected to train for Peace Corps service arrived in January 1968. I was to be one of hundreds of English-as-a-second-language teachers the Peace Corps needed in a country called

Micronesia. I was majoring in history with a minor in geography but had never heard of such a place. The letter gave no clues. First I thought I had read "Malaysia," so I looked that up in a world atlas. Close by, on a map of the Pacific Ocean, I located Polynesia, Melanesia, and Indonesia. Micronesia was nowhere to be seen.

Finally, my finger found the letters of "Micronesia," spread out across an area on the map so large it was easy to overlook that they even spelled a word. But there they were, tiny dots located somewhere north of the equator and west of Hawaii. I learned that "Micronesia" means "tiny islands." And tiny they were, scattered like a couple thousand lily pads across an expanse of ocean the size of the continental United States. If you could gather up and paste together all 2,100 of the Micronesian islands, you would have an island half the size of Rhode Island, the smallest state in the United States. Just one hundred of the islands were inhabited with a total population in 1968 of about 100,000. It was to one of these microscopic places I seemed destined to go.

After the Peace Corps acceptance letter came, I still felt in limbo about my decision. One snowy, winter morning between classes, I made one of my frequent visits to Heritage Hall and the office of my aunt, Anne Springsteen, who was now the university editor. The oldest building on campus, Heritage Hall served as the university library when Anne and my mother were sorority sisters and kindred spirits in the early 1940s, but it now held classrooms and a dozen offices. Whenever I entered the building I could smell a whiff of history, but on this day my thoughts were on my future.

Anne was always happy when I stopped by for a quick hello, and as she listened this day, she heard my uncertainty about what to do. Anne knew I was considering graduate school as well as the Peace Corps. She shared with me her belief that no one can teach someone else how to teach. You just have to learn by doing, she said, noting that the Peace Corps was the perfect place for that learning to occur. Two years in the Peace Corps would help me decide if I liked teaching without the costs and commitment of a graduate teaching degree, not to mention the opportunity to travel somewhere completely new. Her comments made a lot of sense to me, but I also needed to hear from my parents.

The university's annual Parents' Weekend was coming up in February, when my parents and sisters planned to travel from Cleveland for a visit. This plan gave me the opportunity to discuss the Peace Corps assignment with Mom and Dad. We sat together in the living room of the Springsteens' house. Snow covered the ground outside the large picture windows, and the frigid air of the night before laced the windows with frost. I showed them the materials I had received, told them what I knew about the Peace Corps and Micronesia, explained what I'd be doing, then waited. I was anticipating their questions and concerns. All that Dad said to me was, "Well, son, it's your decision." My mother nodded her assent. I was crestfallen. I had been looking for their guidance and wise counsel on such a major decision. I wanted them to ask me questions that might help me better understand the implications of this decision. I needed their blessing on this huge step. I could not see it then, but they had given me exactly that.

Dad's response was a strong affirmation of the man he felt his second-born son had become. By leaving it up to me, my parents were giving me permission to cut loose from the family circle. Only in retrospect have I been able to appreciate what a loving and courageous gift this was. Seven years earlier, my parents had lost their first-born son. Now, their only surviving son was planning to disappear across the ocean for two years.

VALPO'S GRADUATION took place on Sunday, June 9, 1968. It was one week after Robert Kennedy was assassinated in Los Angeles and two months after the Reverend Dr. Martin Luther King was shot in Memphis. After the graduation ceremony, I happened to see my friend and classmate Peter Lutze, Karl and Esther's son. Our paths didn't cross a lot on campus, but I enjoyed his company and respected his opinion. He had been president of the Valpo Student Senate during the past year, and, like his parents, was very active in the civil rights movement. Peter and his father had taken part in the voting rights march from Selma to Birmingham, Alabama, in 1965.

Peter knew I was heading overseas in a few days with the Peace Corps. When he saw me, he said, "Man, I wish I was leaving the country, too." His words surprised me, but I also heard a touch of envy as well as an almost cynical resignation with the state of United States politics. But my motivation was not to escape the protest, violence, and endemic cacophony of 1968 United States. To me, joining the Peace Corps was less a matter of leaving the United States than simply going in a new direction that was not a foregone conclusion, as so much of my life had been. I simply needed to go somewhere, anywhere new, and the Peace Corps was buying my ticket.

Here I was, a child of winter bound for the heat and humidity of the tropics. I was twenty-one years old, fresh from college graduation—an unseasoned entrant into the big wide world. With my suitcase, my guitar, my new camera, and my deeply buried tale of grief and sibling loss all packed, I was set to venture off to what I would soon discover was a Pacific Island culture of laughter, lightheartedness, and fun. I had not yet learned how to listen for the cosmic laughter of the angels. My lessons were about to begin.

MICRONESIA, ROTA, SAIPAN, AND PALAU

6 Moving On

AT SIX O'CLOCK on the morning after graduation, my entire family set off from the Springsteens' house in Valparaiso in Dad's new Buick sedan for my designated reporting site in Escondido, California, near San Diego. We had five days to cover over 2,000 miles and deliver me to the Peace Corps training site by Saturday noon. As a road-trip family, we were used to this type of challenge. I prepared for the long hours in the car by bringing along some reading material about this territory of tiny islands to which I was bound.

A *National Geographic* cover story the previous year on "Micronesia— The Americanization of Eden" detailed the United States' role as trustee of the island territory. Photos showed some of the contrasts between modern development and traditional island ways: a topless woman, wearing only the traditional *lava-lava* wraparound skirt, looked through a rack of blouses in a small department store; a fisherman sat in his outrigger canoe with his hand on the tiller of a small outboard motor as he made his way across the lagoon.

I had gathered other materials in advance of the trip that helped to pass the hours and to acquaint myself with a bit of history of this island territory known at that time as the Trust Territory of the Pacific Islands, or Micronesia, for short. The territory came into being two years after the end of World War II. The Mariana Islands played key roles in bringing the war to an end. United States armed forces waged a bitter, bloody battle to wrest control of Saipan from the Japanese in June and July 1944. A year later, in August 1945, the B-29 bombers Enola Gay and Bockscar took off from an airstrip on the nearby island of Tinian to drop the atomic bombs that destroyed Hiroshima and Nagasaki and brought a swift end to the Pacific war.

After the war, the United Nations declared the area a "strategic trust" and appointed the United States government as trustee. The United Nations trusteeship agreement contained an explicit provision that the "trustee" was to educate and equip the people of the islands towards political self-determination. For the next fifteen years, however, United States policy towards the islands has been described by some observers as "benign neglect."

In the mid-1960s, the United States administration began a shift towards a more proactive approach to development in the islands, driven in large part by a United Nations report that was highly critical of the United States' neglect of its responsibilities as trustee of Micronesia. A key aspect of that policy shift was the introduction of Peace Corps volunteers in 1966. Most of the first groups of volunteers were recruited to teach English as a Second Language, but there were also nurses, engineers, lawyers, and agricultural advisors.

I ARRIVED WITH MY FAMILY at an Escondido motel on Friday night right on schedule. Mom explored the motel grounds and reported that there were other Peace Corps recruits staying in the motel. She was eager for me to meet them. "No thanks," I said. I wanted this break with my family and my past to be clear and distinct. The next morning, we all rode the final leg of our journey up into the hills north of San Diego to the training site, a well-concealed former nudist camp that was a collection of brown, one-story wood-frame buildings nestled among the chaparral and sagebrush-covered hills.

Dad parked the car and helped me unload my gear. I gave each of my sisters a hug, then wrapped my arms around my mother and planted a kiss on her cheek. She held on for a few extra seconds. I looked at my dad and walked to him with my arms spread wide. We embraced, and memories of his farewell on my first day at Valpo rolled around in my head.

With my guitar, trunk, and suitcase on the ground around my feet, I waved good-bye as the Buick slowly disappeared in its own cloud of desert dust. It never occurred to me then to wonder how this playing-it-safe kid with latent Eeyore tendencies made this seemingly bold departure from all that was safe and familiar. I can only think that there must have been a low simmer of desperation to get away, so deep as to remain invisible to me at the time.

In that moment, I knew that for the next two years, I would see no one I had known up to that point in my life. Every social encounter, every friendship, every casual acquaintance would be brand new. There would be no "before" people; the only way the topic of my brother's death could come up was if I chose to mention it. As I stood there, alone in the dry, dusty parking lot, a deep sense of relief washed over me. I felt free. The only familiar facet of the coming two years would be me; my faith, self-doubt, perfectionism, self-pity, intelligence, people-pleasing, musical interests, and athletic abilities were coming along for the ride. It was a new beginning, a fresh start, a time of turning.

AFTER WATCHING THE FAMILY CAR disappear, I surveyed the scene, my first moment as a Peace Corps trainee. I walked a short distance over to several other trainees, who were gathering at a registration table. I joined the make-shift line-up and introduced myself to a couple from Seattle, Dave and Lynda Crutcher, who had been married just one week earlier and were recruited as English as a Second Language—or ESL—teachers like me. I met other new arrivals who had different assignments, like Bev and Ralph Chumbley, a couple from Florida who had signed on as a nurse and a guidance counselor, respectively. There were a couple other guys in the line who had also brought their guitars; we talked about getting together later for a jam session.

When I reached the Peace Corps staff sitting at the table, I introduced myself and said, "Mine'll be the last name on your very last page." She leafed quickly through her list of the names and found mine: "Tom Zink. Well, Tom, welcome to the Peace Corps. You're in Cabin Four this week. And you've been assigned to the Marianas District." The Marianas. All I knew was that it was one of the six districts in Micronesia and was home to the territorial capital on the island of Saipan.

Fifty-five of us were assigned to the Marianas, about the same number of recruits slated to go to each of the other five Micronesian districts. Our 1968 group in Escondido was the seventh group recruited for Micronesia. Known as Micro VII, we were the largest cadre to be sent to the islands. By the time our Marianas group was sworn in as volunteers in late August 1968, the Marianas District of Micronesia had on average one volunteer for every 100 Micronesians, the highest per capita density of volunteers in the world before or since. A similar Peace Corps density in a country like India would have required five million volunteers.

Peace Corps staff filled our staging week with group discussions, psychological assessments, immunizations, slide shows, and films about the islands. The schedule allowed us free time for basketball games, volleyball in the swimming pool, hiking in the nearby hills, and sing-along jam sessions at night. The ten-week training for our Marianas group was to take place on an island called Rota. We would live with Rotanese families to help us acclimate to the culture and to the dominant language in the Marianas, Chamorro. Frank Chong, a Saipanese Chamorro who worked for Peace Corps/Marianas, led several question-and-answer sessions to prepare us for life on Rota.

With a twinkle in his eye, Frank assured us that, yes, in the Marianas they use silverware, they sit on chairs, and they swim in the ocean. The Rotanese, he explained, referred with affection to their island as *mamis Luta*, which is Chamorro for "sweet Rota." On a more practical note, Frank told us that the only place to spend our dollar-fifty-per-day allowance was in one of the two bars. But he warned us to steer clear of the bars on Pay Night, every second Friday night, when government pay checks came out, and the bars filled up with drinkers flush with cash. Then, there was no telling if or when a friendly argument might turn violent.

We also learned more about Marianas geography. The Mariana Islands chain arcs like a mid-ocean parenthesis in the western Pacific. Easy to miss on a global map, it's 1,500 miles south of Japan, 1,500 miles east of the Philippines, and 1,500 miles north of Australia. The north-south island string extends 500 miles from Guam in the south to Farallon de Pajaros in the north. Volcanic in origin, the islands are mountain peaks that rise above sea level from the depths of the Marianas Trench, the deepest ocean trench on the planet. Although geographically part of the Marianas, Guam is a separate political entity from the rest of the Marianas archipelago.

After dropping me off in Escondido, my parents and sisters continued their vacation trip, making their way north to Portland, Oregon, to visit the Bensons, the family of Mom's younger sister Irene. On the night before I was to depart for Micronesia, I called my parents in Portland. We knew it was most likely the last time we'd be able to speak by phone for the next two years. When Dad got on the phone, he asked again how long the Peace Corps term of service was. Two years, I told him. Then he asked how long I was planning to stay. Two years, I told him. To achieve a successful separation from the nest of parental dependence, I was determined to make whatever adaptations were necessary in order to complete my two-year commitment. We were a family of letter writers, and I assured my parents that I would write soon and often.

The next morning was filled with final preparations for our fourteen-hour flight to Guam. The Peace Corps health care team gave all of us a farewell gift, a final inoculation before we headed off to the tropics. To ward off hepatitis, we all received our gamma globulin shot, administered in the fleshy area of the gluteus maximus. This guaranteed us the uniquely shared experience of sitting on sore inoculated posteriors for the entire flight to Guam.

OUR FLIGHT LEFT LOS ANGELES at sunset on a Saturday and arrived at Guam International Airport on a Monday morning. Sunday was swallowed up when we crossed over the International Date Line. I joined the line of trainees making their way down the aisle to the exit door and the gangway down to the tarmac. My first impression of Micronesia hit me full in the face and lungs as I reached the open doorway: humidity so thick and heavy I felt like I could squeeze my fist and wring the air like a damp sponge. The tropical air became a constant, vexing companion for the next two years. Child of winter indeed!

We disembarked from a stretch DC-8 aircraft, the largest passenger plane in the world at the time. Our next flight was on one of the smallest: a twin-engine Beechcraft that would ferry our Marianas training group forty miles north to the island called Rota. The plane constituted the entire rolling stock of the ambitiously-named Micronesian Airlines. Its capacity was ten passengers, provided one rode in the co-pilot's seat. At that rate it took six round-trip flights to shuttle all fifty-five Marianas trainees plus Peace Corps staff to Rota. Groups were arranged in alphabetical order, so I was on the last flight of the day.

Ten of us, and two years' worth of luggage, squeezed into the tiny plane. Luggage was piled shoulder high in the aisle. All of us rode with a suitcase on our laps. There were no safety cards in the seat pockets in front of us, nor did seat belts seem necessary, jammed in as we were. The Beechcraft's name, Spirit of Faith, aptly fit my mood. As the plane taxied toward the runway, I whispered a prayer: "God? It's me, far off on a Pacific island. I sure hope you work out here, too. Please! Get us to Rota safely." The engines roared, the plane rattled and shook. It trundled down the runway for what seemed an eternity before lifting off, carrying us up and over the deep turquoise expanse of the Pacific.

In a short while, the island of Rota came into view. Our pilot, Emmett Kay, circled north of the island and brought Spirit of Faith down safely on the crushed coral landing strip that was Rota's airport. A fleet of recycled military Jeeps and Japanese-made pick-up trucks awaited our arrival. The luggage was loaded onto the vehicles, along with the ten bodies that emerged from the plane. Frank Vogel, Dan Zebo, and I climbed onto one truck's luggage pile for the half-hour ride into Songsong, Rota's lone village. We hung on tight as the truck clumped over or swerved around potholes in the crushed coral road. I was filled with an exhilaration and sense of anticipation like I'd never known before. The breeze I felt riding on the back of the truck was no match for the withering heat of the afternoon sun. We rounded a final turn and headed down a slight hill into Songsong, returning the waves and greetings from children who had run to the roadside to greet this caravan of white-skinned strangers.

As the truck slowed, entering the village, the breeze stilled, and I could feel the beads of sweat forming on my forehead. The main road through the village took us past the brilliant yellow Rota Hotel. Rolling past the Rocky Bar, I heard Dan call out, "Hey, check it out! There's one of the bars Frank Chong told us about!" We passed the village ball field on our way to the Roundhouse, an open-air, corrugated-tin-roofed structure across the road from the large whitewashed Catholic church of San Francisco de Borja.

At the Roundhouse, we were given our housing assignments. I was paired with a trainee named Mark from Baltimore, and our host family's name was Barcinas. The young Rotanese man who was in charge of housing greeted us with the Chamorro words of welcome, "*Hafa adai.*" He introduced himself as Tommy Mendiola. Hey, cool, I thought, one of the first people I've met has the same first name. In the next few months, I would learn that the Chamorro word for guys with the same first name was *kadzu*. As I met more of my *kadzus*, I wondered why they were all called "Tommy" and not "Tom."

A Peace Corps training staff member then told us that we had about twenty-four hours until the first training session on Tuesday. Time to unpack our belongings, explore our new surroundings, sleep off a bit of the jet lag, and experience the first of the digestive disruptions that were bound to ensue from the island delicacies our host families put before us. My roommate Mark and I found ourselves eating hard-cooked fried eggs with rice for breakfast, roast beef chunks with rice for lunch, and greasy pan-fried chicken drumsticks with rice for supper. Always, there was rice.

One of my first explorations upon moving my things into the small bedroom Mark and I shared in the Barcinas' house was to determine the shortest route to the *benjo*, the Chamorro word for outhouse. The Barcinas' house, like the vast majority of houses on Rota, was a wood-frame construction with walls of worn, weathered plywood. The corrugated tin that had become ubiquitous with the arrival in these islands of the Americans, towards the end of World War II, covered all the roofs, much of them rusted to an ugly brown from the rain and humidity. Scattered throughout the village were a few single-story concrete houses with flat concrete roofs.

Mark and I stomached our first supper, then set out to walk the main village road. The arrival on Rota of our Peace Corps entourage was like a human tsunami washing up on the shores of this tiny, thirty-three-square-mile island. Rota's population of just over one thousand meant there was one Peace Corps volunteer for every twenty Rotanese. We would soon find out that it was next to impossible to go anywhere in the village without running into someone we recognized—other trainees, Peace Corps staff, or our Chamorro language teachers.

On this first evening, Mark and I joined three other trainees, Fay, Andy, and Linda, for a walk down to the beach on the west side of the island. We sat and talked and watched as the first of countless spectacular Pacific Island sunsets unfolded before us. We waded into the calm, clear water of the lagoon in our brand new Japanese-made plastic *zoris*, the term used in Micronesia for flip-flops. In the fading light, we caught sight of marine creatures we'd never seen before. Andy pointed out the sea cucumbers, dark blue starfish, and, further out in the lagoon, a small reef shark swimming lazily back and forth.

LIKE CHILDREN WHOSE PARENTS try to teach them to swim by dropping them into the deep end of the pool, we were tossed a couple days later into a pool of learning called HILT, High-Intensity Language Training. HILT started as a ten-hour-a-day slog with the first class at six thirty in the morning. The staff of indigenous language teachers rotated on a daily basis among the ten groups of a half-dozen trainees each. We were immersed twenty-four hours a day in this strange, new language called Chamorro. We heard it in our host families' homes (*gimat-niha*) at breakfast, lunch, and supper. We heard it when we walked through the village, had a beer (*setbesa*) in the Rocky Bar, tried out our new words with the little children (*famagu'on*), or collapsed in bed at night listening to our host families chatting on the front porch. And we had it drilled into us ten hours a day under the patient tutelage of our language teachers.

The levity, animation, and laughter of many of our language teachers alleviated the more tedious parts of this daily routine of repetitive drills and dialogues. There was Louis Tenorio, who took great delight in making sure we learned some of the most common Chamorro swear words, then warned us *never* to say them outside of language class. The tricky part was that certain English words, like "chili" or "sing," with their obscene or scatological meanings in Chamorro, could become embarrassing booby traps for novice Chamorro speakers like us.

Our language teachers used the so-called "oral-aural" method of language instruction: You learn to hear and imitate the sounds of the new language before you are taught grammar rules. For example, they taught us verbs by demonstrating the action while saying the words. "I am walking," they would say in Chamorro, as they walked across the room. Two of our teachers, Catholic nuns named Sister Rosa and Sister Trinidad, were remarkable examples of this method. Their enthusiasm for teaching was infectious. On the days my group had one of the sisters, we knew a surprise or two was in store. Most memorable was their lively illustration of *gumugupu yo'*—I am flying. They flapped their arms like birds' wings, white habits trailing behind them, calling out the words. We knew them ever after as The Flying Nuns.

One day after supper, I was sitting on the Barcinas' front porch when Leon Taisacan, a Rotanese man, drove up in his pick-up truck with the four male trainees he was hosting. "We're heading out to my farm to shoot wild chickens," he called to me in English. "You wanna come?" I jumped into the truck bed with the other guys, and off we went on a forty-five-minute ride up into the hills north of Songsong on a one-lane, double-rutted dirt road with jungle overhanging on both sides, so it felt like we were passing through a canyon of green.

Leon stopped the truck when we emerged from the jungle at the crest of a hill. He pointed behind us and said, "Look at that!" We turned back to gaze at the expanse of ocean and marvel at yet another stunning Pacific sunset. We arrived at the farm, and Leon nosed the pick-up through his pasture, past his half dozen cows, and among the trees, looking for the sleeping chickens. Two perfect shots—"Buena!" he exclaimed—netted him two birds that he stuffed into a sack in the back of the truck. He picked several cantaloupes from his melon patch and offered me one to take home to my host family.

All of our Chamorro language classes, English as a Second Language training sessions, and group meetings were held in the Rota Elementary School. The school was comprised of three one-story wooden buildings with louvered windows and tin roofs with four classrooms in each. Halfway down the covered walkway outside the middle building was a little concession window, from which a Rotanese couple sold bottles of ice-cold Coca-Cola and deep-fried doughnuts, known as *bunuelos*, during our morning and after-noon breaks.

Most evenings were devoted to something the Peace Corps called Area Studies, a series of discussions and talks designed to introduce us to histor-ical, political, and cultural aspects of serving in Micronesia. In these Cold War years, all such programs were required to include a session describing the "evils of communism." The man who presented our anti-communism session was a Peace Corps/Micronesia staff member, former Peace Corps vol-unteer in the Philippines, and a vintage iconoclast named Dirk Ballendorf. He had visited our training site once or twice before from Saipan so his was a familiar face. He kept it short and sweet. He held up a large blank piece of poster board and said, "This is my presentation on communism." He turned the poster board around. Large black handwritten capital letters spelled out "FUCK COMMUNISM." He sat down to raucous applause.

MOST OF OUR LANGUAGE TEACHERS spoke Chamorro as their first language. Lino Olopai and Louis Wabol were two teachers whose mother tongue was the Carolinian language. Lino was a twenty-eight-year-old husband and father of four boys who had been a Saipan police officer before coming to work for the Peace Corps. Louis, a husky, athletic high school student from Saipan, was an animated teacher who played the guitar and loved to sing. I found myself drawn to their ready laughter, friendly teasing, and easygoing manner. As we got to know Lino and Louis, they talked about their history and culture, how in the early 1800s their ancestors had sailed their outrigger canoes northward in search of a new home, after a devastating typhoon had destroyed their home atolls in the eastern Caroline Islands (thus, the name Carolinian.)

These Carolinians navigated across five hundred miles of open ocean, relying solely on the sun and stars, wind and clouds, seas and swells. They made landfall on the shores of the island that is now called Saipan. By the mid-twentieth century, the Carolinians were a minority subculture on Saipan. They had darker skin, broader noses, and stockier builds than the Chamorros, and they remained more closely tied to their traditional ways. Of the nine villages on the island at the time, only two—Tanapag and Oleai—were predominantly Carolinian.

As the training weeks passed, Lino and Louis were always ready to share their language, customs, and culture with us. They were the first to introduce several of us trainees to the beauty of Micronesian music with its simple chord progressions, relaxing rhythms, vocal harmonies, and lilting melodies. Louis played the guitar, Lino the ukulele; their singing evoked the welcoming spirit of the islands. A couple songs were in English and easy for us to learn.

One folk song that became a favorite of many Peace Corps trainees began with the line, "Upon the hill lies the village of the place that I love best, in my home in Saipan." One evening Louis wrote out the words to a Carolinian song called "*Sugi, Sugi,*" ("Open, Open" in English) sung traditionally before weddings. I managed to imitate the words he was singing but had no clue what they meant. But it didn't matter. The literal meaning of the words was secondary to the way in which Louis freely shared his culture. We shared North American folk songs with them. It was an early example of a process I think of as "cultural swapping," a temporary blurring of cultural boundaries in which music and language are shared on an equal basis.

Toward the end of August 1968, as our training program was winding down and our Chamorro lessons were finished, Lino and Louis took the initiative to offer to interested trainees what they called "tough Carolinian lessons." A handful of us joined them for the first lesson, among them the Florida couple, Ralph and Bev Chumbley, who had become trusted friends. The "tough" part became clear in the very first lesson. To respond in Carolinian to the question "How are you?" you had to say two single-syllable words—*ghatch schagh*—meaning "very good." Both words started and ended with sounds that simply do not exist in English. On our *Americano* tongues, the words were unpronounceable, but our attempts were good for plenty of laughs.

On one of the final nights of our training, the Peace Corps program put on an evening of skits at the Roundhouse for the people of Rota—so many of whom had warmly welcomed us, served as host families, and invited us to share their lives at picnics on the beach, wedding receptions, and softball games. To add some Carolinian culture to the show, Lino and Louis taught a group of us guys a traditional Carolinian men's stick dance. Trying to make us look as authentic as our pale skin would allow, they dressed us up with grass skirts made from palm fronds (with shorts underneath), flower leis around our necks, flower crowns (known as *mwarmwars*) on our heads, and palm fronds strapped around our arms and ankles.

It took longer for us to get in costume than it did to perform the dance. The audience in the packed Roundhouse hooted and hollered its approval all the way through the dance and then demanded an encore. The samplings of Carolinian culture I encountered on Rota made me eager to learn more. It was the fourth component of our training program—daily physical education, or PE—that offered the opportunity for me to do just that.

THE PE PROGRAM got us off our seats in the school rooms every afternoon and down to the playing fields in the village center. In the first week on Rota, I noted in my Peace Corps journal, "for a truly enjoyable and satisfying two years here, I'll need in some way to be connected with recreation and PE." I soon found that my knowledge, abilities, and enthusiasm for team sports all came together on Rota's playing fields.

During the course of the summer, I had several encouraging conversations with Kurt Barnes, the PE coordinator for Saipan's eight elementary schools and one high school. A tall man with an athletic build, a shock of dark hair, and an affirming, take-charge attitude, Kurt had first arrived in Micronesia in early 1967 as an English and PE teacher on Saipan. He soon became very involved in Saipan sports, coaching basketball, softball, and volleyball teams to island championships and constructing a running track where Saipan's elementary school students competed in the Junior Olympics.

As we became better acquainted, I heard Kurt speak highly of the many talented Saipanese athletes he felt privileged to coach and play alongside. His men's volleyball team, the Breakers, was the best on the island. He also coached the top women's softball and volleyball teams from the village of Oleai. My ears perked up when he shared with me his opinion that some of Saipan's best grade-school athletes were Carolinians who went to Oleai school, one of several schools with a PE teaching vacancy Kurt needed to fill.

When our teaching assignments were posted, I was thrilled to learn that

I was assigned to my top choice—Oleai Elementary School. In addition to my primary role as an English as a Second Language teacher, I was to teach physical education classes and coach the school's boys' teams and girls' teams in volleyball, softball, and track and field.

Training days on Rota were full. I kept in touch as I'd promised with my family, writing a detailed letter home every couple of weeks. I felt so completely engaged in my new adventure that the thought of missing my parents and sisters rarely entered my mind. For others in our training group, the decision to join Peace Corps did not work out well. Several trainees chose to return stateside during the ten weeks of training. Seven others were sent home—"deselected" was the Peace Corps' term—at the very end of training by a team of Peace Corps psychologists. By the end of August, forty-one of the original fifty-five Marianas trainees were sworn in as Peace Corps volunteers. We packed up, said our farewells to *mamis Luta* and to our host families, and prepared to depart to our new assignments.

I FIRST CAUGHT SIGHT of Saipan from the window of the Peace Corps charter flight that departed Rota on August 25, 1968, and headed north to ferry our group of newly minted volunteers—teachers, nurses, engineers, architects, business advisors, and agricultural advisors—to our new home. In less than an hour, the island of Tinian came into view. Five miles beyond Tinian, across the Saipan Channel, lay the green, somber hulk of Saipan. The rolling hills blanketed with lush tropical vegetation climb up to the 1,500-foot peak of Mt. Tapochau, the highest point on the island.

The island is about thirteen miles long and five miles wide, making its forty-eight square miles about the same size as the island of Nantucket off the coast of Cape Cod in Massachusetts. Approaching from the south, the thin white line of ocean surf broke onto the barrier reef on the western edge of Saipan's lagoon. On the island side of the lagoon was the beach—five uninterrupted miles of white sand from Saipan's southern tip to Micro Beach, mid-island in the village of Garapan. On the east and south sides of the island, the white line of surf ran tight along the coast line, an incessant pounding of Saipan's fringing reef.

The drive from the airport to the Peace Corps office took us along the western edge of the island. Strung out along Beach Road, Saipan's main traffic artery, was a succession of villages—San Antonio, Chalan Kanoa, Susupe, Oleai, and Garapan—that made this the most populous part of the island. Garapan had been the capital between the two world wars, when Saipan was a Japanese colony. Sugar cane, cultivated in fields that covered the lowlands, was hauled on an extensive network of narrow gauge railway tracks to the Garapan sugar mill and then to the docks for shipment to Japan. Of the countless concrete buildings that typified the Japanese era, only a few had survived the bombardments of the war, among them a hospital and a jail in Garapan, and a communications center in Oleai.

During our training on Rota, we also heard tales of the super typhoon named Jean that struck Saipan in April 1968. Evidence of the destruction was impossible to miss. Jean's 200-mile-per-hour winds had demolished ninety percent of the island's housing. Damage estimates reached sixteen and a half million dollars. United States President Lyndon Johnson declared the island a major disaster area, and the United States Office of Emergency Preparedness shipped construction materials for five hundred typhoon-safe emergency shelters to Saipan. The materials were free to Saipanese families, as long as they provided a concrete pad and the labor to construct their emergency houses.

One puzzle we faced on our arrival as brand-new volunteers was to locate housing. I bounced around for a couple weeks between several temporary solutions: the Peace Corps/Marianas office floor, an abandoned grocery store, an apartment with a nocturnally active rat as a roommate, and a second-floor apartment in Susupe village shared with four other new volunteers. This apartment was rat-free, typhoon-safe, a twenty-minute walk from Oleai school, and too much like the life I'd left behind. I had joined the Peace Corps for something new, and this was not it.

The day after the five of us moved into the apartment, I made my way to Oleai to find a place to live. Ralph and Bev Chumbley, whose friendship I had come to value, were about to settle in Oleai and encouraged me to join them. I was eager to find my own niche in my new surroundings, and Oleai beckoned.

By the time I began my house search, many Oleai families had nearly completed building their typhoon-safe emergency houses. Some planned to vacate the houses that had survived Typhoon Jean. The local administrator drove me around the village to help me find a family who might be willing to rent me an empty house. This is how I met Carlos and Olympia Borja (*BOR-ah*), who lived a two-block walk from Oleai school. They had lost most of their house to Typhoon Jean. The part that did survive left the family of eight cramped for space.

Within a few visits, the Borjas and I came up with a plan for me to move into their small 400-square-foot house once they moved into their new government-issued home with nearly double the space. I agreed to pay them my monthly Peace Corps rent allowance of fifteen dollars. Just before I moved in, though, I stopped by one day, and Olympia came out to see me. We exchanged greetings, her English far better than my rudimentary Chamorro. She said that they did not want me to pay any rent when I came to live there because I was teaching their children English. I protested.

"The Peace Corps gives me money for rent," I said. "I can pay you rent every month."

Olympia persisted. "No, Tom," she said. "You live here, you hep our childrens." I protested again but to no avail. Olympia was firm.

Typhoon Jean had been a devastating event for the people of Saipan. No lives were lost, but the destruction affected everyone on the island. Had it not been for the small silver lining of the United States' emergency housing program, I would never have happened upon this corrugated-tin gem of a home in Oleai.

THE SCENE, AS YOU ENTERED OLEAI, was a combination of wood-framed houses with tin roofs and walls, the government emergency houses in varying stages of completion, and assorted piles of housing debris salvaged in the wake of Typhoon Jean. The Saipanese used these reclaimed sheets of corrugated tin, intact two-by-fours, and pieces of plywood to frame low-cost, temporary tin sheds to shelter showers, *benjos*, and the ubiquitous outdoor cooking shelters, known as "Chamorro kitchens."

The villagers augmented these reused materials with sturdy poles of *tangan-tangan*, a species of fast-growing tree that was seeded by the United States military after the war to prevent erosion of the bombed-out, deforested hillsides. The trees grew quickly and spread throughout the island. Vast tracts of the island were covered by *tangan-tangan* trees, often forming nearly impenetrable thickets. Harvested with machetes, *tangan-tangan* was used for fence posts, shed rafters, and firewood for the "Chamorro kitchens."

These covered backyard cooking enclosures were like oversized barbecues, fueled not by propane or charcoal but by *tangan-tangan* wood. The women or girls standing at the six-inch-deep metal-encased stove could control the heat by adding or removing sticks from the fire. The smoke from the Chamorro kitchens permeated the village and gave it the feel of a rustic summer campground. Only here on Saipan, summer lasted all year. Saipan has been listed in the *Guinness Book of World Records* as having the least fluctuating temperature in the world, averaging eighty-one degrees Fahrenheit every day of the year.

MAP OF OLEAI VILLAGE

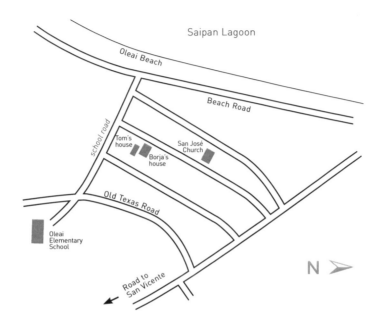

On a map, the village resembled a crudely-drawn trapezoid. At the top was Beach Road, one of only three paved roads on Saipan at the time. On the bottom was Old Texas Road, a notoriously pot-holed route that barely merited the designation of "road." The left side of the trapezoid was a coral street that led from Beach Road to the elementary school. A paved road angling across the bottom of the trapezoid carried traffic to San Vicente village on Saipan's east coast. All the streets within the village were made of crushed coral, a paving material with a split personality depending on the season. In the July-to-December rainy season, the surface turned to muck and was riddled with potholes. In the dry season, a thin film of coral dust, as fine as flour, could be disturbed by car tires, footsteps, or a slight breeze.

Oleai Elementary School was set well back from the corner where Old Texas Road met the school road. The school building was a long two-story concrete structure that had served as a Japanese communications center before and during World War Two. The United States administration opened the school in 1958. Over the main entrance was a concrete portico that sheltered the children if a sudden downpour fell during recess. Right next to the portico was a large Poinciana tree (also known as the "flame tree" for its vivid red flowers), which afforded additional shelter from showers as well as shade from the hot sun. The grassy fields surrounding the school were the places where I taught PE classes and coached the softball, volleyball, and track teams. The school building also served as the Oleai typhoon shelter when the highest level of typhoon warnings forced the closing of stores, government offices, and schools.

The house I moved into had no indoor plumbing. An above-ground water line ran behind the house to a standpipe located next to one of the backyard coconut palms. One extension pipe led to a makeshift shower shed, where warm showers were available only in mid-afternoon after several hours of direct sunshine on the water line. Saipan's water pressure was unpredictable at best and occasionally non-existent. The Borjas' back-up water supply was a fifty-five-gallon drum that caught the run-off from the sweeping curve of a coconut palm trunk.

During the rainy season, the downpours drumming on the tin roof of my house drowned out all other sounds. Dry season weather was quieter. On a lazy February afternoon, I sat in the shade of my tin-roofed dirt "patio" just outside my front door and listened to the sounds that told tales of village life. Somewhere a refrigerator door opened, then slammed shut. The church bells clanged, breaking the calm, calling the faithful to five o'clock Mass. Perched in the small plumeria tree in front of my house a rooster flapped its wings, crowed raucously then fell silent. Fish sizzled in the hot oil over a crackling, smoking *tangan-tangan* fire in the Borjas' Chamorro kitchen.

"Will-*Yam!*" came the crisp, firm call from Doris, the oldest Borja daughter, to her younger brother William to shoo a stray dog out of the house. The rhythmic sweep of a broom—one of the younger Borja girls cleaning house. A billy goat bleated and a little child cried—no way to tell the difference. A big yellow Chevy sedan crunched down the pot-holed coral road, spitting rocks from under its tires, leaving a dusty cloud in its wake. The car's radio rasped with a throbbing country music beat from KJQR, Saipan's lone radio station. A two-wheeled wooden ox cart creaked under the weight of a load of *tangan-tangan* firewood. The old man who lived next door was coming home from his farm up in the hills. Again the church bells rang out with the message that you were now late for Mass. A rotary lawn mower roared to life, the swish of grass losing its last legs.

In my front yard, two goats munched grass, an environmentally-friendly lawn maintenance alternative. Dogs barked—vicious, frightened, retreating in whimpers. A sudden soft tapping sounded on the hot corrugated tin roof as a rain cloud passed over, dropping its pellets. They simmered on the sun-soaked roof and disturbed the dust on the road like micro-bombs landing on a coating of flour. The rain passed, the dust settled. And I went inside to start my supper of rice and canned beef stew.

MY MOVE TO THE BORJAS' HOUSE opened the door for me to the Carolinian community. I found myself in the midst of a culture of laughter and light-heartedness and a people whose unhurried, welcoming, hang-loose attitude slowly eased its way under my skin. At first it was itchy and a bit annoying, but, over time, it worked its way in to loosen me up enough to laugh at myself and accept mistakes as part of the fun. I learned this from my Carolinian students, friends, and neighbors in Oleai who welcomed me as one of their own almost as soon as I arrived. They encouraged me to speak their language and "forget that Chamorro language." The sense of belonging to a community became as strong as any I had known before and fastened my heart to the island of Saipan and the village of Oleai in ways I could neither foresee nor ever undo.

I learned all this most directly from the Borjas, a family that was a micro-cosm of Saipan's two main cultural groups. Carlos was Chamorro, his Spanish surname a reflection of the influence on the Chamorro culture of Spanish language, religion, and cuisine, beginning with Magellan's landing in the Marianas in 1521. Olympia's Carolinian surname, Selepeo, was passed on to her children as their middle name. Carlos and Olympia were both about five-feet-four-inches tall, but beyond their height, there were marked differences in their appearance.

Olympia had the darker skin, broader nose, and stockier build character-istic of the Carolinians. Carlos' hair was straight, well-slicked with pomade, and neatly combed; Olympia's, a frizzy mound of curls framing her round face. Like most Carolinians, Olympia was fluent in both the Carolinian and Chamorro languages and had better command of English than Carlos, who knew only a smattering of English and Carolinian. Their children, who attended Oleai school, were becoming trilingual: Chamorro and Carolinian spoken at home, English at school.

Carlos worked as an auto mechanic, and Olympia was a homemaker, looking after their six children: Doris, the oldest at thirteen; William, eleven, their only son at the time; and four daughters under the age of ten—Lourdes, Rosalia, Bernadetta, and Jesusa. The children helped Olympia with the house-hold tasks of laundry, cooking, cleaning, and tending to younger siblings. At times, the Borja household included Olympia's sixteen-year-old younger sis-ter Florence, who stayed with them in Oleai because it was closer to her high school. At other times, Florence stayed with her parents in Garapan.

The girls' comings and goings afforded me impromptu language lessons that were often over before I realized what they were. I was sitting at my desk one afternoon, finishing up lesson plans, when Jesusa, the Borjas' youngest daughter, came into my front room.

"*Hafa adai, Susa,*" I said, using the customary greeting we'd practiced endless times in training. I asked how she was. Chamorro small talk. Silence. Susa was on a mission from Mom, and I easily gleaned that helping this Peace Corps neighbor practice speaking her language was not it.

"*Tom, gwaha penis butter?*"

"*Hafa ilek-mo?*" I asked, startled. What did you say?

"*Penis butter,*" she repeated softly, her hands behind her back.

"Oh," I said, quickly cluing in. "You mean pea-NUT butter, *abwo?*"

Susa's head tilted a little to one side, and she looked me in the eye. "*Hunggan, yes, peanut butter.*"

"Well, *that's* something I *do* have," I replied. I walked over to my kitchen cupboard and put the peanut butter jar on the counter. Not sure how much she wanted I asked her, "*Quanto malago-mo?*"

Susa then showed me the small bowl she was holding behind her back. Without another word, I filled the bowl. She turned and walked quickly toward the doorway. "*Adios,*" I called after her, grateful for this surprising Chamorro lesson.

I SOON NOTICED that the boundaries between "mine" and "yours" were more porous here in Oleai than back home in Ohio. I grew accustomed to an ethos of communal reciprocity—"What's ours is yours, what's yours is ours." This was true of the house. Before I moved in, it was theirs. Now, I was staying in it, so it was mine, yet I rented it from them, so it was still theirs.

Almost every day the younger Borja children were in and out of a house I thought of alternately as mine, theirs, ours. When I was doing some minor improvements just after moving in, they came in to watch—and to giggle and point when I bent a flooring nail or got paint in my hair. I bought a five-gallon can of kerosene for my one-burner cook stove and kept it on the side porch of the house that the Borjas still used for storage. A few days later the can was noticeably lighter. I knew they had taken what they needed and no more. The kerosene-sharing was a small in-kind rent payment.

Nick was a high school boy in the village who was in a rock band with a couple other youths. They came over sometimes to play my guitar, sing, and hang out while I ate supper or finished lesson plans. I showed them the chords for "Proud Mary," a Credence Clearwater Revival song, and a couple of Beatles songs. Sometimes I'd ask them to sing "Upon the Hill Lies the Village" that Louis Wabol had taught us on Rota.

One day, Nick said, "Hey, Tom, can we borrow our guitar?" "Our" guitar? I thought. That's not the way *I* think of it. But, hey, I figured here was a chance to make a small token gesture to show I wanted to be part of this village and to understand the unwritten rules of reciprocity. I said yes, trusting that the guitar would make it back. I was not disappointed. A few days later I spotted the guitar at someone else's house. It was making the rounds of Oleai. A week or so later it came back to me in the same shape it had left.

This mutuality carried over to the joking banter and ready laughter that was part of every gathering of Carolinians. For me, laughter defined the Carolinians. They laughed on a volleyball court when a teammate made a great play. They laughed when a teammate goofed up. They laughed together at the antics of a young child. They laughed together at the antics of a drunk on Pay Night. They laughed as they sang together, drank together, ate together, played together. They laughed when my attempt to pronounce a simple Carolinian word or expression made it sound obscene. It took some time for me to adjust to their light-hearted sensibilities. I didn't get it right away that their laughter was inclusive, inviting this newcomer into their camaraderie. Here was *gemütlichkeit* on a tropical island. It seemed I could give my trusty old Ridiculometer a rest.

IN MY FIRST YEAR ON SAIPAN, Oleai school had a team of four Peace Corps English teachers. Wayne Hill, Teresa Maebori, and Elayne Halpern were all in their second year as volunteers. Teresa and Elayne taught the primary grades; Wayne and I the fourth- through seventh-graders, who were grouped according to English ability. Pre-adolescent boys whose voices were changing were placed in the same classroom as precocious little fourth graders. All the other Oleai teachers were Saipanese. The only other American was our principal, Neal Baker, who was employed by the Marianas District government.

I soon became aware that the buzzing sound of the letter "Z" did not exist in either Chamorro or Carolinian. It came out sounding like a "J." So when the children wanted my attention and called to me at recess, it came out as "Mistah Jink." My new nickname was picked up by my three fellow Peace Corps teachers at Oleai, who, to this day, still refer to me as Mistah Jink.

I soon decided it was time to guide my classes toward correct pronunciation of my last name. To do this I used a "minimal pair drill," a teaching game we had learned in training. Minimal pairs are two words that differ in only one sound, like "ship" and "sheep" or "pat" and "bat." The students' first step is to be able hear the difference between the two sounds. For this drill to train their ears in the "Z" sound, I chose to use the minimal pair of the name "Sue" and the word "zoo," oblivious to the linguistic minefield that lay ahead.

I said the two words together: "Sue-Zoo." If the students thought the sounds were the same, they placed both hands on their heads; if different, they raised their hands in the air. I varied the minimal pairs—"Zoo-Zoo," hands on head; "Zoo-Sue," hands in the air. The first time I pronounced the pair "Sue-Sue" a few titters broke out in the room. The next time I said those two sounds together, giggles rippled across the room. I was flummoxed. What was going on? I checked my fly. It was zipped. Just then a bright fifth-grade boy saved me. I happened to glance over at Ramon just as he took his hands off his head, cupped them, and very rapidly touched his chest two or three times. Then it hit me. Louis Tenorio. Rota language training. Chamorro words you should never say, like "*susu*," the Chamorro word for "breast." I was basically standing in front of my class and saying "boobs." I quickly changed my minimal pair to "Sea" and the letter "Z" and began again. The room calmed down. Note to self: no more *susu* in the classroom.

My first name was another story. Ever since I had first met Tommy Mendiola on Rota, I wondered why all of my *kadzus* were called "Tommy" and not "Tom." A hotshot Carolinian teenager named Miguel was persistent in trying to rouse my Ridiculometer back into action. Every time he saw me near the school or at a picnic at the beach, he walked over, and with a knowing grin on his face and a suggestive nudge, very slowly pronounced my name, "Hello, Tommmmmm," drawing out the second word and giggling as he did. There had to be something embarrassing about it, but I was clueless.

One day when Louis Wabol, our language teacher from Rota, stopped by on his way home from school, I decided I had to know what was going on with "Tom." He looked around to make sure none of little Borja girls was within earshot, sat me down, and said quietly, "In our language, the word *tom* means 'your testicles.'" All at once being called "Mistah Jink" didn't seem so bad.

CLASSROOM DISCIPLINE was a challenge, especially in the class with the lowest English proficiency skills. To restore order in the room, I often had to raise my voice. On rare occasions I resorted to sending disruptive students out into the hall. One of these students expressed his opinion about my disciplinary tactics with a short work of free-verse graffiti on the hallway wall. It looked like this:

    stupid
    stupid
    stupid
    Mr. Zink
    Mr. Zink
    Mr. Zink
    You are
    very stupid man
    Mr. Zink is the
    stupid man
    his the one
    is very stupid man
    all the man are
    very good
    and Mr. Zink is
    the one
    is very stupid man

The grammar left a bit to be desired, but the spelling was quite good.

Some days, I walked home alone after school, lost in my thoughts about my shortcomings as a teacher and a coach. I questioned whether I would ever understand how to handle the cultural and language differences that caught me off guard (like the *susu* incident). The lackadaisical attitudes of the kids on the Oleai sports teams I coached could get under my skin. Some felt they needed no instruction from me at all; others seemed more intent on talking a good game than making the effort to play it.

The searing heat and humidity were especially oppressive on these lonely walks home. By the time I had covered the two blocks to my house, my shirt was soaked. Drowning in sweat and self-pity, all I wanted to do was collapse on the floor and hope the power was on so my little electric fan could cool me down.

With Saipan's random unannounced power outages, electric clocks were not a reliable way to tell time. But within the Micronesian perception of time, stopped clocks were of little concern. The rhythm of their unhurried pace was a clear cultural message I sometimes struggled to keep time with. Four of the teachers at Oleai school were Carolinian women who lived in the village. Every day after school, they walked out under the portico and the spreading Poinciana tree and down the crushed coral driveway of the school to their homes. One Friday during the dry season, I found myself heading home at the same time as these colleagues. I understood a pitifully small amount of the Carolinian language, but I began walking with them, listening, and trying to follow the gist of their conversation. I was walking as slowly as I knew how, yet I kept getting ahead of them. I'd stop and wait for them to catch up but in another couple minutes, found that I had again gotten ahead of them.

If "keeping up" means not lagging behind, my problem was that I could not seem to "keep down." I looked at their *zori*-clad feet in the dusty driveway. It occurred to me that I was walking with a group of people who were so unfocused on a destination that they actually seemed to be lingering on each step, all the while chatting away. Though the words they spoke were still somewhat mystifying to me, the message in their lingering footsteps was clear. I think of the lesson I learned that day—on the Oleai Teachers' Walk— as simply: How you get where you're going is often more important than where you wind up.

DURING SCHOOL BREAK for the Christmas holidays in my first year, two events took place that showed me how effortlessly this Carolinian community was taking me in. At the center of each of Saipan's nine villages, built of typhoon-safe concrete, stood the Catholic Church. San José Church in Oleai, a two-minute walk down the road from my house, sponsored a group for youth and young adults called the Oleai Civic Youth Organization. We all knew it simply as The Civic. As my first Christmas on Saipan approached, Florence Selepeo, Olympia's younger sister, invited my friends Ralph and Bev Chumbley and me to practice with The Civic for its annual carol sing. I wasn't sure when to walk over to the church on the day of the first practice. I went next door to see Florence when she came home from school.

"When's the practice?" I said.

"This evening," Florence said.

"I know, but when is it?"

"This evening."

"But when?"

She was getting impatient. "I *told* you, it's this evening."

"Yes, Florence, but *when* is it?"

We were both speaking English but in different languages. I needed the clock as a reference point to keep me from being late. Florence's perception was free from the tyranny of the clock; she was on Micronesian time. Once the caroling practice did get started, Ralph, Bev, and I did our best to follow along on the mimeographed word sheets we were given with the Carolinian and Chamorro words for familiar carols.

We rehearsed "O Come All Ye Faithful," in Latin ("*Adeste Fidelis*"), Chamorro ("*Fanmatto manhenge*") and Carolinian ("*Au ito ma lugelug*") as well as English. The Carolinian carols we learned were exquisite with counterpoint harmonies, driving rhythm on the guitars and ukuleles, and a collective energy that pulsated through the evening air. I couldn't wait for the next rehearsal and the caroling tour of the island.

On the evening before The Civic's caroling tour, the children of Oleai school presented their Christmas concert. A four-foot high outdoor stage was built against the wall of the school and decorated with pine branches and Christmas lights. Sitting near the front of the audience with a tape recorder, I was awestruck by the four-part acapella harmonies sung by the choir of fifth to eighth graders on carols like "Joy to the World" and "Silent Night," sung in English and Chamorro. Next came the primary grade children whose Saipan version of "Santa Claus is Coming to Town" told of Santa coming to each of the villages close to Oleai and evoked appreciative giggles and laughter from the audience. The concert highlight, though, was the delicious irony of hearing forty Saipanese schoolchildren singing, "I'm dreaming of a white Christmas, just like the ones I used to know."

On the Friday evening before Christmas, forty-five youths and adults from The Civic, lots of guitars and ukuleles, and three Oleai Peace Corps volunteers boarded a chartered school bus and headed out to sing at key locations around the island. We stopped at the Royal Taga, the island's only modern hotel, at the hospital, the Trust Territory High Commissioner's house, the Nursing School, the United States Coast Guard station, and at the clubhouse of the Saipan Golf Club, where all the Marianas Peace Corps volunteers and staff were gathered for a Christmas party.

The enthusiasm, joy, laughter, and vocal cords of The Civic carolers continued unabated whether we were on or off the bus, through six hours of singing. For my first Christmas away from home, I discovered a brand new and enduring meaning of the spirit of the season. The absence of snow, cold winds, icicles, and frosted windows did little to diminish my joy that Christmas.

On the night of January 1, 1969, The Civic had a holiday party in the Quonset hut next to the church. I was not in a partying mood, but I went anyway and sat outside the Quonset on a bench, sipping a Coke. One of the Carolinian boys came over and sat down next to me. "Mistah Jink, there's three Chamorro boys from Oleai who said they're going to beat you up."

"Oh, you don't say," I replied. Idle threats were bandied about in the village from time to time, and I was too tired from the week of holiday goings-on to show much concern. Two of the guys from The Civic volleyball team came up and told me to call on them if anything happened. A couple seventh-grade boys I coached on the Oleai school softball team got all agitated on my behalf: "We'll go and fight those Chamorros, Mistah Jink." They walked over to the road, like sentinels, waiting for something to happen.

That was when Olympia Borja's younger sister Florence came by and said that Placido was going to drive her to Garapan, the next village north, where she was staying at her parents' house and that I should ride with them. I finished my Coke and climbed into the back seat. When Placido and I got back to Oleai later, the coast was clear. There was never another word of the reported threat, but just in case, I slept with a baseball bat next to my bed for the next few nights. Whether or not the threat had been real, I felt well-protected by my Carolinian friends.

WHEN I SAID GOOD-BYE to my family at Escondido, I had sixteen years of parochial Lutheran education behind me. Joining the Peace Corps began to dilute those concentrated doses of religion and church I'd received like medicine in my earlier years. The after-supper devotions, Sunday morning church, confirmation class, and my parents' Bible passage discipline were all like scaffolding within which my faith in God could grow. My faith came with me to Saipan, but doubts traveled alongside.

Ever since Steve died, I had been following along with the prevailing wisdom of my elders that his death was God's will. This Christian overlay, the only way available to make some sense of an incomprehensible event, served to silence my grief so I could get on with my life. But it also held my memories and my pain frozen in the past. I was accustomed to keeping my emotional life opaque to others. On Saipan, I kept a lid on my occasional bouts of loneliness, the times when I doubted if I had any real friends, questioned my effectiveness as a teacher, and wondered how I was going to survive the stinking heat in my corrugated-tin oven of a house. But my faith was my back-up. When I needed it, I found it in unexpected places.

One afternoon late in my first year, I was descending into a pit of personal angst. I was pushed to the end of my rope by the constant presence of chattering children around my house, the fruitless efforts to rid myself of the sheen of sweat on my forehead as I worked to finish marking eighth-grade English papers before a school deadline, and a pervading sense that when all was said and done, I was still just a stranger in a strange land. I left the unmarked

English papers on my desk and lay down on my bed. The stink of my own sweat seeping out through every pore made it all worse. Something had to change. I got up, slipped on my *zoris*, and headed out the door to my personal place of refuge just two blocks away, Oleai Beach.

Oleai Beach was the section of the five-mile stretch of white sand on Saipan's west coast that fronted Oleai. Typically, it was an un-busy place. Although an easy walk from the village, it was rare that anyone came to swim. The shallow bathtub-warm water of the lagoon afforded scant respite from the enervating heat and humidity. Because it was usually quiet, the beach near my house was the place for me to be when I was dangling from the end of my rope. Under the shade of the palm trees and tropical pines, I sat down on a log and dug my toes into the sand.

Several hundred yards out at the far side of the quiet, sun-drenched lagoon, the undulating movement of the white line of surf marked the reef. A breeze whistling through the tropical pines above me took me back to a family vacation in the Great Smoky Mountains in North Carolina, where we had heard the pine trees whistling at our campsite. I breathed in the warm air and relished the slightest wisp of breeze. I moved to lie down in the sand, resting my head on the log, my hands clasped behind my head. Looking up at the cotton ball flotilla of clouds carried west by the trade winds, I sensed a presence, a companion I could not see but recognized as the God of my childhood faith, a guide I knew I could count on at times like this.

Oleai Beach was one place I was occasionally reminded of God's presence on this island so far from home. But church it was not, and I did not warm easily to the church options on Saipan. Early on, I attended a service at the only Protestant church at the time, the non-denominational Saipan Community Church, with services conducted in English and attended largely by Americans who worked for the Trust Territory government.

The service was somewhat familiar and the people friendly. But I couldn't shake the feeling that I was back at St. Thomas church, enmeshed in the proper, polite, prescribed churchiness I wanted to leave behind. Over the next two years, I returned just a couple more times when a wave of Sunday morning guilt washed over me. I'd grown up in an environment in which physical attendance in church was perceived as the key indicator of your faith. In my new home, I went to church far less often but began to find new ways to think about faith and spirituality.

The other church option was San José Catholic Church, just down the road from my house in Oleai. Raised Missouri Synod Lutheran, I had internalized Catholics as "different." They prayed to the Virgin Mary. We didn't. They crossed themselves. We didn't. They couldn't eat meat on Fridays. We could. These inbred barriers were soon revealed as part of my religious scaffolding. They may have been vital to my family's religion, but I discovered they were not part of my own personal faith.

Ninety percent of the people in the Mariana Islands were nominal Catholics. Mass at San José church was Catholic and said in Chamorro; I was neither Catholic nor Chamorro. The service felt foreign to me, and I attended just once my first year, more as a social choice than religious. It was midnight Mass on Christmas Eve, and I went with several other volunteers so as not to stand out. In the after-Mass mingling and exchange of Christmas wishes out on the lawn by the church, I realized how many students, friends, teaching colleagues, and neighbors I knew in this mostly Carolinian congregation of Catholics. My Christian connection with them, and our shared celebration of this religious festival, superseded my long-held aversion to all things Catholic. Part of the scaffolding began to dissolve.

One midweek afternoon a few months later, another piece of scaffolding fell. The church bells were ringing out their call to five o'clock Mass as I crossed the lawn next to the church on my way home from a visit on the other side of the village. I was wearing my after-school, dress-down Peace Corps uniform—an old T-shirt, shorts, and my beat-up *zoris*. Sister Rosa, one of the endearing Flying Nuns from our Rota training, saw me passing by and called out, "Tom, come to Mass!"

"I'm not dressed properly. I can't go like this."

Rosa responded with a line I had never heard growing up in St. Thomas Lutheran Church: "God doesn't care how you're dressed. Come on!" I went to Mass that day, feeling a bit awkward, dressed as I was. But going to church was not where I typically looked for redemption. I looked to sports, a big part of my everyday life on Saipan.

I TAUGHT GRADE SCHOOL and junior high school physical education, coached grade school sports, played in a Saipan basketball league, helped build volleyball and basketball courts, and joined pick-up games of basketball, soccer, softball, and touch football with other volunteers and Saipanese. But it was the game of volleyball that was the crucible of the sharpest cultural jolt I would experience. The skills and knowledge I'd gained playing on the Valparaiso Volleyball Club were my calling card in Saipan sports circles. I gladly took on many different roles to promote the game. But my appreciation of the easy laughter and unhurried style of the Saipanese faded when it came to sports. Too often the island sentiment of "No beeg teeng, brudda" grated against my Protestant work ethic.

A few months after our Micro VII group arrived on Saipan, plans were beginning for a historic sporting event in Micronesia. Saipan was to play host to the first Micronesian Olympic Games (Microlympics) in July 1969. Teams of seventy-five athletes from all six districts of the Trust Territory would gather to compete in ten different sports, including men's and women's volleyball. Gold, silver, and bronze medals would be awarded for the top three finishers in every event. Kurt Barnes became the coach for the Marianas women's volleyball team, and I was chosen to coach the men. I saw this as my big chance—to coach a team to Olympic glory. It didn't matter that it was on a tiny Pacific island. Winning was winning.

Nine of the best players in the Marianas District were selected for the team. I took a tough, no-nonsense approach, and practices got off to a good start. The skill drills, physical conditioning, and clear expectations set an agreeable rhythm. Very soon, my demands got out of step with the players' needs. I was so intensely focused on what my players lacked, I was not able to appreciate their skills and motivation. My failure to take sufficient notice of the fact that I was now in a very different culture was the start of my undoing.

Attendance at practice became haphazard and unpredictable. Excuses for not showing up ranged from "I forgot" to "I couldn't get a ride" or "I had to look after my auntie." I learned from a friend one day that one of the players was at the Oleai Bar during a practice. In five months of twice-a-week Microlympic volleyball team practices, only three times did all nine players show up. Weeks passed. My frustration grew. My eagerness and enthusiasm slowly morphed into resentment and resignation.

By the time the Microlympics came, I had lost my rapport with some of the players but didn't know who to blame. I'd begun to admit my role—the harder I pushed, the less effect I seemed to have—but I wasn't ready to overlook what I saw as the players' apparent lack of commitment. The team had moderate success in the Olympic competition. We lost three matches and won two, just missing the bronze medal. I felt disillusioned and completely spent when it was all over. The women's volleyball team coached by Kurt Barnes won the only gold medal of the games for the Marianas District.

I needed a break. My Peace Corps friend Andy Pavley had coached the Marianas track and field team and shared my frustration over the Olympic experience. Over the last two weeks of July 1969, the two of us traveled to three other Micronesian districts on a vacation. I returned to Saipan for my second year, unaware that I was about to learn, in a very personal way, the reason that Peace Corps service is a two-year term, not one. Year one had seen progress and success in teaching and becoming part of the Oleai community, but it ended with disillusionment over what felt like my very personal

Olympic failure. In my second year, I gradually allowed my attitude to shift in order to live more in tune with the rhythms and harmonies of my new home.

In my first year, I was a player-coach with the Oleai Civic team in the island-wide men's volleyball league. We lost as many matches as we won. During that season, I noted in my journal the continuing minor annoyance that "these Carolinians, more so than Chamorros, have a tendency to laugh at the humor of their mistakes rather than work to correct them." After what I considered the fiasco of the Olympic volleyball team experience, I decided there might be some merit to the phrase heard so often on Saipan, "No beeg teeng, brudda!"

Indeed, in my second year, our Civic team adopted the saying as our team motto. I would have bristled at the idea the year before, but this time around, it really was "no big thing, brother." I still played as well as I could but felt less urgent about trying to avoid losing. I was learning that the playing of the game might possibly be of more value to the players than the final score. By looking through the eyes of my friends and teammates, I began to see that the zero-sum approach to games—for every winner there has to be a loser—could be combined with a focus on playing just for fun.

My second-year teaching assignment at Hopwood—Saipan's 750-student junior high school with grades seven, eight, and nine—gave me the opportunity to put my amended attitude about competition into practice. After the Christmas break, I began holding practices for a girls' volleyball team in anticipation of playing teams from the Marianas High School. In my first year, I had fallen into a habit of expending a lot of energy to coax Oleai Civic players to come out for practice. For this Hopwood team, I shed the earlier habit and applied my new "no beeg teeng" motto.

Instead of begging girls I knew to be good athletes to be on the team, I simply announced at school that girls should show up after school if they wanted to play. And show up they did: two dozen girls from all three grades. And they kept coming back. Our twice-a-week practices focused on skill improvement and fun. A majority of the girls were Carolinians, and I was, by this time, able to throw an occasional bit of Carolinian into the constant patter at practices and maintain a good-natured tone. We played with six on a side, and the girls all understood that if they messed up in a practice game, one of the girls waiting on the sidelines would be happy to replace them.

Our final practice before the big day when we would take on the Marianas High School teams took place during non-school hours at a municipal court some distance from the school. The girls lived in villages all over the island. Because of the Peace Corps' "no-vehicle" policy, I was in no position to offer anyone a ride. I had no idea if any of the girls would show up. With my new "no beeg teeng" attitude and my customary bag of practice balls in tow, I walked from my home in Oleai to the practice site.

I arrived fifteen minutes early and was overwhelmed by what I saw. More than half the girls were already there, sitting in the shade of the tropical pine trees that edged the court, talking and waiting for me. The rest of the girls arrived soon after. On game day, the high school coach and I each had enough players for four teams. We decided to play four games so that every girl had a chance to play. In light of my changed attitude, the results were startling. Our Hopwood Junior High teams won every game, two by scores of 11-2 and 11-1. If this lesson didn't make the point, the conclusion of the Saipan men's volleyball league a couple months later certainly did.

Our Oleai Civic team built on the previous year's experience and finished in a second-place tie with a team from the east side of the island called the Sun Raisers. The play-off match took place two weeks before I was due to leave Saipan. One of our teammates was ill, so we had only five players—Sam Iginoef, Dino Tebuteb, Jesus Mettao, Louis Wabol, and me—to the other team's six. We lost the first game, 17-15, and trailed 14-10 in the second but rallied to win it, 16-14. After trailing 5-0 in the third game, we hung on to win it 15-12. We were exhausted but deliriously happy. We laughed and hooted and patted each other on the back and shook hands with our friends on the Sun Raisers. The league president handed the second-place trophy to Louis. It was a dime-store variety trophy about ten inches tall with a volleyball player on top and a small plaque on the base that simply read "SECOND PLACE."

The five of us repaired to the familiar setting of Oleai Beach. Soft breezes coursed through the tropical pines. The sun had set. The lagoon was calm. We drank some beer and rehashed our victory. We had played our hearts out and risen to the challenge. Success was sweet. My teammates chatted briefly in Carolinian. Louis then turned to me and handed me the trophy. "We think you are the one to keep the trophy. You taught us and coached us, and this is our thanks."

Sitting there on the beach with my friends, having a beer and laughing together about our unexpected success, I marveled at the fact that by giving up my obsession with winning and my fear of losing, I had just received the first sports trophy of my life. It was almost too funny to be taken seriously, as moments of grace often are. I had arrived: I had a trophy for my imaginary trophy case. The boyhood memories of epic sports losses that I clung to as though they alone defined me faded from sight that evening just like the last lingering colors of the sunset.

MY EXPERIENCE IN THE PEACE CORPS, particularly in the village of Oleai, fundamentally altered my sense of being a stand-alone isolate in a world full of people I perceived as belonging. Yes, I had high school friends, college fraternity brothers, cousins and aunts and uncles, and my parents and sisters, but I clung to the fact that I was different from all of them, because I had lost my brother Steve. When I entered the Peace Corps, I chose not to accentuate that difference. If someone asked, "How many siblings do you have?" I took their use of the present tense literally and simply said, "Three sisters." I saw no point in troubling my many new friends, both Americans and Micronesians, with this tragic tale of grief and loss. My heart had moved on from October 1961. Or so I thought.

The hearty, good-natured welcome I received in so many ways gradually wore away my shell of isolation; it was replaced with a sense of inclusion. I had frequent visitors at my little house in Oleai—the Borja children, kids I taught in school and their older siblings, Kurt Barnes, the Chumbleys, and other volunteers. If the degree of privacy I was used to in North America felt compromised by all this company, it was more than balanced out by my growing sense of belonging. In my final week on Saipan, that sense allowed me to receive a gift of surprising grace. It happened a week after The Civic volleyball team had won the second-place trophy. On my last Sunday on Saipan, The Civic had a farewell picnic for the Chumbleys and me—the three Micro VII volunteers in Oleai—at Micro Beach, Saipan's largest beach. I borrowed a Peace Corps pick-up truck to cart some of the Oleai youth to the picnic. Later, when we packed up to leave, Angie hopped into the front seat with me.

Angie was an athletic, feisty seventeen-year-old. She was one of the more consistent players on Kurt Barnes' Oleai women's volleyball team and had played on the Marianas' gold medal women's volleyball team in the Microlympics. No moody prima donna, she played volleyball with determination and skill, a fact that endeared her to me when Kurt first introduced her at a practice the previous year. You could spot her on the court by her dangling white earrings, her long black hair braided down her back, and her random sexual innuendos in Carolinian followed by bursts of laughter from her teammates.

Her fifteen-year-old brother José jumped into the truck bed with a couple younger boys, and we headed back to Oleai. Angie and I talked about my imminent departure from Saipan. My flight was to leave the following Friday.

"Are you leaving for good, Tom?" Angie asked. I wondered how the term "good" could apply to leaving a place I had grown to love.

"I love it here too much to say there's anything 'good' about leaving,"

I replied. I stared ahead, concentrating on my driving, avoiding her gaze.

"Why go then?"

"Because."

"Because why?"

"Because," I paused, knowing that anything I said would sound like an excuse. "My two years are up on Friday. Besides, I'm going to graduate school in the fall, my family misses me, and I've already bought my plane tickets."

"*Lanya dai*, Tom. You're the *mwowesch*," Angie said, using the Carolinian term for "the one you feel sorry for." "But maybe you'll come back to Saipan."

"Maybe. I don't know. It's hard to leave."

We rode on in silence. The chattering of the boys in the back of the truck flitted in through the open windows. I turned off Beach Road into Oleai. I pulled up at a house near the church, and two of the boys climbed out.

"Bye, Mistah Jink!" they called as they ran off.

"Good-bye," I hollered back.

José moved to the front of the truck bed, leaned out, and spoke to his sister in Carolinian. The only words I caught were "school" and "house." "He wants you to drop us at Oleai school," Angie told me. "We're staying at our auntie's now."

Driving the last two blocks on the dusty roads towards the school, I recalled the many Sunday picnics I'd enjoyed on the beaches of Saipan: the Oleai women's volleyball team celebrating another winning season, the picnic for the altar boys from the Catholic Church, the Oleai teachers' picnic at the end of the school year. These picnics were festivities at which guitars and ukuleles were strummed, and I felt privileged to share the lively island music with friends gathered in the shade of the palm trees and tropical pines.

These were also the places I learned, for the first time, to dive, float, and relax in water that was over my head. Memories of the skinny seven-year-old who shivered in the cold water at the YMCA in Cleveland were fading. Swimming in salt water buoyed not only my body but also my spirit as I reconsidered the time my father seemed displeased about the ninety-six on a high school math test; maybe ninety-six was actually good enough. And maybe taking the role of equipment manager and statistician for that victorious junior varsity basketball team in high school was good enough.

I parked under the shade of the sprawling Poinciana tree that graced the front entrance of the school where I'd taught in my first year here. Even though I had stopped to drop off riders, I opened the door and got out of the truck. Angie got out, and José hurdled out of the back, kicking up a puff of coral dust as he landed. I did not want this day, this time, this stay on my island home to end. I tried some idle chit-chat to keep them around a bit longer.

"Where's your auntie's house?" I asked them.

"Just beyond that breadfruit tree," answered José.

We talked about aunties and uncles and families. Then Angie asked me if I had any brothers and sisters. "Three sisters," I replied, "all younger than me. And I had an older brother named Steve, but he died when we were teenagers. He was fifteen when he died."

"*Lanya dai*, same age as José, *abwo*?" said Angie. "How did he die?"

"In a traffic crash. He was hit by a car while he was riding his bike. He was here one minute and dead the next." I snapped my fingers. "Just like that." The words came out before I had time to think about them. It felt as easy to talk about Steve with Angie and her brother as telling them what I'd had for breakfast.

Our conversation drifted to other topics, and soon they were saying goodbye and walking across the schoolyard towards their auntie's house. When they turned and looked back, I waved and hollered the Carolinian farewell, "*Ulelah abwo!*" Literally it means, "You're going, yes?"

I watched them go and thought about this moment of secret-telling that had come and gone so quickly. I considered the possibility that this clear sense of belonging I had grown accustomed to in Oleai—that I was in the right place at the right time in my life—allowed me the safety to tell the story I had kept buried in winter's frigid cold for nine years. Perhaps the warmth of my tropical island home had, for that brief moment, melted my heart enough to let my secret out, like the short mid-winter thaws I remembered from boyhood that set icicles to dripping from the gutters. But I was due to leave the islands in a few days, and this brief thaw would be a mere memory when I returned stateside to the snow and cold of winter.

Carlos and Olympia Borja.

Tom, at home in Oleai village on the island of Saipan in the Mariana Islands.

The three youngest Borja sisters enjoy a sweet, juicy sugar cane snack. Left to right, they are Jesusa, Rosalia, and Bernadetta.

7 Itchy Feet

I TOOK A WINDOW SEAT on an Air Micronesia Boeing 727, the first leg of my long journey home in June 1970. As the plane rose and banked to the west, I watched the green rolling terrain of Saipan rotate slowly beneath me. The salty sting of nascent tears rimmed my eyes. I felt surprised and not a little embarrassed at my feelings. I kept my face turned towards the window to hide this quiet show of emotion. Saipan soon disappeared behind us. This did not feel like leaving "for good"; a part of me would remain on the island. I hoped for an early return to this home I'd grown to love, but I knew that was about as likely to happen as a white Christmas on Saipan.

On that departure flight, I was part of a small group of fellow Marianas volunteers whose plan was to travel home the long way, beginning by heading west to Japan instead of a direct return stateside via Hawaii. Peace Corps policy allowed us to use the cash in lieu of our direct plane ticket home plus a portion of the so-called Readjustment Allowance for travel. Our travels took us to Osaka, Japan, for Expo '70, and to Kyoto and Tokyo. After two weeks in Japan, we rode the train to Yokohama, where we boarded the Soviet passenger ship *SS Baikal* for a two-day voyage to the city of Nakhodka on the Soviet Union's east coast. There, we boarded the Trans-Siberian Railroad. Eight days and 10,000 kilometers later, we arrived in Moscow. Visits followed in Leningrad (now St. Petersburg), Helsinki, Stockholm, Copenhagen, Amsterdam, Munich, Switzerland, Paris, and London.

Eight weeks after departing Saipan, my adventures with my fellow volunteers came to an end. I flew from London back to Cleveland, where Mom, Amy, and Judi met me at the airport. My sisters had grown taller while I was away and were now the same height as Mom. I suppose I might have expected this, but the changes still stunned me. I was grateful to be home again, but "home" was now a different house. My parents had sold 3250 and the Back Acres and moved to a different suburb, to which my parents and sisters were delighted to welcome me.

In the twenty-six months I'd been away, we had only been able to communicate through letters, a couple recorded tape cassettes, and an occasional package of color slides. I was back in familiar surroundings, but I had changed, and the changes left me feeling uneasy. I had many tales to tell, but mere words did not have the power to convey the essence of the gifts I had received while I was away and the depth of my connection to Saipan and its people. I felt frustrated and more than a little annoyed that family and friends weren't more curious and intrigued about my adventures.

After dinner that first day home, I went upstairs to the room where the gear I had shipped ahead from Saipan was stored. In the first box I opened, I found the second-place trophy my Oleai Civic teammates had presented to me. This simple object that symbolized victory paradoxically became a talisman to remind me that there was more to sports than who won or lost. Life did not always have to be an either-or, win-or-lose, zero-sum game.

Next I found the storyboard that Danny Olaitiman had hand-carved for me to take home. A storyboard is a Pacific Island scene or traditional tale carved into a rectangular slab of wood. Danny's carving on an inch-thick board, eighteen inches wide and six inches high, depicted a traditional village in the Yap district with palm trees, banana trees, a taro patch, and a men's meeting house, known as a *faeluw*. The curved pathway that ran through the middle of the scene was wide at the bottom and narrow at the top, making it seem to disappear in the distance. The scene was framed by an intricately carved border. Danny finished the carving with brown shoe polish to bring out the three-dimensional relief in the scene.

Danny was a Carolinian man I first got to know as the janitor at Oleai school. The older two of his eight children were students in my classes. Danny's skin was dark brown, his cheeks and belly rounded, the body shape typical of most Carolinian men. Danny was soft-spoken, easygoing, and skilled in a variety of ways. When I needed plumbing help to bring running water into the kitchen sink of my house in Oleai, Danny came over on a Saturday morning to show me how to do it. A task I had procrastinated for ten months took all of two hours to complete. This mundane convenience, always taken for granted prior to the Peace Corps, was thrilling to behold. It was a "Kodak moment." I snapped a picture of Danny as he stood at my kitchen sink and turned on the water.

Unwrapping his storyboard reminded me of Danny's generosity, kindness, and helpfulness—qualities I regard as Christian, in a man who, as far as I knew, seldom went to church. Was being a regular churchgoer the primary requirement of living a life of faith, I wondered. The gift I received in Danny's storyboard was simply that I was now asking myself this question.

My Japanese-made Akai M-10 reel-to-reel tape recorder had also arrived safely from Saipan. While in Tokyo, I'd purchased a set of Pioneer SE-30 headphones that resembled bloated white ear muffs. I turned on the M-10, put on the headphones and played one of the Micronesian music tapes I'd recorded with my Oleai friends just before I left Saipan. The headphones let me immerse myself in the island music I had come to love. Music was a large part of my connection to Saipan and to Oleai—picking up the words, harmonies, and rhythms of Carolinian and Chamorro songs, learning to play Hawaiian slack-key, finger-style guitar, and singing familiar carols on the Oleai Civic Christmas caroling tour of the island.

I was back in Cleveland, but I felt pulled in opposite directions. Prior to our departure for home, Peace Corps staff in Micronesia had prepared us that many returning volunteers found readjusting to life back in the United States even more difficult than adjusting to life overseas. We could expect a form of "reverse culture shock," they said. For me it was the feeling that I now had one foot back in the land of my birth and citizenship while the other lingered in a distant place that for two years had felt as much like home as any place on earth. I felt like a wishbone.

MY MOSTLY POSITIVE EXPERIENCES on Saipan in sports and recreation had erased the disdain I'd felt at Valpo toward sports and recreation as legitimate subjects of academic study. In the fall of 1970, I enrolled in a two-year graduate program in recreation administration at George Williams College, a small YMCA school near Chicago. Through friends in the program, I landed a job the following summer as a counselor at Camp Herrlich, a co-ed camp operated by a Lutheran social services agency in New York City and located in the rolling hills and farmland an hour north of the city.

Within the first two weeks at camp, a letter from Micronesia arrived for me. The postmark intrigued me. It said "Palau," one of the three Micronesian districts that my friend Andy Pavley and I visited right after the Microlympics in 1969. I recalled the boat ride with some Palau Peace Corps volunteers among the fairy tale-like scene of hundreds of small, uninhabited islands, known as the Rock Islands.

The letter came from my Peace Corps friend and mentor on Saipan, Kurt Barnes, who was now the physical education and recreation coordinator at the Micronesian Occupational Center, a new vocational school for post-secondary students from throughout Micronesia. Kurt asked if I was interested in taking a job as a dormitory manager: a two-year contract, full benefits, travel expenses paid, and a regular salary far exceeding a Peace Corps living allowance. I felt my heart pause for a split second, zapped by a mix of elation and disbelief.

I read the letter again, held it loosely in my hands, and looked up at the

blue July sky, my eyes focused far away. The contrail of a passenger jet flying west drew my imagination upward. I was on that plane, window seat,
leaving all this behind—camp, graduate school, America, my family—ready
to go tomorrow. I folded the letter and put it in my pocket, my body fairly
abuzz with excitement. I needed to let this possibility percolate. Camp was
my immediate concern.

My experience in the Peace Corps, working with children of another culture, suited me well at Camp Herrlich, where most of the campers were from
lower-income black and Puerto Rican families in New York City. The skill I'd
developed on Saipan of allowing other people space to be themselves served
me well at camp, whether I was patiently helping ten-year-old boys learn to
fish, a pastime that I loathe, or gently but assertively talking a young, homesick Latino boy out of walking back home to the city.

The camp job reinforced my decision to move into the field of recreation
and was a refreshing break from graduate studies, but the letter from Kurt
Barnes was always on my mind. The initial flash of excitement did not fade.
Was I ready, I asked myself, to drop everything and return to Micronesia?
The job, the culture, and the setting would be different from Saipan, but Kurt
knew my skills, work ethic, and love of Micronesia well enough to take the
chance that I'd be interested. I wrote him back for more details about pay and
responsibilities. The job was to start in early September, a few weeks after
the end of summer camp. I sent a letter to my parents, not so much seeking
feedback or permission, but informing them of this opportunity that I was
seriously considering.

Making that summer at camp vastly more interesting—and complicated—
was the fact that I met—and quickly fell in love with—a twenty-year-old
college student named Naomi. Naomi had long, dark hair, a ready laugh,
and a keen interest in me I didn't fully understand. It was a first love for us
both, something I did not handle as well as homesick campers, overnight
backpacking trips with pre-adolescent boys, campfire sing-alongs, and bait-
ing fish hooks with wriggling worms. By summer's end, I had already decided
to accept the job in Micronesia. My desire to return to the islands trumped
this first love. My third trans-oceanic move in three years was about to cure
me of my longing for the islands in a difficult, sometimes dangerous, but
altogether successful, way.

BARELY FIFTEEN MONTHS after leaving Saipan "for good," I was back, having
scheduled a stopover of several days while in transit to my job in Palau. At
the airport to meet me were Carlos and Olympia Borja, Danny Olaitiman, the

man who carved my storyboard, and Neal Baker, an American who was my school principal both years I was in the Peace Corps. I had written to Neal from camp of my plan to visit Saipan, and he offered me a place to stay and loaned me his Jeep.

Just before sunset on that first evening back, I drove down from Neal's house on Navy Hill towards Oleai. Below me lay the island's west coast, the reef, and the lagoon, glistening with the colors of the sunset. I was smitten with the resplendent, redundant beauty of Saipan. Was I merely watching a diorama of a scene I had dreamed of countless times in the past year, I wondered. Or was I really back on the hills of Saipan? The warm, humid evening air erased all doubt that this was real. Again, I was enveloped by my infatuation with this island and its people, which had only grown stronger in my absence.

I drove to Oleai and stopped first at the Borjas' house. Rosalia and Jesusa saw me pull up in the Jeep and ran inside, calling to Olympia, "*Ma, ngeli Tom*. Tom's here." I was soon wrapped in an Olympia-sized hug and surrounded by smiling faces. It felt as if I had never left. "*Tolung munggo, Tom*," they said, "Come in and eat." I followed the family inside for some rice and fish and the strong, bitter Saipan coffee I could only survive by adding spoonfuls of sugar.

I left the Borjas' house and walked the village lanes and soon found some of my Oleai Civic volleyball teammates gathered outside next to Jesus Mettao's house. These were the guys who had decided I was the one who should keep the second-place trophy. They shared their beer. Pete came by with his ukulele, and we sang and laughed together and reminisced. Always, there was the laughter of the Carolinians, one of the most enduring and endearing gifts they'd given me. We talked long into the night. Life was good. But it was about to change.

My deflation began the next day in Neal Baker's office in the Marianas District Education Department. From the time I first heard about the job as "dorm manager," I pictured dorms like those I had lived in at Valpo— two or three students to a room. The pictures Neal showed me of the two Micronesian Occupational Center dorms jolted me into reality. The students lived barracks-style in large open rooms with twenty-five students housed in each. Bunk beds lined the walls, with metal lockers for the students' personal belongings. With two of these rooms on the ground floor and two on the second floor, each dorm had space for 100 students. The two dormitory buildings were sturdy concrete structures with a small apartment at the front for the dorm manager. There were students from all six of Micronesia's districts: some came from tiny, remote atolls in the Marshall Islands or Yap; some from

Saipan, the territorial capitol; others from the high islands of Ponape, Truk, or Kusaie, now known as Pohnpei, Chuuk, and Kosrae.

One day later, I arrived in Palau and was welcomed by Kurt Barnes, Pete Espinosa, and Pete's wife, Rita. Pete, a Peace Corps volunteer I worked with on Saipan, was the manager of the other dorm. At that time, Palau's airport consisted of a coral landing strip, three small thatched-roof huts to shade greeters from the blazing sunshine, and an old concrete Japanese building repurposed for travelers to clear customs and claim baggage. Neal Baker had alerted me that the leadership style of the American director of the occupational center set a tone of hard-nosed discipline based on a literal, punitive application of rules and policies.

I SOON LEARNED that everyone referred to the Micronesian Occupational Center as MOC, pronounced phonetically as "em-oh-see," and that MOC offered skills training in automotive mechanics, small engine repair, drafting, construction, electrical, plumbing, shorthand, diesel mechanics, and culinary arts, among others. I also figured out I had signed on to an untenable situation. The school was only two years old. Orientation for new dorm managers was paper thin. The students addressed Pete and me, their dorm managers, as *Papa-san*, a term borrowed from the Japanese to refer to a person of authority, usually an older person, which, in many cases, Pete and I were not. The students were high school graduates, many of them older than us, some with wives and children back on their home islands.

At the front of each dorm was the dorm manager's small apartment. Outside our louver-covered windows, students tended to gather to chat, sing, tease, smoke, argue, and laugh. Open the louvers to let in air or daylight, and students walking by could look in. On paper, our work schedule was forty hours per week, but our fishbowl location in the midst of student comings-and-goings made a joke of the schedule; if we were at home in our little apartments, we were on duty, whether we were scheduled to be or not.

To add to the fun, the MOC administration had a strict bed check policy. All students had to be in bed at ten fifteen on school nights and at midnight on weekends. Pete and I were in charge of enforcing bed check every night. Most nights, this was not a problem; students were studying, writing letters home, sitting outside chatting, playing guitars, smoking. Bed check came, lights were turned out, and all was well.

Weekends were a different story. On weekends, students could leave campus, and many went drinking in local bars, down at the docks or in the boonies. Micronesians were known for their ability to consume excessive quantities of alcohol. The bed check policy guaranteed that dozens of students, many in exaggerated states of intoxication, would all find their way back to the dorms at the same time.

The night before Halloween that year was a Saturday. I remember it now as the "Battle of Halloween Eve." The number of drunken students returning to campus that evening was higher than usual. Three guys from the Truk District had polished off two cases of beer. One of them, Franky, roamed the dorm inside and out in a fit of rage, hitting, slapping, and shoving anyone who got in his way. One sober student, whom Franky had hit, took off after Franky with vengeance in his eyes. At one point, Pete approached Franky to try to calm him down. Franky shoved Pete to the floor.

Someone called the local Palauan police. In the best of times, there is a wary truce between the Trukese and the Palauans. This night was not the best of times. In rapid succession, the police tried to arrest the enraged sober student who had been chasing Franky. While trying to take him into custody, the officers were jumped by three other students. The police managed to get back to their Jeep and drive away. Minutes later, they returned carrying rifles with the safeties off. By this time, Wilhelm Rengiil, the Palauan deputy director of the school, was on the scene at the dorms. He calmly inserted himself between his students and the police, assuring the latter that the school could handle this disturbance, and the situation was under control.

The following week, half a dozen students who were drunk and out of control that night were expelled and sent home on the next flight. Franky, a smart, well-respected student, was warned but not suspended by the school administration, a decision out of step with their reputation for hard-line enforcement of the rules. Such inconsistencies in administrative judgment made Pete's and my job on the front lines much harder. This uncertainty, coupled with growing resentment, made me extremely careful to make sure I was working within the rules in dealing with student behavior.

By the time New Years' Eve approached, I was wary of permitting students to plan a celebration. I did not want to be seen by the school administration as having sanctioned a New Year's celebration that was likely to get out of control. My stance against a student celebration made no difference to the students, though. Around midnight, I heard the clatter and clang of students banging on garbage can lids, drumming on empty oil drums, smashing garbage cans into crushed metal carcasses while parading around the school's athletic track located just behind my dorm.

An hour later, several students reported to me that a drunken Palauan high school student had walked onto the MOC campus and was yelling obscenities, carrying rocks, and threatening students. It was my job to approach him and tell him to leave. This teen walked ever closer to me and dropped the rock from his left hand. He grabbed the front of my shirt. With another rock clenched in his right hand and his arm cocked behind him, he screamed, "Fucking Americans!" He was so close he could have broken my head open without throwing the rock. Before he made another move, a Palauan MOC student who knew the younger boy stepped between us and said something in Palauan. The boy released his grip and was led away by the MOC student.

I was beginning to see an alternate interpretation of Palau's "rock" islands. Rock-throwing was apparently a form of self-expression and even entertainment here. Several months later, on a calm, normal, sunny morning I stood in front of my dorm and watched the MOC students leaving the cafeteria after breakfast and heading for class. A group of Palau High School students passing by on their walk to school started yelling taunts at the Trukese MOC students. As I watched, rocks began to fly in both directions. The distance between the two groups was such that the rocks fell harmlessly to the ground. Next to me stood Aiwo, a big Trukese guy. He was laughing out loud. I was dumbstruck. This was entertainment? Apparently so, and par for the course.

But my life at the MOC was not all rocks, drunks, and close calls. Every evening, the school's large cafeteria was transformed into a recreation hall with ping-pong tables, a trampoline, movie nights on Fridays, and a student-run snack bar, where I could get a chocolate sundae and French fries for forty cents. Many students took part in the volleyball, softball, and soccer leagues as well as the competitions in waterskiing, table tennis, and trampoline. Once every month or two, MOC's fifty-passenger picnic boat, the *Miss Micronesia*, would ferry students and staff to the Rock Islands for Saturday picnics. On some evenings, I could hear students sitting outside the dormitory, playing guitars and ukuleles, filling the evening with songs from their home islands. Some of my musical friends from Saipan were MOC students, and, as often as I could, I brought my guitar and joined them singing the songs we'd sung on Saipan.

The difficulties and dangers of my job far outweighed the recreational diversions and the considerable salary I was earning. But there was an additional distraction. I kept in touch with Naomi, the young woman I had met at summer camp, a relationship that seemed to prove the maxim, "Absence makes the heart grow fonder." Not long after the New Years' Eve melee, my strategy shifted: Instead of trying to survive to the end of my two-year contract, I began making arrangements to leave before my contract was up, which meant paying my own way home and giving up on life in the islands. My year at MOC significantly bulked up my savings account back home, which became my own personal "readjustment allowance." And it cured my island fever through a combination of my cynicism and resentment at the MOC leadership's style of management, the absence of a sense of belonging in a welcoming community I'd found on Saipan, and my desire to see Naomi again.

In the final weeks of my stay in Palau, I wrote a song called "A Day in Micronesia." (See page 234.) With a leisurely island rhythm, the verses move through the phases of a day, linking the movement—and stifling heat—of the sun and the rise and fall of the tide to the growing questions in my mind about the downsides of changes I was seeing in Micronesia. In the simple, idyllic morning scene, the "hours pass by unnoticed" when you're on "Micronesian time." But in the afternoon, the children "return from school carrying books made far away" and at night, their "new diversions are delinquency, dances, and drugs." The song's final line conveys the uncertainty with which I was leaving the islands this time: "And the question keeps re-echoing: What will tomorrow bring?"

I left Palau in early July 1972. My first stop was a farewell visit to Saipan. I knew this would be my final visit on Saipan, so I wanted to capture as many island sights as I could with my camera. I'd written to Carlos and Olympia to tell them I was coming. They met me at the airport and insisted I stay at their house. They went out of their way to cater to my photographic wishes. One afternoon, with four of their children and me tucked into the back seat of their little Datsun sedan, they drove me to many of Saipan's scenic highlights, among them the Old Man by the Sea, an eroded limestone block on the east coast that looks like a man's head with eye sockets, hollow cheeks, and a large bulbous nose—a must-see photo attraction for tourists.

After stops at several other scenic viewpoints and historic landmarks, Olympia had Carlos stop the car so she could treat me to a sight few visitors ever saw. She stood next to me and pointed to a jagged formation along the top of an exposed limestone ridge that resembled a man's profile looking up at the sky. When I finally was able to see the profile, Olympia laughed and said, "That's called the Old Man in the Sky."

In my time with the Borjas as a Peace Corps volunteer, I often felt more like a visiting amateur anthropologist—camera always at the ready—learning about island culture through their eyes, rather than a cherished family member who was always welcome. It was only much later I realized that Carlos and Olympia considered me an adopted son, an older brother to their children. I had barely a hint of the impact I'd had on them. On the day I was leaving, the Borjas draped an embarrassment of flowered decorations around my neck and my head. I was drowning in the fragrance and brilliant color of plumeria, ling-y-ling, hibiscus, and ginger. And in the Borjas' affection for me.

IN THE FALL OF 1972, I returned to George Williams College to complete my master's degree in recreation administration. In January, there came a welcome but unexpected twist in my relationship with my father. Dissatisfied with his job in Cleveland, he had begun looking for a new employer. He was fifty-six years old, but was not a man who was able to stew in his discontent and survive until retirement. The engineering firm that offered him the position he sought was located, ironically enough, in Chicago. After thirty years in Cleveland, my parents began a five-month transition to the Windy City.

Dad worked in Chicago during the week, staying in a bachelor's apartment on the north side, and flew back home to Cleveland most weekends. For the first time in the eight years since I'd left home to attend Valpo, I was less than an hour's drive away from my father. When our schedules allowed, I'd make my way into the city to meet him, check out his tiny apartment, and help him figure out some of the basic tasks of bachelorhood. He was a rookie at it, while I was a veteran at independent living. What was new for me was providing tips and reassurance to my own father about shopping and cooking. He spoke once or twice about how much he missed Mom's companionship, homemaking skills, and meal planning. Sometimes he'd just say to me, "C'mon, I'll take you out to dinner."

While my father was adjusting to temporary bachelorhood, I arranged my required, second-year field placement at a nearby pre-school that enhanced my understanding of the more playful attitude I'd learned on Saipan that "It ain't no beeg teeng, brudda." At the request of the school director, I developed and led a music and movement program for the children that provided me valuable insights into how children learn through play. I initiated activities by asking them movement questions like, "How long can you balance on one foot?" or "Who can hop ten times on one foot and not fall over?" There was no one "right" way to respond and only two rules: Give each activity a try, and be safe while you do it. Most of the time, the activity room was a scene of controlled chaos, with children crawling about on all fours, mooing like cows, while I played the guitar and sang "Old MacDonald Had a Farm."

Two small tumbling mats allowed the children to take turns trying somersaults and log rolls. When not in use, the mats were folded and stored; in this way, they resembled a small tunnel, a feature whose appeal to young children I failed to recognize. One day, the youngsters were scrambling about the main activity room like zoo elephants while I sang Tom Paxton's "Going to the Zoo." Two of the "elephants" wandered off towards the overturned mats. They started poking their heads under the rolled mats, then backing out again, giggling and chattering as they did. This was a little too chaotic for me. In my urgent attempt to curtail their antics, I blurted, "If you don't stop playing around, you can't play!" I'm sure I was the only one in the room who recognized the inane redundancy of my scolding.

My words were significant to me, though, as they went to the heart of what I was trying to understand about play, an unwieldy, unpredictable yet essential component of human behavior and learning. The two children exploring the tumbling-mat tunnel had shown me that the rules of a game could sometimes be changed to sustain the fun for the players. I realized those two tunnel-crawlers had a great idea that opened the way to a new game. A few days later, I set up the mats in tunnel form and asked the children, "Who can crawl from this end of the tunnel through this *darrrrk* passage all the way to the light at the other end?" This soon became one of the children's favorite games.

By the time I finished my master's degree in June 1973, my parents had completed the move to the Chicago area, where they would live for the next ten years. I turned down three unappealing job offers because I was yearning to hit the open road for parts of the country I'd never seen. Naomi had just finished her college degree and agreed to accompany me. We made our way west in my 1965 green two-door Ford Fairlane. Along the way, we visited places I'd only been able to dream about as a youth in Ohio: the Black Hills of South Dakota, the Beartooth Mountains of Montana, Wyoming's Yellowstone and Grand Teton National Parks, Yosemite National Park, and the majestic redwood and sequoia forests in California. Our final stop was Seattle, Washington, the home of Dave and Lynda Crutcher, my good friends and fellow English teachers on Saipan. They were generous in providing a home base while I looked for an apartment and a job.

THIS WAS A TIME when I was living out a post-Peace Corps phenomenon a fellow volunteer had once called the Itchy Feet Syndrome. The Peace Corps had taken me 8,000 miles from home to an unknown place in which I had a profoundly life-altering experience that lasted precisely two years. For better or worse, that experience not only primed me to have positive expectations about long-distance moves to brand new places, it also set a pattern that consumed the next phase of my life.

In the decade after I finished my master's degree in 1973, I made four cross-country moves, had a dozen different mailing addresses, and moved from job to job—and at times to no job at all—as interests, convenience, and opportunity led me. I did not stay in any one place much longer than two years. I was, among other things, a daycare center director in Seattle, Washington; a casual laborer on a dairy farm in western Washington; a YMCA soccer teacher; a student activities director at a community college in Hartford, Connecticut; director of the Activity Truck, a mobile urban arts and recreation program; a freelance recreation leadership consultant in Vancouver, British Columbia; and a child care counselor at the Children's Foundation, a residential treatment center for children in Vancouver.

I was between jobs in late 1974, when my friend Dave Crutcher, recently hired as the city manager in Sweet Home, a small town in western Oregon, encouraged me to apply for a job as Sweet Home's first full-time parks and recreation superintendent. The work, blending park maintenance and recreation programming, was challenging but deeply satisfying and kept me busy, especially in the summer when my days began before dawn, setting up sprinklers to irrigate the parks, and ended twelve hours later when the playground programs closed.

My relationship with Naomi had become an enigma. For better or worse, I loaded onto it all of my hopes, dreams, and illusions about long-term romantic bliss, but none of them stuck. Our connection was an on-again, off-again negotiation in which we lived close to each other at times, far apart at others. We slowly drifted away from each other, and by 1976, when I was working in Sweet Home, Oregon, Naomi moved back east from Oregon to live with her parents in Connecticut and look for work. I had little trouble reading this part of my story into a Tom Paxton song I'd learned ten years earlier: losing this love was "the last thing on my mind." Our relationship had run its course, living beyond its "Best Before" date. While others could see our relationship slipping away, I tried to hang on to it for dear life. I might as well have been trying to grasp a fistful of water.

IN THE SPRING OF 1976, about a year into my job in Sweet Home, at an otherwise unremarkable regional conference of parks and recreation professionals in Spokane, Washington, I was introduced to a brand new concept in recreation that would significantly alter my life's direction in the coming years. Reading the numerous workshop titles in the conference brochure, I noticed a session, called "Promoting New Games." The workshop description, with phrases like "cooperative games that everybody wins" and "play for the fun of it," caught my eye. I decided it was worth a look-see. If it turned out to be true that anyone, including me, could play these "new" games free of the "loser" anxiety I had carried around since childhood and could also capture the spirit of playfulness and fun that I had learned to appreciate in the Peace Corps, I could not afford to pass this up. Little did I imagine how this brief two-hour introduction to New Games would change my life by elegantly connecting my past with my future.

It was clear almost immediately that this was not going to be a typical conference session. One of the leaders asked everyone to help move all the chairs to one side and stack them along the wall. She said her name was Anna, then motioned us all to gather in a large circle around George, her co-leader.

"This is New Games," said George. "If you're expecting research, charts, and hand-outs, you're in for a surprise because we are here to *play*." This was different. The session was beginning with no recitation of the academic degrees and qualifications of the leaders and no cursory review of goals and objectives. "To help everyone get acquainted, we'll start with a name game." Nervous giggles rippled around the circle when he said the name of the game: Zip-Zap-Zorch. On the surface the rules were simple. "If I walk up and point to you and say 'Zip,'" he told us, "you have to say the name of the person on your right before I count to three." "Zap" meant you had to say the name of the person on your left; "Zorch," your own name. If you couldn't spit the name out in time, you moved into the middle and became the leader.

The leader began to zip, zap, and zorch people at random around the circle. The tension was palpable but playful. Some blurted the name out in time, some stuttered a syllable and then giggled or bent over in laughter; others stood speechless, unable to connect their brains with their mouths. Flustered players who couldn't get the correct name out in time changed places with the leader. In a few minutes, more players were tapped to go into the middle. Soon four or five leaders were moving about, zipping, zapping, or zorching others. The leader who introduced the game blended into the circle and allowed his role to be taken by other players who had never even heard of the game ten minutes earlier. He pointed out later that this game illustrates key elements of New Games: rules are kept simple, mistakes are welcome, and distinctions between winners and losers, and leaders and players, are intentionally blurred.

We were warming up to this idea of New Games and to each other. Men started loosening their neckties and rolling up their shirt sleeves. Women shed their high-heeled shoes and stowed them under the stacked chairs. Anna then arranged us into smaller groups of about a dozen each. Each group formed a circle, standing shoulder to shoulder. The instructions—to clasp hands with two different people across the circle from you—were simple, but the objective was not. We were to attempt to unravel the "knot" we had created without letting go. Smiles, giggles, and groans ensued as we considered our task. We began solving the problem together. Some stepped gingerly over others' lowered arms; some reached behind bodies and twisted themselves into pretzel shapes; others did the limbo under raised arms. Slowly, our knot began to unravel. Cheers broke out as we emerged into a single hand-holding circle.

In the space of twenty minutes, we had seen an orderly circle of adult professionals dissolve into the controlled chaos of Zip-Zap-Zorch, then a confusion of arms and hands tied up in a human knot resolve into a unified circle. Every game had a specific objective—to learn names, to problem-solve. But it was the play—the inclusiveness, the implied permission to let go of our professional roles, to laugh, to join hands with people who were complete strangers twenty minutes before—that made this a New Games experience. The only "final score" that mattered was that everyone relaxed, took part, and had fun.

After a full hour of novel, fascinating games and a brief discussion of the New Games philosophy, I left the session with a couple new friends, new program ideas to take back to Sweet Home, and a brochure from the New Games Foundation. The foundation had been organized a few years earlier in the San Francisco Bay area to foster and communicate a style of play that emphasized inclusion, creativity, and community. New Games leaders were called "referees," and the New Games motto, "Play Hard, Play Fair, Nobody Hurt," emphasized the primary concern with the safety, both physical and psychological, of everyone playing. The foundation offered weekend trainings in the Bay area to provide the skills, knowledge, and experience needed to lead New Games.

Six months later, I boarded a bus from Sweet Home to San Francisco to learn more about this fascinating phenomenon I had discovered in Spokane. The training site was a typical school gymnasium, but within the training's first two hours of non-stop games it became clear there was nothing typical about the space we had entered. The team of three trainers made sure there were at least three games going at any one time. Games flowed seamlessly, one into the next, with no whistles, penalty flags, or fouls called. Some games were strenuous, others quiet. Some used equipment like a giant Earth Ball or a parachute; most needed no equipment, like Zip-Zap-Zorch or Knots. Taking a time-out was up to us individually if we wanted a break to step back and observe.

Giggles, laughter, and excited shouts punctuated the atmosphere in the gym that morning. The mix-ups, confusion, and surprising new rules for familiar games built a strong sense of camaraderie. When we gathered to talk about what had just happened, the key point was that New Games was not just about the games. The games were a means to an end, not the end itself. The "end" was to invite others into the games and give them permission to play, to laugh, to run, to chase and be chased, to act silly if the rules of a game required it, to be surprised and to embrace kinship with people they'd only recently met.

I was hooked. For a guy who had grown up expecting to lose and was surprised to win, I was attracted at a deep level to these new games that blurred the lines between winners and losers.

The emphasis on inclusion, community, and creativity was like an oasis in what I had long experienced as the win-at-all-costs desert of traditional team sports. I returned to Sweet Home and within a month, I was organizing a New Games program for children, led by high school students I had trained using the principles learned in the Bay Area New Games training. A valuable resource I brought home from the training was *The New Games Book* that described sixty new games and included several essays on the origins and philosophy of New Games. One essay, called "Creating the Play Community," reflected many of the principles I valued. I wanted to find out more about the author, a games designer and play facilitator from Pennsylvania named Bernie DeKoven.

In the spring of 1977, as I approached the two-year mark in Sweet Home, the Itchy Feet Syndrome kicked in again. The Peace Corps pattern reasserted itself: two years in, then move on. I had accomplished a lot in my two years and had done all I could with New Games in a small town. I was eager to become more involved in New Games and knew that living in a city would offer a greater variety of opportunities to do that. Family ties were drawing me east. My parents were living in the Chicago area, Judi in nearby Peoria, Illinois, and my sisters Kelly and Amy near Washington, DC. The destination that drew me was Hartford, Connecticut.

The New Games Foundation had earlier sent me the names of New Games connections in the east, and one of them was Bernie DeKoven, who was planning to be in Hartford that summer to teach a graduate education course based on a New Games approach to social interaction. Bernie's course had already begun by the time I arrived in Hartford, but a few weeks later, I went to meet him at the house he was renting for the summer with his wife and two children. His personable, welcoming ways made me instantly comfortable. We spent the whole afternoon together, getting acquainted. Bernie was a forty-something man with a beard, a balding head, and an impish grin. His conversation was liberally sprinkled with wise insights, playful words, and infectious giggles.

When I told Bernie I was eager for more involvement in the New Games program, he began trying, in his seriously light-hearted way, to convince me of the absolute, life-or-death necessity of attending the five-day intensive New Games training camp in Pennsylvania in August. The hundred-dollar fee was daunting. I was still trying to settle in to my new location. I had neither a job nor prospects in sight to staunch the outflow from my savings account.

After much discussion about the camp with Bob Gregson, a Hartford artist to whom Bernie had introduced me, Bob and I decided to sign up. I had a hunch that the investment might prove to be worthwhile. It was a heady investment at the time, but, like my brief introduction to New Games at the conference in Spokane, Washington, I was soon to find doors opening to me I could not imagine. Not long after I sent in my registration fee, I found success in my Hartford job hunt. The two part-time jobs that would begin in September were enough to sustain me.

The five-day New Games camp expanded on the experience of the introductory weekend trainings and allowed participants time for a deeper look at implications and applications of the New Games philosophy. By the end of the camp, Bernie and the two co-directors of the New Games Foundation had taken note of my evident enthusiasm and aptitude for leading New Games. Two weeks later, Bernie called to invite me to become an apprentice trainer with the New Games Foundation.

At this same time, the New Games Foundation was awarded a substantial grant from a private foundation to expand from its base in the Bay Area to a national training program. I was in the right place at the right time. It was a dream come true to be asked to be part of this significant growth for the New Games Foundation. I started as an apprentice trainer in the fall of 1977, working alongside Bernie and other trainers and learning the tricks of the trade in places like Springfield and Cambridge, Massachusetts; New York City; and Charlotte, North Carolina. At each training, we met dozens of interesting and engaging people eager to make New Games part of their personal and professional lives. I returned to Hartford after each training, feeling a mix of gratitude to have met these professionals and regret that our paths would never cross again.

AROUND THE TIME I BEGAN my work with the New Games Foundation, a reminder about the loss of my brother arrived in a September 1977 letter from my mother, addressed to my three sisters and me. Mom wrote:

> A strange kind of milestone passed recently, which I wanted to mention to you all, with a request. At the end of August, enough years had rolled around that Steve had been gone as long as he was with us. I realize that for you kids, his presence was both less and more than for Dad and me. None of you knew him for fifteen years and forty-five weeks, but on the other hand, he'd been a part of your whole life up until that day in 1961, when he was suddenly taken away. It made me

wonder whether you think back sometimes to the years when we were seven [the "Zinkseven"], and what his life meant for your life. I would appreciate it very much if you would write down for me some things you remember about him, both positives and negatives, and whether his personality and doings, and/or his death, provided any learnings and growing experiences for you.

I thought very little about Steve during these Itchy Feet years of traveling and learning and growing. That early part of my life was still a frozen tundra. My mother's words brought me back and made me realize that Steve was still very much present for my parents. My mother's precise calculation of the number of years and weeks Steve was alive gave me a clear idea of the source of my own propensity for calendrical calculations. I don't remember what I said in reply to her, but she later wrote, "We were delighted with your card and grateful for your remembrances of Steve. Your paragraphs reminded me again how private and individual any reactions always are. Another person can never know someone's reaction to an experience until told."

EIGHT MONTHS LATER, in April 1978, I helped lead a New Games training at George Washington University's athletic center in Washington, DC, with Bernie DeKoven and a veteran Bay Area trainer named Todd Strong. By lunchtime on the first day, I had taken notice of a woman named Beth Hewson, a spunky, playful, and engaging participant whose infectious laughter brought smiles to everyone around her. As we talked at lunch, I learned that she was born and raised in a city called Sudbury in northern Ontario, and she was working towards a master's degree in therapeutic recreation at George Washington University.

Ever since my three years in Micronesia, I was drawn to people who made the choice to leave home to live and work or study in a different country. Over the course of the weekend, I noticed Beth's ability to laugh at herself and exude a sense of joy, as if life was a series of new exclamation points. This New Games trainer gig I had landed had its high points and low points. My farewell to Beth on Sunday afternoon was one of the lowest. I gave her an arm-around-the-shoulder squeeze. The only thing I could think of to say was, "I like the way you play." Beth then became one of those many attractive, interesting training participants I knew I would never see again.

My first scheduled training in the fall of 1978 was in Columbia, Maryland, a planned community located halfway between Washington, DC, and Baltimore, Maryland. On Friday, October 20, my two fellow trainers and I arrived in Columbia to make plans for the weekend. The next morning, we were at the Columbia community center early, opening the equipment bags and setting up a registration table to greet and welcome participants as they entered the gym. I was sitting at the table, checking names off the list. I looked up and was stunned to see Beth walk in. I stood up and walked over to greet her, surprised that she remembered my name, just as she was surprised to hear me introduce her to my fellow trainers, using details I recalled about her graduate thesis project using New Games with patients in a mental hospital.

At the break after the morning games session, I approached Beth and said I was interested in hearing more about her master's project. I suggested we could skip the next item on the day's agenda, a New Games slide show she'd already seen. We sat on the edge of the stage in the empty community center auditorium and talked about her master's degree project and about my work in Hartford, where I led a mobile arts and recreation program called the Activity Truck.

This training in Columbia included an experimental third day on Monday designed to explore ways of incorporating playfulness into everyday life. That Monday found us in a community room in a small shopping mall in Columbia that had an open-air plaza in the center. The plan for the afternoon was to divide into groups of two or three and to explore the opportunities for play in the rather business-like environment of the shopping mall. Somehow, I managed to wind up in a twosome with Beth. Beth took the lead as we moved out to assay stores for playful possibilities.

We wound up browsing the aisles of a store that sold bar accessories— corkscrews, cocktail glasses, ice buckets, wine racks—and, we discovered, nose-squeezers. Beth was a non-drinker, but I didn't know it at the time, so there was either a touch of irony or mischief in her choice of store. In an aisle full of small gadgets, Beth picked up a pliers-like contraption. Squeezing the handle caused the small flat jaws to close together. One of the jaws had holes in it, apparently to drain juice from whatever fruit was being squeezed. In the grip of this woman with whom I was becoming increasingly enamored, the gadget became a nose-squeezer. She held it up to her nose and gently squeezed until it compressed her nostrils.

"Here, try it," she said, her face set with serious intent. Playing along, I leaned closer while she held it to my nose and lightly squeezed.

"Hmmm," I said, "You're right. It *is* a nose-squeezer."

"Let's leave it here and ask the clerk if they sell nose-squeezers," she said, our conspiracy begun.

We walked to the check-out counter. With an innocent sincerity, Beth said to the young man, "Do you sell nose-squeezers?"

The clerk hesitated, looked at Beth, then at me. He'd been invited into a new game called Find the Nose-Squeezer. He seemed up for the challenge. As he moved out from behind the counter, he said, "Well, I'm not sure. Let's go have a look."

It took him less than three minutes to find his way to the aisle we had just left. His eyes searched the racks of gadgets and stopped on the lemon squeezer. He took it off the rack, showed it to Beth and said, "Here. This might do."

"Oh, thank you," she said without a hint of sarcasm. "We've been looking all over for one of these."

I was smitten by her *chutzpah* and her playful way of using humor to include, rather than exclude, a concept New Games continued to impress upon me.

Beth and I said our farewells at the end of that training day. On my flight back home to Hartford, questions filled my mind. Would I ever see Beth again? Did she have any interest in seeing me again? How would we ever be able to arrange a get-together? I figured the odds of us meeting again were slim, but I did have her address, and I could at least send a card. I found one with a child's drawing on the front. It showed two children playing catch and the words, "Get out…" and on the inside of the card, "…and never let anything interfere with play." With the card I enclosed a short letter asking for her feedback on the training and letting her know how much I appreciated her insights. And at the very end, I hinted that she'd be welcome if she ever thought she'd like to visit Hartford.

I mailed the card and thought about tai chi. I had learned the basics of this Chinese martial art form some years ago when I was a student at George Williams College. Tai chi involves a continuous flow of movements with your weight shifting slowly and smoothly from one foot to the other. Inherent in all tai chi moves is the concept of "stepping empty." With all of your weight on your back foot, you first touch the other foot to the floor in front of you without transferring any weight to it. The weight on your back foot then slowly decreases as the weight on your front foot increases. It is the stepping style you would use to cross a rock-strewn stream by stepping from rock to rock. With solid footing on one rock, you would "step empty" onto the next to make sure it is solid before committing your weight to it. In empty-stepping, you make your move only when you're confident that it won't send you sprawling into the water.

I found myself empty-stepping my way forward with Beth. I was concerned she'd think it presumptuous of me to send her a card and that my words would disappear into the sullen void of relationships that never materialized. Sorting through my mail a few days later, I felt a heady mix of relief and elation. There was an envelope from Beth. Our cards had crossed in the mail. She ended her note by including her phone number. I called the next day, and we talked about getting together, another small stepping stone across what felt like a formidable stream. She was nearing the end of her master's program and had her final thesis to submit in December, but she thought she could make a short visit to Hartford towards the end of Thanksgiving weekend in late November.

The Amtrak train from Washington to Hartford on that Saturday night ran late. Scheduled to arrive at midnight, it didn't actually materialize until four in the morning. I took a catnap at my apartment to fill the extra time, and I wondered, and I worried. Would Beth walk towards me with her hand extended for a handshake? Were we still just friends who would spend time together talking about New Games, the main thing we had in common?

Greeting Beth on the Hartford train platform felt like another pivotal moment, a stepping stone. I was nervous. I got to the station, parked the car, and climbed the steps to the platform. There I joined others who awaited a parent, a spouse, a lover, a son or daughter. While I waited for . . . what? I would soon learn the answer. I watched her step down onto the platform, look around, and catch sight of me. She smiled. As we walked towards each other, I knew right away that this was not to be a handshake greeting. We hugged and exchanged pleasantries: Did you have to wait long? How was the trip? Boy, am I tired! Are you hungry? I took her bag and slipped my arm around her waist, leading the way to the car. When she put her arm around my waist, I thought of stepping stones and shifting weight and progress across this stream of unknown depth and width.

Beth brought with her a piece of news that startled me into realizing I had big decisions ahead of me. In the month between the training in Columbia, Maryland, and her visit to Hartford, Beth had applied for a job to become the first director of a new therapeutic recreation training program at a community college near Vancouver, British Columbia. In November, she had flown out to Vancouver, interviewed for the job, and was hired. Her start date would be January 2. My heart was split in two. I was unsure if this surprise was the beginning of the end of something that seemed so promising or if it was a very long stride onto a new stepping stone across a very wide stream. We walked together in downtown Hartford that gray Sunday afternoon, around the Old State House, and across to the Phoenix Insurance Company building where we danced a quiet waltz to the music in our hearts across the empty concrete plaza.

I saw Beth off on the Monday morning train, just twenty-seven hours after she had arrived, but not before we made plans for me to visit her in Washington three weeks later. During this subsequent visit, I saw evidence of Beth's grace under pressure as she submitted her master's thesis, defended it in her final oral exam, and packed up everything she owned for her move across the continent to start her new job.

Somehow, Beth made time for me such that I didn't feel like an imposition. I learned that Beth had three younger siblings: two brothers, Ric and Ben, and a sister Margie. I mentioned that I also had three younger siblings, all sisters—Kelly, Amy, and Judi—and that I had an older brother named Steve who had died when we were teenagers. I spoke briefly about Steve's death and then changed the subject, asking Beth about her home town of Sudbury. We discovered both of our birthdays were on the twentieth of the month—hers the twentieth of May, mine the twentieth of March. This somewhat trivial discovery was meaningful to me, as it fed into my fascination with calendrical calculations and was another small nudge forward towards the stream's distant shore.

On the last day of my visit, Beth and I walked the few blocks from her apartment to the Washington National Cathedral, the largest Episcopal Church in the United States. Beth had been baptized and confirmed in the Anglican (Episcopal) Church in her hometown of Sudbury, Ontario. But for me, it was the first time I had set foot in an Episcopal church; it would prove to be far from the last.

It was mid-afternoon on a weekday. The cathedral was empty. As Beth and I entered through the fifteen-foot tall bronze entry doors, I felt like a tourist, here to observe a neogothic architectural masterpiece and to marvel at the grandeur of the gothic arches, the loftiness of the high ceiling, and the splendor of the stained glass windows. We entered the nave and walked slowly, silently down the central aisle together. I felt strangely changed. Church buildings have always been special places for me, and I felt invited, enveloped, and somehow cared for by the vast space around me. I sensed also in Beth a kind of quiet reverence, as if we were in the presence of something beyond the two of us. We sat down together halfway up the nave, near the large baptismal font located dead center in the aisle. To be touched so deeply in this cathedral with my new-found companion next to me brought me to tears. Looking up in silence, a wordless prayer formed inside me, and I sensed a renewed confidence in our next step together.

Before she moved to Vancouver for her new job, Beth planned to be with her family in Sudbury for Christmas. She invited me to come up after the holiday to meet them. I rode the overnight bus from Hartford and arrived at five in the morning. Beth met me at the bus station, and we drove to the

Hewson home, where I soon met Beth's father, Geale, as he came downstairs to start the morning coffee. Beth's mother Peg came down soon after, and, although she had just woken up, she asked me if she could fix me something for breakfast. The gracious hospitality of Beth's parents was a constant during my visit. I also met Beth's sister Margie; Margie's fiancé, Dale; and Beth's brothers Ric and Ben.

On this visit, Beth and I explored the possibility of closing the distance between Hartford and Vancouver, seeing if there was a way to step across to the stream's other bank. Beth had a full-time job with a good salary and benefits. Back in Hartford, my colleague Bob Gregson and I were freelancing as a play leadership consultant team to human service agencies, day care centers, and community groups. I was therefore virtually unemployed and hustling for income, not the economic lifestyle most suited to my personality. I knew that if Beth and I were to get together, it would be me who would need to move.

For a child of winter, northern Ontario in late December was cold, white, and frosty with a certain ineffable feeling of home. My visit with the Hewson family was to be five days. Beth and I were both planning to fly out on New Year's Day—she to Vancouver and me back to Hartford.

A northern Ontario blizzard struck on New Year's Eve and changed the plan. My flight to Hartford was cancelled. Beth's flight to Vancouver was not. She left in the morning. This unexpected turn of events left me with an extra day to get better acquainted with her family. Margie cooked me a breakfast of bacon, eggs, toast, and fresh-squeezed orange juice. Dale and I went out cross-country skiing on the hilly snow-packed streets in the neighborhood. We ate well, played board games, and watched old family movies and slides of Beth and her siblings as young children. I learned more about Beth and her family than I ever could have if the blizzard hadn't cancelled my flight.

I returned to Hartford on January 2. Things quickly began to snowball. On January 3, I walked into a United Airlines ticket office to inquire about flights to Vancouver in March. By late January, I had begun to contemplate the possibility of relocating to the far side of the continent for the third time in six years. I knew my next step was to visit Beth in her new surroundings and assess my employment options in Vancouver. I had made such long-distance moves work before. I was confident I could do it again.

My flight left Hartford the day I turned thirty-two. I made a three-day stopover in Chicago for a family reunion at my parents' home. My sister Kelly and her husband Hal were both in the United States Army and would be departing soon for a three-year posting in West Berlin. Amy came from her home in Washington, DC, and our youngest sister Judi drove up from her home in nearby Joliet, Illinois.

Hanging on the wall next to the fireplace in Mom and Dad's family room were framed pictures of their five children, one above the next in the familiar stair-step I remembered from my youth, with Steve's yearbook photo at the top. We still did not discuss Steve or his place at the top of our family "stairs," but we enjoyed our time together, each knowing this would be our last visit together for at least three years. As we gathered for dinner on the final night, I remember an intuitive sense that this could well be the last time I would be with all of them as a single man.

The week in Vancouver with Beth strengthened our resolve to make our relationship work. We both had independent, stand-alone lives that were meaningful, rewarding, and challenging. We had much in common: our Christian faith, the importance of our families, staying physically active, making time for fun, and having birthdays on the twentieth of the month. We both were seeking the companionship of a fellow traveler and were ready for the changes that would require.

Beth and I have sometimes joked about our "one-three-five-seven" courtship: one day together in Hartford, three days in Washington, five days in Sudbury, and seven days in Vancouver. Those visits were the highlights, but the stepping stones drawing us closer to each other relied just as much on the phone company and the postal service: I mailed nose-squeezers to Beth for her twenty-ninth birthday in May.

In June, Beth traveled home to Sudbury for her sister Margie's wedding to Dale Lougheed on the same weekend I was in Chicago to lead a New Games training. Beth arranged a three-day stopover there on her way back to Vancouver. On a walk one day in the neighborhood of my parents' suburban home, Beth mentioned that a colleague of hers at Douglas College told her a wedding is "a public declaration of a private intention." By this time, we had become quite clear with each other about our intentions and were ready to let our families know that we planned to be married.

Less than a month later, Beth and I chose a wedding date that suited us both. The third Saturday in October preceded a scheduled mid-semester practicum week for Beth's therapeutic recreation students. Free of her teaching duties that week, she could take the week off for our wedding and a brief honeymoon. The date's calendrical symmetry also appealed to me; it was exactly halfway between our birthdays—five months after Beth's on May 20 and five months before mine on March 20. This sense of inherent balance gave the date a feeling of inevitability. And so it was that the date we chose was Saturday, October 20, 1979, exactly one year after the surprising grace of our paths crossing a second time in Columbia, Maryland.

I left Hartford two years after I had arrived and moved to Vancouver in August 1979. Plans moved quickly over the next two months. The wedding was to be small; we invited only extended family and a few friends. Beth's sister Margie would be our maid-of-honor, and my cousin Rob Springsteen, the oldest of Bob and Anne Springsteen's children, best man. Pastor Lutze, my theology professor and friend from Valpo, accepted our invitation to present the homily at the service.

Beth and I took a red-eye flight from Vancouver, arriving in Sudbury at seven in the morning, two days before the wedding. Beth's mother, Peg, met us at the airport. On the ride into the city Beth sat up front with her mom, while I rode in the back seat, barely awake from jet lag and the nearly sleepless flight. I scanned the scenery: hard, dark, igneous rock as far as I could see with barely a tree in sight. The only other time I'd been here, the landscape had been covered in snow. I remarked to no one in particular, "Boy, it sure is rocky around here."

Peg was quick and forthright, with a reply that spoke volumes about the landscape and this northern Ontario family I was about to join: "We like to think of it as rugged."

The next day was Friday, the nineteenth of October. My parents arrived from Chicago with all three of my sisters in the car. Bob and Anne Springsteen and their two sons, Rob and John Peter, arrived from Valparaiso as did Pastor Lutze and his wife, Esther. I was met with warm greetings, hugs, and congratulations by all. The rehearsal that evening in the chapel was simple and brief, and the rehearsal dinner a relaxed, enjoyable blending of Hewsons and Zinks. This time of rejoicing and celebration, the day before our wedding, also marked the day eighteen years earlier when Steve had died.

The week after the wedding, Beth and I had a short honeymoon at a resort not far from Sudbury, then flew to Chicago, where together our parents hosted a second reception for friends and relatives in the United States who were not able to make the trek to northern Ontario. My Peace Corps friends in Oleai, Ralph and Bev Chumbley, now the parents of two little girls, drove up from their home in Memphis, Tennessee, for the occasion. To share our news with our many friends and relatives throughout Canada and the United States, Beth and I sent a brief wedding announcement:

> In a small, simple ceremony in Sudbury, Ontario, (Beth's home) on October 20, 1979, we joined our lives together, dedicating ourselves to gracefully growing old together. Our joy is full and we want to share it with you, the good friends and companions who have shared

life's path with us. As partners, we're both keeping the names you've known us by as individuals.

AFTER OUR SUDBURY WEDDING and the reception in Chicago, Beth and I returned to Vancouver, a thriving coastal city of spectacular beauty, framed by the glistening ocean to the west and snow-capped mountains to the north and east. Known as Canada's "Lotusland" or "Hollywood North," Vancouver was a mecca, a destination for those seeking all the best that life had to offer. Locals liked to boast of being able to go sailing on English Bay in the morning and downhill skiing at Grouse Mountain in the afternoon.

But some illusory end-of-the-rainbow notion about the idyllic lifestyle in this laid-back metropolis was not what had landed us here. Living in Vancouver was not a particularly comfortable fit for a couple of just–married easterners. We were instead drawn by Beth's job at Douglas College. The fact that we were now living on the western fringe of the continent, while our families all lived in the eastern half, exerted a strong tug in that direction. On occasion, Beth would drop hints about one day moving back east, as if, for her, it was a foregone conclusion. I was newly arrived and found this a bit disconcerting. Also unsettling was the vague unease of living in an earthquake zone, a place where, far beneath the surface, continental plates could collide without warning and cause great destruction. A Vancouver friend, and fellow easterner, once spoke about his wariness of "the spirits in the earth," a feeling that resonated with us.

We led very busy lives in those first few years of marriage. Beth worked long hours as coordinator of the Douglas College therapeutic recreation program. I started a freelance recreation leadership consulting business called PlayWorks and continued my New Games training work. After two years, I took a full-time job as a child care counselor at the Children's Foundation, a residential treatment center for children with behavioral problems. Beth and I still talked in vague terms about moving back east, but were unsure how we would know when we had reached the point of actually planning to move.

That point made itself known one evening in mid-December 1981. Before work that morning, Beth had gone to see her doctor for a pregnancy test. Later in the day, I had supper ready and waiting when I heard her car pull up at the curb. I hurried outside knowing she might have news that would change our lives. My question was answered before I could ask it. Beth's first words as she got out of the car were, "Well, hello, Papa Zink." I had lived and worked with youngsters from pre-schoolers to teenagers for most of the past fifteen years. And now, at last, I was going to be a father. It was a dream of mine that began to be crystal clear from the moment in 1974 when I first heard Harry Chapin sing, "Cat's in the Cradle." The song's story of a father too busy to play ball with his son was one I was determined to rewrite. Beth and I hugged and held on to each other. Our parenting adventure was about to begin.

In August 1982, our son Jesse was born, the first grandchild on the Zink side of the family and the second on the Hewson side. We were awash with love for Jesse and learning more deeply than I could ever have imagined the full meaning of two words: contentment and exhaustion. The distances to our families in the east immediately felt much larger. Our move became a matter of when, not if. In late December, Beth and I opened our new 1983 calendar books and together made a tai-chi-like, "stepping empty" decision. We drew a circle around the last Sunday in June—in pencil—as the day we might possibly depart. We had no way of predicting how this would work out. We felt a sense of relief, knowing we now had a timeline, even though our eventual destination was still in process.

Beth and I wanted to be within driving distance of her parents in Sudbury, Ontario, and my parents, who would be relocating to Roanoke, Virginia, in September, 1983. I had been thinking for some time about doing research that would synthesize the key themes that had informed my life and my work since my graduation from Valpo: the inclusive laughter of the Carolinians on Saipan, the play of pre-school children, the playfulness of New Games, and the often challenging dynamics of families at the Children's Foundation. I was curious about the role of laughter, humor, and playfulness in families, and knew it would be hard to fit this topic into a standard doctoral program.

When I'd been living in Hartford, I had heard that the doctoral program at the School of Education at the nearby University of Massachusetts at Amherst was flexible enough to allow students to design their own course of study. When I learned that my application had been accepted, I made an exploratory visit in March 1983 to the UMass campus, where I learned that my research goals and the flexibility of UMass' doctoral program requirements would be a good match.

On June 26, we loaded our bicycles onto the front bumper rack of our GMC van, strapped Jesse into his car seat in the back seat, and hitched up a U-Haul trailer that was stuffed with all our worldly belongings. At ten in the morning, we drove away from our rented Vancouver house. One mile later, we stopped for coffee and doughnuts and a quick haircut for Beth and me to ensure we would be traveling in style. Driving east along the Trans-Canada Highway and United States interstates, we were modern-day pioneers, heading in the reverse direction from the nineteenth-century wagon trains.

We made stops on our way east to visit my parents in Chicago, the Springsteens in Valparaiso, Beth's parents in Sudbury, and Beth's Aunt Buzz and Uncle Ted in Niagara-on-the-Lake, Ontario, a short distance from Niagara Falls. The last leg of our journey took us eastward across New York state to our final destination, a region of western Massachusetts known appropriately as the Pioneer Valley.

We arrived in the dripping, drenching heat and humidity of late July, undaunted by the challenge of settling in a brand new place. It was not the first time for either of us to take on such an adventure. With our customary frugality and our accumulated savings, we were confident we could make this venture work, and we were right. Starting basically from scratch, we found an apartment in one week, a favorite swimming hole in two weeks, part-time jobs in three weeks, and three families with children of Jesse's age in four weeks. I didn't know it at the time, but our four years in Vancouver would prove to be the final stage in my fifteen Itchy Feet years. The Itchy Feet Syndrome had run its course. This trans-continental move would last me twenty-three years.

Beth, holding ten-month-old Jesse, and Tom—ready to begin the journey east from Vancouver, British Columbia, to the Pioneer Valley of Massachusetts in 1983.

Tom and Beth in Vancouver, a week before their
wedding on October 20, 1979.

8 Settling

THE APARTMENT WE FOUND was in Northampton, a small city of about 30,000 in western Massachusetts, about two hours west of Boston. Northampton is the center of a region referred to as the Five College Area, with four small private colleges and the University of Massachusetts all located within ten miles of each other. We lived on South Street, a main traffic artery that led into Northampton's downtown area from the south. Our apartment was located in a precise section of roadway in which semi-tractor trailers approaching downtown from the south had to downshift. The noisy truck traffic was intermittent at all hours of the day or night.

On October 7, 1983, we were jolted awake around five in the morning by a brief rumbling that rattled a few objects on shelves. A fleet of eighteen-wheelers cruising by perhaps? Or did the guy in the apartment above us drop a load of bricks on the floor? And at five in the morning? A few hours later we heard the news: an earthquake had struck in the Adirondack Mountains of New York state, measuring 5.2 on the Richter scale. Our wariness about the "spirits in the earth" in British Columbia had been a minor but contributing factor in our decision to leave and move to the supposedly rock-solid ground of New England. We never felt an earthquake in Vancouver; it took just two months to feel one in New England.

The earthquake hit on Friday of the three-day Columbus Day holiday weekend. Beth's family had made plans to gather in Niagara-on-the-Lake, Ontario, on that same weekend, when Canadians celebrate Thanksgiving. So, a few hours after we were awakened by rumbling, we packed up the van and set out. One of the main reasons Beth and I had moved east was to be able to make weekend trips like this to be with family for these special occasions. With Jesse in his car seat and me resting on the bed in the rear part of the van for the first leg of the drive, Beth took the wheel, and we were off.

Within a few moments, I sat up. Something didn't feel right. I noticed we were heading north on Interstate 91 towards Vermont and Quebec. "Beth, where are we going?" I said.

"To Canada, of course," she said, barely able to conceal her excitement. She well knew that, generally speaking, Canada *is* north of the United States.

And we were indeed headed to Canada, but it was the long way around to Niagara-on-the-Lake.

I pointed out that if we headed west through New York state, it would take far less time. Soon we were on the Massachusetts Turnpike—westbound—to the New York Thruway and on to Niagara-on-the-Lake. By dinnertime we reached the home shared by Beth's Aunt Elizabeth Hewson, whom we all knew as "Buzz," and Buzz's brother Uncle Ted. The rest of Beth's family arrived soon after from their homes in other parts of Ontario.

The false start on our first trip to visit Beth's family in Ontario was never repeated. The westbound route from Northampton through New York state into Ontario became as much of a family habit as our Zinkseven westbound road trips from Cleveland to Valparaiso in the 1950s and 1960s. We made the Ontario trip two or three times every year: to celebrate Easter and Canadian Thanksgiving at Buzz and Ted's and to enjoy summer vacations further north in Beth's hometown of Sudbury and at the family's cottage on a lake not far from Manitoulin Island.

Our apartment in Northampton was within walking distance of St. John's Episcopal Church. On one of our first Sundays at St. John's, the incumbent priest announced his retirement. That's how we got to know the Reverend Jim Munroe, who came to St. John's soon after as interim priest and was installed nine months later as the full-time priest. Father Jim was about my age, a Vietnam War veteran, a rock-climbing, mountaineering outdoor enthusiast whose leadership helped grow the church in more than just numbers. Many people were drawn to his inclusive preaching style, which brought the Gospel to life in unique ways.

One Sunday, to illustrate his sermon topic, Father Jim brought a step ladder into church and corralled about a dozen parishioners to help. We had a short pre-service session to practice our roles: We were to catch a falling priest, fully robed in his vestments. I recognized his plan as a game we called Trust Fall at New Games events.

During the sermon, Jim lined us up in two rows of six, facing each other, with our hands extended out in front of us, knees flexed, palms up, ready to catch. He climbed to a step on the ladder that was about as high as my head. He crossed his arms on his chest and fell backwards—as straight and stiff as a board—into our waiting arms. Jim was a short, stocky fellow and landed with definitude. Accompanied by the sound of the congregation's collective gasp, the twelve of us caught him and safely lowered his feet to the floor. He returned to the pulpit and continued his sermon on the true meaning of faith. Father Jim and St. John's church would play a central role in our family as we gradually put down roots in Northampton and settled in to life in Massachusetts.

FOR MOST OF MY ADULT LIFE, I'd dealt with differences with my dad by placing distance between us, but I now saw new commonalities we shared. We
had both undertaken significant moves in the summer of 1983, and I was also
beginning to notice skills and attitudes I could trace directly back to my father.
I recalled how I used to watch him work at home, laying out what he called
a "critical path" for completing an engineering job. He showed me how he
listed tasks in a column on the left side of a chart and matched them with a
timeline across the top of the chart. I had already used that same tool in planning New Games trainings in Vancouver and had started similarly charting the
numerous requirements of my doctoral program. There were also intangible
qualities I attributed to growing up as Al Zink's son, like a natural ear for
music and harmony, a deep sense of faith, and a strong work ethic.

Dad was dedicated to his work, both professionally in the engineering
business and at home, where minor car repairs, leaky faucets, blown fuses
and broken windows were dealt with promptly and skillfully. One of his
maxims was, "Don't be afraid of getting your fingernails dirty." His actions
communicated his work ethic so clearly he seldom needed words, but one
incident stands out when his few words spoke volumes to me about the value
of responsibility and hard work.

One year, when I was a Valpo student, I took a part-time job over Christmas
vacation at the Cleveland post office. Our beloved Cleveland Browns football
team had an important playoff game on television on Christmas Eve at the
same time I was scheduled at the post office. Cleveland sports teams rarely
advanced to the playoffs, and I was bummed about having to miss the game. I
was heading out to the car to drive to work when Dad said to me, "Remember,
this is just a football game. Tomorrow it'll be over. But what you're doing is
showing that you take your responsibilities seriously, and you'll show up for
work when you're scheduled. And that will last you a lifetime."

Easy for you to say, I thought. You get to watch the game. His thoughtful
words of encouragement did indeed linger far longer than memories of the
game: The Browns were routed 52 to 14.

Now that Jesse was part of our lives, I wanted to remove some of the barriers our distance had created between my parents and me so they could watch
their first grandson grow up. I did this by providing them with a steady supply
of photographs. As any new father with a camera, I took an abundance of
pictures of my firstborn and made copies to send to Roanoke. Two shots taken
on Jesse's first birthday, at the swimming beach we discovered soon after arriving in Northampton, proved to be a catalyst for a new, mutual understanding
between Dad and me. Jesse was crawling on the beach, wearing only his diaper, inching this way and that, away from the camera, towards the camera,

back and forth while his father clicked away. I mailed copies of these shots to Mom and Dad. In a phone call soon after, Dad, in his familiar jocular manner, said, "It looks like he doesn't know whether he's coming or going."

It was an innocuous enough remark, but it reopened an old wound and reminded me of my once-trusted Ridiculometer. I said nothing during our phone call, but the sting made me recognize that what I'd wanted to hear from Dad was a simple acknowledgement of how vibrant and happy our child was. His comment may indeed have been his best effort to do just that, but what I heard instead was something I was more accustomed to: humor that was neither adoring nor approving.

I let my reaction simmer awhile as I decided how to respond. I was determined that the thoughtless teasing Dad dished out to his own children was not going to be fed to mine. In a letter to him a few weeks later, I reminded him of his comment and stated in as clear and friendly a way as I could that he should henceforth consider Jesse off-limits for his teasing. When his reply came in the mail, I read with relief words that told me he had gotten the point. Acknowledging my request "that the pictures of Jesse at the beach not be used as a basis for comments of a belittling nature," he admitted his propensity "towards remarks that are meant to be funny and harmless and yet turn out to be not very funny and occasionally harmful."

While I was a doctoral student at UMass, I worked with several colleagues to develop and lead humor, laughter, and creativity workshops for parents and human service agency staff with titles like "How to Take Your Job Seriously and Yourself Lightly" and "The Lighter Side of Parenting." Our workshops were upbeat, affirming, and participatory, and we wanted to add some light-hearted music. I wrote a song called "Good Enough for Me," with three verses about children whose best efforts get squashed by adult "shoulds." The sing-along chorus has alternative words those adults *could* have used: "Oh, you're doing just fine, and I like you like you are. If you trust your own thinking, then you really will go far." The chorus ends with a self-assertive, "So there!" line—"I'm good enough for me." (See page 236.)

I wrote the song as a positive, affirming expression for other people to enjoy singing in our workshops. The fact that one of the verses was autobiographical and the song's message was relevant to me had little effect on me. After years of absorbing my father's "comments of a belittling nature," I had made a kind of uneasy peace with the feeling that I didn't measure up to his standards. At the time I wrote the song, I was unable to absorb the fact that the "good enough" message was more for me than for a workshop audience.

Near the end of my first year in the doctoral program, I began my search for a faculty advisor by introducing myself to Dr. Janine Roberts, a UMass professor who had finished her own doctorate a couple years earlier and headed the university's training program for marriage and family therapists. Our first meeting was instructive. I told Janine about my personal experience living with both the hurtful, teasing side of humor in my own family and the inclusive, good-natured laughter of the Carolinians on Saipan. My research goal, I explained, was to find out if and how other parents with young children used humor and laughter in positive ways in their everyday lives. My interests leaned more towards strengthening families through education than to treating family dysfunction through therapy. A short while later, Janine agreed to chair my doctoral committee and recommended that I take her series of family therapy courses to deepen my understanding of family dynamics and to provide context for my research.

THE VERY FIRST ASSIGNMENT in the first course I took with Janine provided an opportunity to remember Steve. From a list of two dozen novels that dealt with family relationships, we were to select one book, analyze the family in it, and compare that family to our own. I studied the list, weighing my options, and selected a familiar story, *Ordinary People* by Judith Guest, a story about the sudden death of a teenaged son and its impact on the family. I had twice seen the movie that was based on the book and already knew the story's resonance with my own family's similar experience. In retrospect, I wonder at times if I chose the book or if the book chose me.

Under the guise of "doing my homework," this assignment gave me permission to ask some of those questions I'd been afraid to ask in the past. Looking back, I wonder if my growing sense of settling into our new home in Massachusetts allowed me some slack to take on this potentially unsettling topic of family loss. I could not be sure where a project like this might take me, but, like the empty stepping that is so fundamental to the practice of tai chi, I sensed that it was time to find out.

The ordinary people in the book were the Jarrett family—with parents Calvin and Beth and their two sons Jordan, or "Buck," and Conrad, who were fourteen months apart in age. The book described the day that Buck and Conrad were boating on Lake Michigan when a violent storm erupted and capsized their boat. Both boys were good swimmers, but Buck lost his grip on the boat and slipped down into the angry water. Conrad was not able to reach him, and Buck drowned. A rescue boat operator made a call to the frantic parents waiting on shore, saying only that one of their sons had survived without saying which one. Conrad, who often felt overshadowed by Buck, carried the weight of survivor guilt. A few months after the accident, Conrad attempted suicide, was admitted to a mental hospital, and later began seeing a psychiatrist. The novel was an in-depth study of the psychological impact of the older brother's sudden accidental death on the surviving family members.

Producing a similar analysis on the psychological impact of Steve's death on my own family seemed too difficult to do on my own. The lack of engagement we'd had around the loss was so pronounced that I didn't know how it had affected individual members of my family or the family as a unit. So, I mailed letters to my parents and my three sisters, asking for their help with my assignment. The message within was couched in research terms—I was simply trying to complete a school assignment.

It was not my intent to upset the equilibrium each member of my family had managed to establish in dealing with their grief over Steve's death. I phrased the letter in the most non-threatening, open-ended way I could. I posed three questions: "What do you remember about Steve? What do you remember about the day he died and the days and weeks right afterwards? What do you think were the effects of his death on our family?" I concluded my letter by acknowledging that I knew this was not easy territory for us. I asked them to respond in any way they chose or to not respond at all if they preferred.

Replies from my father and youngest sister Judi came within a couple of weeks. Ironically (or intentionally), the date on my father's letter was October 19, the anniversary date of Steve's death. Both of their letters recounted detailed memories of Steve as well as moments from his funeral and our family life in the weeks that followed the funeral. I gleaned more information from those two letters than I had in the twenty-three years since Steve's death.

I learned for the first time about Dad's harrowing high-speed cab ride to the airport in Rio de Janeiro after he had received the telegram to "hurry home." Judi recounted how Steve helped her learn to ride a two-wheeler and how difficult the first Christmas was after he was gone. Question three—the effects of Steve's death on our family—stumped them both. Dad wrote, "I'm afraid I must pass." Judi's response was "I have no ready answer. Off the cuff I'd say it had no effect but obviously that cannot be."

My mother's response came after I submitted my assignment, but she and I did have several meaningful conversations about Steve—in person and by letters—in the coming months. My sisters Kelly and Amy were not yet ready to respond, which confirmed my initial intent with this project to avoid a sense of intruding on any family member's personal grief journey.

At Christmastime that year, my family—parents, sisters, spouses, grandsons—gathered at Dad and Mom's new home in Roanoke, Virginia. Altogether, we were a family of ten in a house that could sleep eight. Mom and Dad had arranged for two of us to stay at the home of neighbors who were away, but it surprised us to learn it would be them. At ten o'clock on our first night together, Mom and Dad said good night and carried their pajamas, toothbrushes, and alarm clock across the street. An hour later, the phone rang. After a brief to-do over whether we should answer, I picked up the receiver and said, "Hello." A voice that sounded suspiciously like my father's said, "It's eleven o'clock. Do you know where your parents are?"

On the morning that Beth, Jesse, and I were getting ready to head back to Massachusetts, Mom told me that she wanted to talk with me about the *Ordinary People* paper. It was not the first time that a difficult, emotionally-laden family topic was saved for the tail end of a visit when the car was packed, and we were eager to get on the road. But this was an opportunity I could not pass up.

Mom and I sat down together on the day bed in their guest room, out of earshot from everyone else, and talked about Steve. She was curious about what I had learned from writing the paper. Who in our family had replied to my letter? How was our family similar to and different from the Jarretts? What was my professor's reaction? We each had tears once or twice, but because the conversation was framed around my academic and intellectual comparative analysis of the Jarrett and Zink families, we both remained distant from our own feelings of grief and loss. I couldn't see it then, but it was a beginning, a small stepping stone forward, that allowed a bit of warmth into this long-frozen story.

As I look back now at our loss and the ways in which we all buried it, I notice certain ironies. My parents and I were all fairly decent communicators, for instance. I had become a skilled training leader in New Games, teacher trainings, and humor workshops. Dad was often the project engineer brought in to improve communication on a construction project that was snarled in misunderstandings and hard feelings. He once organized a skit for a company banquet using a hefty dose of humor to illustrate that good communication was good business. Mom was a trained parent educator, helping parents practice skills for positive communication with their children. One of her favorite admonishments to us as children when a misunderstanding created strife was a single word, enunciated syllable by syllable for emphasis: "*Com-MYUN-i-cate!*" Yet, we had great difficulty communicating with each other about Steve.

I mailed my parents a copy of my final paper a few weeks after returning to Northampton after Christmas. It took Mom almost a full year to bring herself to read it, but read it she did. In January 1986, she wrote me a letter that gave me my first real glimpse into her internal grief process; I knew from her 1977 letter to us, for instance, that she was processing Steve's death but not what her feelings looked like. She wrote that her first reaction to the theme of distance in the family was, "Yes, we separate so as to reduce the frequency of family gatherings where we are reminded that someone is missing—like avoiding the sight of the 'empty chair.'" She said she was surprised that she didn't feel weepy while reading the paper "because I really was taken up intellectually with your development of the theme." After her first reading of the paper, she "cried, as much for our ignorance of how to deal with it more wisely as for the memories of the great loss."

She then read it again and wrote, "I realized that I probably never spoke to the family about some of the help I got in working through the grief (from several sources) and recognized that through all those years I have often quelled a sad remembrance with the thought, 'I haven't got time to cry about that now.'" My mother also told me she intended to do her own investigations into the emotions around Steve's death: "I got a tablet [of writing paper] and started listing some of the incidents of the following months [after Steve died] that were significant. I plan to describe them in writing in the hope that opening up the locks on this box of gloom will be helpful for me and maybe for others."

In a subsequent letter to Mom, I expressed my interest in reading the list she hoped to start, but I never saw it and am not sure she ever managed to write it. Nor did I ask her about the help she got after Steve died, in deference, I suppose, to our habitual, historical pattern of avoiding the pain. But the conversation did continue, slowly and over time.

Four years later, in 1990, an article in the national Sunday *Parade* magazine grabbed my attention. With the title, "Can a Marriage Survive Tragedy?" the story described the difficulties couples face trying to sustain their marriage after the death of a child. I knew for certain that my own parents' answer to the question in the title was, "Yes, with the help of God." I was also well aware that my parents' grounding in the Christian faith made all my travel adventures and long-distance moves possible. I never doubted I would always find welcome and stability at their home. I clipped out the story and mailed it to my parents with a short letter, saying the article "made me even more appreciative of the two of you for how you did manage to weather the shock and keep us all together."

Mom responded a few months later:

> Thank you for the kind words about our holding together after Steve's death, but I must say there was no inclination toward splitting up at that time... As for our family, I know that the good Lord was both shielding and sustaining us through that shock and the gradual

re-structuring of our family life. What I regret a lot is that we didn't help each other with the grieving process. In those days nobody was recommending that people express and share feelings in order to get through a disturbed time, and I think each of us did our mourning in complete solitude.

The *Ordinary People* project had been like a warm February breeze, bringing a brief thaw to the unyielding frigidity that surrounded my family's pain. But my attention was drawn away by the demands of completing my doctoral dissertation. Dripping icicles froze again, puddles iced up, and our collective "memories of the great loss," as Mom had written, once again became my life's backdrop.

JANINE ROBERTS ENCOURAGED her doctoral students to form small peer support groups to counterbalance the on-your-own solitude required to complete the research, analysis, writing, and editing for a dissertation. I was fortunate to meet and form a group with two women, Nancy Fisk and Linda Johnson, both of whom were psychotherapists focusing their studies on alcoholism in families. Our support group met nearly every month for four years. The mutual exchange of practical and emotional support was indispensable along the way. We became familiar with the focus of each other's work, our family backgrounds, and other issues in our lives.

My dissertation research focused on humor in parenting. I gathered small groups of parents of young children and listened as they talked about their families' lives. In response to my questions about humor and laughter, I collected stories of parenting antics that completely flew in the face of logic. To defuse stressful situations, some parents spontaneously did something silly and unexpected. One dad was getting frustrated in his attempts to cook supper by his two-year-old son's kitchen floor tantrum. He brought it to an abrupt, giggling halt by getting down on the floor himself, throwing his own *faux* tantrum and asking, "Am I doing it right?" The child relaxed, and his dad continued cooking supper. One mom turned her three-year-old's stubborn refusal to wear the shirt she'd picked out for him into a moment of shared laughter by placing the shirt on her own head and saying, in a high-pitched voice, "If you won't wear it, I guess I'll just have to!" Her light-hearted infusion of humor changed their tug-of-war into a cheerful hug where they both won.

With Beth pregnant and due in early fall, I was working feverishly to finish a final draft of my dissertation. On the first Friday in October, I was in deep focus and typing rapidly at my computer when a knock on my office door startled me. It was Beth with Jesse standing next to her. "I need you to take me to the hospital and take Jesse over to Brenda's house. We need to go now." My typing had to wait. We welcomed baby Jody that evening with great joy and not a little trepidation. Our cash flow was strained. I had a part-time teaching assistantship, and Beth's maternity leave pay amounted to only six weeks of "disability" benefits. In January 1988, when Jody was three months old, we found a babysitter to look after him while Beth started a half-time job at a nearby children's museum.

That same month, I made a successful oral defense of my dissertation. My doctoral committee required me to make some revisions before I could submit the final manuscript to the graduate school office. I made the revisions and began to print out the final copy of my 210-page masterpiece. At that time, our Sanyo computer was connected to what was called a dot matrix printer. The printer did one line at a time, the print head zipping back and forth across the paper, which was fed into the machine in a continuous loop from a stack behind the machine. Its operation was similar to a highly automated typewriter. The pages were then separated by hand into single sheets by tearing along the perforated edge at the top and bottom of each page. To achieve the print quality required by the graduate school office, I switched the printer to NLQ—Near-Letter-Quality mode. Now the printer swept back and forth across each line twice. Printing a thirty-page chapter could easily eat up half an hour.

As I watched the pages of the first chapter roll out of the printer, I began to feel rather giddy. The end was in sight! Before I separated the pages, I took one end of the long banner of paper, raised it above my head and walked from my office at one end of our apartment to the kitchen at the other end, proclaiming to all who would listen, "Chapter One is done!" Beth obliged with an appropriate and cheerful "Hurrah!" Jesse clapped a few times, then went back to looking at his library picture book. This celebratory ritual continued over the next couple days as chapters two, three, and four rolled out of the printer. I proudly paraded my fifth chapter one evening just as Jesse, not quite five years old, was finishing his bath. As I walked into the kitchen, the words "Chapter Five is done!" had barely left my lips when Jesse, standing in his pajamas in the kitchen doorway, said very matter-of-factly, "You mean you've been doing this for five years, and you only have five chapters?" An explanation to my son of the demands of graduate school seemed pointless. Maybe one day, I thought, he'll get to find out for himself.

Our support group met again a month after I received my degree in May 1988. By this time, Nancy and Linda knew that I had lost an older brother named Steve and that his death as a teenager had left me as the oldest child.

I leaned back in my chair with my hands clasped behind my head, feeling the satisfied glow of reaching this milestone in my life, and I heard myself say something that caught me by surprise. "Now that this is all done," I said, "I'm ready to once again be a second-born."

The fact that I had completed this doctoral degree felt like I had reached the pinnacle of ersatz oldest child achievement, fulfilling what I had for years perceived to be my role in the family—being the first to achieve significant accomplishments. I'd scaled the doctoral mountain I had set out to climb five years before and had reached the summit. But I was left feeling disillusioned by the ordeal. My anticipated panoramic, 360-degree vista, accompanied by a clear sense of perspective and contentment, was obscured by a dense fog. I had no better vision about my future career direction than I had five years earlier, when I'd arrived at UMass. But one thing was certain: I wasn't going anywhere. My moving days were over. We had already lived in Northampton for five years, longer than I had stayed anywhere since I finished high school twenty-four years before. I had no interest in a nationwide hunt for a dream job that required relocating my family. My priority was to find work that was close to this new home we had made in Northampton.

IN JANUARY 1988, I was hired for a position on the health education team of a Northampton substance abuse prevention program called Prevention One. As a novice in the field of health education, I faced a steep learning curve. I observed my colleagues as they led trainings and workshops for teachers, parents, and high school students that focused mostly on keeping youth alcohol- and drug-free. Topics also included correcting commonly held myths and stereotypes about alcoholics as well as the long-term effects of alcoholism on children and families. I studied substance abuse prevention curricula and other training materials, including educational videos I previewed on my own to understand their content and how to use them in trainings.

One of the videos I watched, "Lots of Kids like Us," portrayed the lives of children of alcoholics. The two children in the story, Ben and Laurie, were confused about their father's drinking. An older boy named Conrad, who had known for several years of his mother's alcoholism, told Ben and Laurie that they were not alone; many children lived in similar family situations. He reassured them that they did not cause their dad to drink.

I sat alone in a small Prevention One meeting room with the lights off, watching the story unfold. Something about these quiet, withdrawn children resonated with me. I had known, taught, and helped many children up to that point in my life. I recalled the African-American and Latino children at Camp

Herrlich. I thought of the troubled family lives of the kids at the residential treatment center in Vancouver, where I'd worked as a counselor. I knew their lives could be difficult. Something about this story hit home, but I could not explain what it was. Before long, my eyes started to fill with tears, tears that made no sense to me. I never thought of myself as a kid, like Ben and Laurie, who'd grown up with an alcoholic dad. Because I felt so outside of their story, the video could easily have been titled "Lots of Kids like *Them*." I dismissed my tears as simply a sign of my empathy for children.

IN THE WAKE of the brief melting period in my family's communication about Steve that ensued from the *Ordinary People* paper, my new interest in keeping Steve's memory alive was shared by other family members. A custom in many churches is to dedicate the flowers on the altar in memory of loved ones who have died. When Steve's birthday came around in 1985, Beth and I donated altar flowers in his memory at St. John's in Northampton; at the same time, Dad and Mom donated memorial flowers at their church in Roanoke, as did Amy at her church in the Washington, DC, area. Steve would have been forty years old that year.

One summer, Kelly and her four-year-old son Ben visited us in Northampton. As she and I talked about Steve one evening, she was surprised to learn that I still had a copy of Steve's funeral sermon, which I'd transcribed years before. Kelly was grateful to receive a copy of her own. Judi had occasion to travel to Cleveland for a high school reunion about this time. In a letter to all of us after she returned home to Chicago, she described her visit to Elmhurst Park Cemetery, where she placed flowers at Steve's grave, recalling how he helped her learn to ride a bike and lamenting that his death meant we were left to wonder who he might have become had he lived.

My own interest in reviving memories of Steve and of my past in Cleveland translated into plans for a family road trip to Cleveland in the summer of 1989. My parents agreed to drive up from Roanoke to meet us there. It had been twenty-eight years since Steve died, and close to twenty years since I'd last visited his grave.

I had a sense of history in the making as we made the two-day road trip to Cleveland. It was a pilgrimage for me, back to the city where I first gained a sense of place. It was my first opportunity to show my wife and our sons the city of my youth and to bring them to Elmhurst Park Cemetery. I began telling Jesse and Jody stories about their Uncle Steve, how he toppled into the pricker bushes, learning to ride a bicycle, how we got busted for our comic book caper in Dicky Olson's backyard, and how Steve once built a giant Erector Set crane and a real go-kart.

My sons' laughter about the stories of my remembered past with my brother lightened my heart as we made our way west to Cleveland. Imagining our visit to the cemetery evoked memories of the solemnity that permeated the place on the day of Steve's funeral. Knowing that Mom and Dad would be there with us added a certain air of gravitas, since they also well remembered that day. The occasion was fraught with meaning: ersatz oldest son returning home to pay respects at the grave of his older brother in the company of his parents, his wife, and his children.

On our first day together in Cleveland, we all took a riverboat cruise on the Cuyahoga River, infamous for being so polluted in the 1960s that it caught on fire, inspiring Randy Newman's song "Burn On." We drove through Rocky River to have a look at our old house at 19517. Our Side Yard had disappeared, obliterated by a new house built on the lot. We stopped at 3250 in Westlake and saw that the Back Acres were gone, built up with luxury homes. One evening, I took seven-year-old Jesse to a Cleveland Indians' game at the Municipal Stadium, where I had witnessed my first major league baseball game at about the same age.

After dinner one evening, my parents, Beth, and the kids, and I drove west in two cars on Detroit Road to the cemetery, just as Steve's funeral procession had done so many years before. The cemetery's sprawling expanse of lawn was graced by the presence of large shade trees, well-maintained garden plots filled with colorful flowers and evergreen shrubs and a long, narrow pond just inside the entrance. Passersby could easily mistake Elmhurst Park Cemetery for a public park. Viewed from the road, the grave markers are not visible due to the cemetery's policy of setting each one flat on the ground, just below the level of the grass.

My sense of the solemn, mystical nature of being in this place quickly evaporated in the realities of the moment. As soon as we were out of the car, things started going haywire. We had neglected to stop on the way to buy flowers. It had been so many years since we'd been there, we had to search to find Steve's grave. The distinct outline of Steve's rectangular marker was obscured beneath years of dried, caked dirt, grass, and dead leaves. "Don't these people maintain this place?" grumbled Dad. "All they seem to care about is cutting the grass once in a while." We had no garden tools, water, or cleaning rag.

While Beth and Mom drove off to buy flowers, my father, my sons, and I set about cleaning up the grave. Using a car key in place of a trowel, I kneeled and scraped off as much of the caked-on dirt as I could. Jesse took his empty orange juice bottle over to a nearby standpipe and filled it with water. He brought it back and poured it over the grave marker. Kleenex from the car served as clean-up rags. Jody, on his knees, did his best to yank off the longest blades of grass intruding on the edges of the marker.

Leaning on his cane, Dad slowly and gingerly lowered himself to the ground to help. As he did, he let go a fart. "A very appropriate, commemorative sound, Dad," I said, "at the grave of a boy you once described as having 'a proclivity for dropping the most lethal SBDs.'" The four of us shared a chuckle about "Silent-But-Deadlies," Dad and I feeling reassured that this quintessential form of Zink humor was being passed on to the next generation. Beth and Mom returned with the flowers. We placed them in the bronze vase mounted on the grave marker, added water from Jesse's juice bottle, took a few pictures, and made our way back to our cars. Our family visit to Steve's grave did prove to be memorable, but not in the way I had imagined.

Annual yardstick photos. At top, Jesse on
his seventh birthday in August 1989. Above,
Jody on his second birthday in October 1989.

Tom and Beth, with Jesse, five, and Jody, seven
months, on the day Tom received his doctorate
from the University of Massachusetts.

The Hewson-Zink family home in Laurel Park,
Northampton, Massachusetts.

9 Closing In

IN EARLY JANUARY 1990, Dad had a mild stroke. When I called him in his hospital room a few days later, he answered my call on the second ring. I was relieved to hear that his voice was still *his* voice, not that of a man recovering from a stroke.

"How are you doing, Dad? Are they treating you right?"

"Yes, yes, and I'm slowly coming out of this." His words were punctuated by his familiar mid-sentence chuckle, an audible sign to me that he was indeed on the mend.

"They've pulled out most of the tubes and needles and got me a recliner chair (chuckle) so I can sit up. It's the biggest one they have so my skinny legs don't hang over the foot rest. With the four-legged walker, I can get myself to the pot when nature calls, but this (chuckle) backless mooning jacket they put on me leaves nothing to the imagination."

He asked about Beth and the boys. I told him we were all busy but doing fine and that the earliest we'd be able to visit was Easter weekend in mid-April.

"Well, that's great, something to look forward to. Give me time to get better."

We talked about the weather, the football play-offs, and the lousy hospital food. I hung up, feeling somewhat reassured about Dad's recovery, although my concern about his health lingered. We heard from Mom that Dad was discharged after two and a half weeks. Dad's doctor continued to notice steady improvement in his health.

Three months later, Beth, our two young boys, and I set out on our two-day, 700-mile drive from Northampton to Roanoke. As we got closer, various scenarios about Dad's condition weighed on me. Mom had told me about the walker Dad needed, so I wondered if he'd still be using it or if he'd progressed enough to only need a cane. More detailed information was not forthcoming from Mom, so I had little sense of how much the stroke affected his mood and energy.

I pulled up in front of Dad and Mom's house and beeped the horn. Beth unstrapped two-year-old Jody from his car seat and opened the car door. I watched in amazement as my father, with neither a walker nor a cane, walked out the front door to greet us. Jody dashed up the front lawn to him. Dad squatted on his haunches to greet his youngest grandson with a hug and his familiar, laughing, "Hello-hello!" The degree to which he had recovered was unexpected. But that was not the biggest surprise of the weekend.

My sister Kelly had driven up from Atlanta with her six-year-old son Ben. Dad told us all that he wanted some time with just Kelly and me, so the next day Beth and Mom loaded the boys into the car for a visit to Roanoke's science museum. Dad plunked himself down in his big, brown La-Z-Boy chair. He rested his head on the back of the chair with a distant look in his eyes. He turned and looked at my sister and me and began to tell us his story.

About a week after he was admitted to the hospital following the stroke, Dad said he started getting irritable and anxious, his hands were shaking and his racing pulse made him sweat. A short while later he began to have hallucinations. He told Kelly and me that it was the most terrifying experience of his life. The medical staff told him he was going through alcohol withdrawal. His symptoms, they said, were a sign that he was alcohol-dependent, that is, an alcoholic.

The news struck me like a whack to the side of the head. My world suddenly lost its rose-colored tint. Naiveté is tenacious, and I was not prepared to be its executioner. Memories of incidents and situations that, up to then, had seemed random began to click into place, clearly presenting to me a pattern of problem drinking I'd been too busy and too far away to notice before.

I thought back to Dad's tale of sampling from his parents' wine decanters with his buddy Bobby Coles when they were teenagers and how he then fell asleep in the bathtub. I recalled the stories Steve and I somehow caught wind of in childhood about our dad being the guy at the church "couples club" parties who got well-lubricated and literally danced with the lampshade on his head. Back then, we thought it was rather comical. There were the family dinners at fancy restaurants to celebrate our parents' anniversary or a special birthday. Dad would order refills of whatever cocktail he was drinking, turn on the charm, and flirt with the waitresses. His obnoxious flamboyance would draw unwanted attention to all of us.

In my adult life, an unfortunate combination of geographic distance from my parents, deference to my father, and denial of troublesome family issues left me with very little sense of how much daily drinking Dad was doing up to the time of the stroke. But his experience in the hospital was evidence that he was drinking enough to provoke the profound symptoms of alcohol withdrawal. I had not heard such jarring news since the day the police officer told me that Steve was dead.

On our walk that evening, Beth and I found a small, quiet park close by. We came to an empty swing set, each sat down on a swing, and, as we watched the setting sun grace the tops of the nearby mountains, I told her Dad's story. Beth was taken aback, but she listened patiently as I spoke about feeling more shell-shocked and sad than angry at Dad. And as I talked with Beth, I was struck by the irony of my recent teacher training on the needs of children growing up with an alcoholic parent.

One goal in all our Prevention One trainings was to debunk the myth that the label "alcoholic" only applies to people who drink too much, pass out, have black-outs, lose jobs, and slowly destroy their lives. My father was a functional alcoholic, someone who lives a relatively stable life and drinks just enough to prevent alcohol withdrawal. Unable to maintain that alcohol level during the hospital stay after his stroke, he experienced the life-altering experience of withdrawal.

I came home to Northampton with Beth and the boys after the Easter weekend, knowing without question that the word "Them" that I had sub-stituted in the title of the video about children of alcoholics was truly now "Us." My siblings and I had indeed been like those kids in the video whose dad's drinking caused problems for his family. The words "lots of kids like us" conveyed the simple truth that our family was not alone in this experience either. But that was a hard pill for me to swallow. I had learned to cope with the loss of my brother by keeping the story secret and moving on with life all by myself. Other than talking on the phone with each of my sisters over the next few weeks, and confiding in a trusted Prevention One colleague about my father's alcoholism, I was not ready to share this story with anyone. I needed time to make sense of this startling news privately.

Through my work at Prevention One, I knew about twelve-step recovery groups and was aware of Al-Anon meetings in Northampton for adults who grew up with an alcoholic parent. But I was not ready to take that step. I was afraid to admit the secret that walking into an Al-Anon adult children of alco-holics meeting would reveal and doubted it would do me any good. I had long been a slogan cynic. For years, I had dismissed with a self-righteous smirk all those Alcoholics Anonymous bumper stickers: "Keep it simple," "One day at a time," "Let go and let God." Human existence—my own precious life, at least—was far too complicated, I told myself, to be helped by five-word gimmicks. "A panacea for simpletons" was my summary judgment. Going the twelve-step recovery route was a last resort. Case closed.

A YEAR AFTER WE ARRIVED in Northampton, we celebrated Jesse's second birthday in our cozy, two-bedroom apartment near downtown. To mark the

occasion, we wanted to record how tall he'd grown. Our method for preserving this family history was to have Jesse pose for a snapshot, holding a
yardstick. The top end was just below the top of his head. These birthday
yardstick photos became a tradition in our household, as my father's stair-
step photos were in my nuclear family.

Taking these photos reminded me that my father once told me that a
child's height at age two would be doubled when he was fully-grown. When
Steve was two years old in December 1947, he measured three feet, three
inches—just an inch taller than Jesse at the same age. I realized that if Steve
had lived, he would have grown to be six feet, six inches, the same height as
Dad and an inch taller than Jesse is now at his full height.

In the summer of 1998, as Jesse approached the age of sixteen, I did a
calendrical calculation similar to Mom's in September 1977, when she noted
the date when Steve had been gone as long as he'd been alive. Steve died
forty-eight days short of his sixteenth birthday. On June 24, 1998, Jesse was
forty-seven days shy of his sixteenth birthday. I had now had a son longer
than I had had a brother. I felt a keen sense of relief and gratitude about this
pivotal moment in my life, but, to spare Jesse the burden of a life passage that
was uniquely mine, I did not mention it to him.

Beth and I became first-time homeowners in 1989. We moved from our
apartment to a small, two-story house in Laurel Park, a neighborhood of
about one hundred homes three miles north of downtown Northampton.
Laurel Park was organized in the 1870s as a Methodist church camp in the
midst of a forest of white pine, eastern hemlock, oak, and maple trees. Dozens
of laurel bushes planted around the park bloomed every year in June. Most
of the church camp cabins had been expanded and winterized for year-round
use. Living in the woods was just one of Laurel Park's attractions for us. It
was a safe neighborhood to raise children with its posted ten-mile-per-hour
speed limit and narrow one-lane roadways punctuated with speed bumps.
The community was a blend of working couples, single adults, retirees, and
families like ours with growing children.

St. John's Episcopal Church continued to play a key role in our family.
Beth and I came to church with our boys nearly every week. The Reverend
Jim Munroe was a jovial man and an inspiring preacher. His gift for relating
to children helped our boys see the church as a welcoming place. Jesse became
an acolyte after he had his first communion and volunteered as a Sunday
school teacher's aide when he was in high school. Beth was active on the
Mission and Outreach Committee, taking on leadership roles in fundraising
activities like book sales and the annual Christmas Fair. At Reverend Jim's
request, I started a children's music program, which meant serving on both

the Music Committee and the Christian Education Committee. Beth and I both served three-year terms on the church advisory board.

IN 1993, DAD AND MOM moved into Brandon Oaks, a life-care retirement community in Roanoke, Virginia, that provided three levels of care: independent apartments and cottages, assisted living in the personal care unit, and a nursing home. When Dad and Mom sold their home and tried to shoehorn as many of their belongings as they could into this brand new apartment, Dad said he felt like they were moving into a telephone booth. It was as if the whole idea of moving into "Phantom Hoax," as he referred to it in his worst moments, told him that his next move would be to his grave. Mom was uncomfortable with what she called the "fussy elegance of the meal service"—long-stemmed glassware, cloth table napkins, and fancy china in the dining room where they had their dinners.

They adjusted reasonably well to their new surroundings, but my concerns about them were heightened when we heard that Dad had a second stroke in the fall of 1995. He spent a week in the hospital and then several weeks in the personal care unit at Brandon Oaks, until he was well enough to return to their apartment. Living apart like that was new to them. The only time they had done so in their fifty-three years of marriage was when Dad started his new job in Chicago in 1973 and rented a bachelor apartment, commuting home to Cleveland most weekends. Familiar aspects of their lives were continuing to unravel.

Dad's third stroke in April 1996 left him almost completely disabled. His hearing was intact, but he had lost his eyesight. The few words he could say seldom made sense. He was moved from the hospital to the Brandon Oaks nursing home when a bed became available. Mom visited him every day, often fed him his lunch and rolled him in his wheelchair outdoors onto the patio when the weather allowed. Since we all lived some distance away from Roanoke, Kelly, Amy, Judi, and I agreed to arrange our visits so that one of us could be there about every four weeks.

My turn to visit came a few weeks after the third stroke. Before I left home, I packed a small cassette player and a tape of the King's Singers, a male a cappella vocal group that I knew Dad loved. I arrived at Brandon Oaks just after supper time. Knowing how disabled he had become, I wasn't sure what to expect when I approached Dad's room. He was leaning back in his Geri chair, a large reclining wheelchair. His eyes were closed, his body still. I softly voiced the words, "Hello, Dad," so I wouldn't startle him. His eyes opened, and he acknowledged me. "Oh, hi," he said. I gave him a hug and kissed him on the forehead, recalling the kiss he'd given me on our parting at Valpo in 1964. I told him I had a surprise for him and started playing the King's Singers' tape. Resting in his chair, eyes closed again, he listened to the traditional Irish tune, "Danny Boy." Near the end of the song, they held a stunningly beautiful chord. Dad turned his head toward the sound and said a wistful, "Ooooh, that's a nice chord."

The next day Mom and I wheeled Dad in his Geri chair to the nursing home dining room. I sat down next to him to feed him his lunch, using some of the same playful tricks he had likely used when I was a baby: "Open up the hangar, airplane's coming in!" "Ooh, here comes a tasty bite of applesauce!" Dad's more vulnerable condition radically changed the quality of my visits. No longer did I need to keep my Ridiculometer on high alert in his presence. It was easier to relax and settle in to simply loving him. Gone were his edgy, joking banter and his interruptions whenever a thought struck him. What remained was my approachable, agreeable father.

Alongside these changes in Dad, the signs of Mom's declining abilities had become unmistakable. On her desk in their apartment I found unopened mail, unpaid bills, and indecipherable reminder notes in random piles of tiny scraps of paper. Being organized was always a source of pride for Mom, and the condition of her desk embarrassed her. She apologized for what she called "this mess," but I reassured her that, together, we would get it back in shape. She was no longer able to manage driving safely, so we decided to sell the family car. Mom was gradually losing her independence. Her world was shrinking.

I returned home from that visit to Roanoke, knowing well that the firm foundation our parents had given my sisters and me was now up to the four of us to sustain. Mom and Dad gave Kelly and me legal power of attorney. With Mom's consent, I began to look after their finances. A few months later, the nursing staff decided that, for her health and safety, it was best to move Mom out of their apartment and into the personal care unit. My sisters and I scheduled a weekend in May 1997 to pack up their belongings to sell, store, or bring home with us.

I arrived in Roanoke the evening before everyone else. Alone in my parents' apartment, I started the sorting process with the filing cabinet in the den. Among the file folders, large envelopes, and boxes of color slides, I discovered a manila envelope with a one-word label: "Steve." With a mix of anticipation and trepidation, I slowly opened the flap. I flipped through the pages, and came across a copy of Steve's certificate of death. Memories of his final morning in 1961 came hurtling back at me as I read Steve's name, the date and location of death, and our parents' names. There for the first time, I saw in black and white some of the details of the collision that had killed my brother. I sat down on the desk chair and wept not only with sadness at my loss but also with a deep sense of gratitude that my parents had kept these details from me when I was fourteen. I jotted down some key items from the death certificate and made a mental note that at some point in the future I would ask a physician I trusted to interpret the medical terminology for me.

ON OUR SEVENTEENTH ANNIVERSARY in October 1996, Beth and I went for a drive through the rolling hills of western Massachusetts. It was a Sunday afternoon—a picture-perfect autumn day. Summer's wilting heat and humidity were past. The first frost had erased the annoyance of all manner of flying, crawling, and biting insects. And the deciduous forests that blanket the hills were stunning in their bright fall colors. But being on this country excursion was not what we'd originally planned.

I was hoping to have an anniversary dinner Saturday night at our favorite Mexican restaurant, then go to a movie, leaving our boys in the care of a trusted friend in Laurel Park. For the plan to work, one of us had to make the babysitting arrangements, but in a scenario that seemed to recur with annoying regularity around our anniversary time, a simple misunderstanding left us high and dry by Saturday afternoon.

"Did you find someone to look after the boys tonight?" Beth said.

"I thought you said you were going to do that," I said.

"No, I distinctly remember talking about it on the way home from church on Sunday. You said you would ask Lisa down the street to come over."

"That's not how I remembered it."

"Let's try her now."

"Naw, it's way too late. She'll have other plans. Let's just forget it."

"Wait a second. Don't give up. We can still do this. Jesse and Jody can stay home on their own tomorrow afternoon. Maybe we can just go for a drive and stop for coffee and ice cream at the Williamsburg General Store."

I was angry and upset at how this was turning out. It wasn't the first time. These feelings seemed to come up for me every year as our anniversary drew near—misunderstandings, bollixed-up plans, resentments, regrets. I'd had inklings in the past that my yearly angst might somehow be linked to the coincidence of our wedding anniversary falling on the day after the anniversary of Steve's death but usually glossed over its relevance. It was on an evening walk in the Laurel Park woods a couple weeks earlier that the reality became crystal clear. The permafrost that had settled over my memories of Steve's life and his death had blinded me to this unfortunate juxtaposition of opposites.

And so as I took the wheel on that anniversary afternoon, I was ready to share my new understanding with Beth. We headed into the nearby Hilltowns—meandering through small New England towns, through forested hills, past an earthen dam, over a century-old steel truss bridge to the Williamsburg General Store, our favorite ice cream stop. October is one of my favorite months, and on this sun-splashed day, the hills were glowing with reds, oranges, yellows, and golds. I drove slowly, taking my time on the numerous turns, up-hills and down-hills. My easygoing pace gave me time to relish the scenery and time for this most-important conversation.

I told Beth I felt responsible for the unwitting juxtaposition of these two very different anniversaries that led to my dissatisfaction every year about our anniversary plans, no matter what they were. I was prepared to accept all the blame for what I saw as my big mistake. Beth reassured me that there was no blame for this: We chose October 20 together because it suited our schedules. The guilt and shame I felt for this thoughtless oversight seventeen years before kept me from forgiving myself, but Beth had already forgiven me.

Our anniversary celebration turned out to be much different than I had hoped, but it was a moment of surprising grace. I felt blessed to be reminded of the depth of Beth's love and compassion.

THE WEIGHT OF WORRIES was piling up on me in the fall of 1996. On top of the guilt I continued to feel about the anniversary glitch was my ongoing worry about my parents' failing health. These tensions exacerbated the everyday strain of full-time work, my mile-long to-do list of projects at home, maintaining our marriage relationship, and raising two active, healthy, growing boys.

I was feeling more and more alone in my struggles even though I was used to reaching out for emotional support and was no stranger to the benefits of counseling and therapy. For more than ten years, Beth and I had been members of a co-counseling community that gave us a safe, structured way to vent feelings through weekly peer counseling sessions. In the wake of my disillusionment after completing my doctorate, I had met with a mental health counselor for a handful of sessions. The topic of Steve's death seldom came up in these co-counseling and therapy sessions because I was conditioned to see his death as a *fait accompli* I could do nothing to change. I now saw that I needed something these familiar forms of support had not been able to provide. Despite my dismissive attitude about simplistic slogans, I began to consider checking out an Al-Anon meeting but kept finding reasons to postpone it.

I might have continued to procrastinate had it not been for Pat, a co-worker I met in early 1996. Pat was a recovering alcoholic and ex-smoker whose affable style and upbeat way of describing the recovery experience in a twelve-step program allowed me to open up about my own life. Our lunch-time chats over several months softened my cynicism enough that I became willing to ask Pat about times and locations of adult children of alcoholics meetings. Pat's attitude—that going to a meeting was not as big a deal as my fear made it seem—was the catalyst for my decision to take a break from co-counseling and try Al-Anon for a while.

The basic Al-Anon principle of anonymity was evident that Saturday morning; it seemed even the meeting location was a secret. Finding the room was like trying to wind through a maze, not the most encouraging prelude for an apprehensive newcomer. No one else was around when I stepped into the entry hall of the church and saw three doors. On one of them, a hand-scrawled sign said, "Al-Anon here." This helped.

I opened the door and walked down a half-dozen well-worn wooden steps that creaked as they led me into a basement storeroom lit only by daylight forcing its way through dust-caked windows. The musty, damp smell took me back to the neighbor's garage in Rocky River where Dicky Olson had tossed that match into an open paint can. In the semi-darkness, I noticed two empty oil tanks, a monstrous natural gas furnace, a dusty derelict piano, three extension ladders stacked against a wall and plastic tubs filled with Christmas decorations. But where's the meeting room, I thought.

On the other side of the storeroom, bright light outlined a loose-fitting door; the hinges squeaked as I opened it. The room was bathed in fluorescent light. Nameless people were setting up chairs. On the back wall was a table of books, another with tea and coffee. I mouthed a perfunctory "Hello" or two, avoided eye contact, and wandered over to the book table. I picked up a book called *Courage to Change* and flipped through it, stopping at a random page and offering my best charade at focused reading.

More people entered, found seats, and chatted with others. Three concentric circles of chairs faced a small table on one side of the room, where the person leading the meeting sat. I found a seat in the back row. A quick tally told me there were more than fifty people, a number that was at once intimidating and reassuring: too many to feel safe talking about myself, and just enough to allow me to hide. Everyone together said the Serenity Prayer to begin the meeting: "God, grant me the serenity to accept the things I cannot change, courage to change things I can, and wisdom to know the difference." Sitting with my arms folded across my chest, I watched, and I listened.

Near the beginning, a card was passed around. One by one, the twenty questions on the card were read aloud to help us answer the question: "Did you grow up with a problem drinker?" It was less a score sheet than a guide to better understanding the source of certain unhealthy attitudes that had been hard for me to admit. I noticed myself thinking, "Yes, that's me," to questions about being overcommitted, hyper-responsible, having a need for perfection, and feeling anxious around angry people. I found out I was not the only person in the room who lived with self-pity, resentments, and self-doubt. At the end of the meeting, everyone stood, joined hands to say a prayer and to voice the closing words, "Keep coming back." I decided it was advice I'd do well to heed.

For the first few months of intermittent attendance, I sat in the back, said my first name in the roll call, and listened as people around the circle took turns sharing thoughts and feelings. Often there was laughter, sometimes tears; listeners were always interested in the person who was speaking. No one interrupted or gave advice. It took some time, but Al-Anon's spirit of acceptance and inclusiveness grew on me and helped lighten the burden of worries I felt were mine and mine alone.

I began to learn two things: I was never obliged to say any more about myself than my first name, and I often heard experiences similar to my own in the words of others. Al-Anon meetings became a new habit, and I began to trust others in the group enough to begin talking about myself. I found myself feeling right at home with the spiritual focus on maintaining daily—and sometimes hourly—contact with God, also referred to as a "Higher Power." This spiritual centering of Al-Anon through prayer and meditation was a reminder to me that my connection to God was not a Sundays-only event. The Saturday morning meetings became an essential counterbalance to Sunday morning worship at St. John's church.

IN EARLY DECEMBER 1997, the Brandon Oaks nursing director called to say that Dad had become unresponsive. His breathing was shallow, and he was eating very little. Mom still visited him every day, managing the short walk from her room in the personal care unit to the nursing home. On the day of the call, we were told that Dad did open his eyes in response to Mom's presence. Beth and I prepared the boys that their grandpa might not live much longer.

My father died in his sleep in the early morning hours of Christmas Eve 1997, five days shy of his eighty-first birthday. At his funeral service several days later, the first Bible passage read was Steve's confirmation verse from the Old Testament book of Joshua that was also read at Steve's funeral in

1961. When I heard the familiar and telling words, "…the Lord thy God is with thee withersoever thou goest…" I found it impossible not to think of my brother at this funeral for my father. My grief about Steve was piggybacking onto my grief about Dad. Bringing Steve to mind in this way felt like a beam of sunshine reaching into the Arctic landscape of my heart. But, just as an ice fisherman's hole freezes up when ignored, the window of light did not remain open for long. I was too busy with life to pay attention to the long-buried secrets that were beginning to insist on being told.

In the next few months, I began to experience random, recurrent head-aches, as if I had a giant C-clamp attached to my head. Every few days, a turn of the handle, sometimes tightening, sometimes loosening. Every few days a headache. Headaches that appeared from nowhere snuck up and set me off-balance. In the middle of the night they came, in the middle of meetings at work, in the middle of washing dishes. Some were stop-me-in-my-tracks severe; others very slight. Some lasted all day; some disappeared if I popped a couple ibuprofens or lay down and closed my eyes for fifteen minutes.

In early June 1998, I stopped at a drug store in need of a fresh supply of ibuprofen. I walked down the greeting card aisle on my way to the pain relief aisle. The display of Father's Day cards caught my eye and stopped me cold. A rush of emotion came over me as I remembered that my father had died. After fifty years, this would be the first year I would not be sending Dad a card in June.

A couple weeks later, I drove with Jody to Cleveland for a weekend gathering my sisters and I had planned for friends and relatives not able to travel to Roanoke for Dad's December funeral. Beth stayed in Northampton with Jesse, whose summer camp counseling job took priority. More than fifty friends and relatives came to pay their respects and to celebrate Dad's life: Mom, Judi, Amy and her husband, Brad; Kelly and her fourteen-year-old son Ben; the Springsteen family from Valpo; and many old and dear family friends from St. Thomas church. I had unexpected feelings of envy and resentment towards Dad as his memorial event drew near; they bubbled up and consumed my anticipation. Here he goes again, I said to myself. He's six months gone, and he's still able to hog all the attention.

My favorite Valpo professor, Pastor Lutze, led the memorial service at Elmhurst Park Cemetery under a large green tent that afforded shade on a sunny June afternoon. We sang Isaac Watts' stirring anthem, "O God, Our Help in Ages Past," a hymn with a verse that echoes the words of Psalm 90 that Dad loved: "Time, like an ever-rolling stream bears all its sons away; they fly forgotten as a dream dies at the opening day." Standing on the same ground where we said our farewell to Steve thirty-seven years earlier, we buried Dad's ashes in the plot right next to Steve's. Now my brother and my father, the other two males in my birth family, were buried side by side.

At the reception following the graveside service, memories both poignant and humorous were shared by friends and relatives. One of Dad's best friends from church regaled us with a tale from the 1950s that brought much laughter and hilarity to the room. Dad, this friend, and several other men from church were sitting around our kitchen table at 19517 drinking beer, swapping stories, and tossing the empty cans out the window. The man enjoyed recalling the high, old times they had together. I kept a smile on my face to match the mostly upbeat tone of this event, but inside I found it hard to ignore the damage that alcohol had caused Dad and our family.

I was a jumble of mixed emotions as Jody and I made our way back home to Northampton. I missed Dad, and thoughts of him kindled thoughts of Steve. My love for both of them wrestled with my grief that they were gone and with my resentments about the years of feeling like their hapless victim. Even though Steve didn't live long enough for us to move beyond our teenaged competitiveness, I felt blessed that my father's long life had given me time to come to terms with our differences and to appreciate how much the man I became was a product of the man he was.

Phrases from my journal that year reflected my inner turmoil:

"I think I have a lot of grief about Dad and Steve."

"I just can't see God at work in my life."

"I think the grief must build up and have nowhere to go. So I sat in the parked car and cried."

"Everything in my life right now feels up for grabs."

"The pretense is killing me."

But there were also bright spots in my life that helped to balance out my painful memories and grief. Jesse and Jody were often able to invite me into play—Frisbee, Trivial Pursuit, or Nerf basketball in the basement—just as I had done with so many people in my career as a pre-school teacher, a New Games trainer, and a juggling, balloon-delivering clown while in graduate school. Beth's regular schedule of jogging, gym workouts, and karate classes inspired me to stay active. On my walks through the Laurel Park woods, the memory of the easygoing pace of the Oleai teachers walking home from school reminded me that slowing my pace led to a greater sense of contentment and gratitude. I sang in a community Gospel choir in which the camaraderie, vocal harmonies, and upbeat rhythms of the songs at weekly rehearsals lifted my spirits. With the acceptance, understanding, and spiritual focus I found at Al-Anon meetings, I was sharing more about my internal struggles and feeling less isolated.

MY HEADACHES CONTINUED off and on. I became an ibuprofen junkie. Every day before I left for work, I packed a few pills into a small container and put it in my pocket, just in case. Getting headaches was one thing. The anxiety about when and where they might strike was an added stress. I attributed them partly to the radical shifts in the foundation stones of my life due to my father's recent death and the dementia that was slowly taking my mother away. Recurring lower back pain added to my physical distress. Unable to figure out how to relieve these symptoms, I was beset by a pervasive feeling of indifference about many aspects of my life. I felt like I was on a roller coaster from moodiness to enthusiasm and back again with small dollops of melancholy and hopelessness tossed in for good measure.

I couldn't see it then, but this painful morass was a mask sitting on top of deep, inexpressible pain. The mask was wearing thin. In the fall of 1999, I finally went to see Dr. Jim Abel, a trusted physician who was also our sons' pediatrician, about my headaches. After a careful exam and assessment to rule out the possibility of a tumor or an aneurysm, he referred me to the University of Massachusetts Health Center's Pain Clinic.

The "headache doctor" at the clinic asked me about my symptoms, told me to keep up the headache diary I had started, and recommended that I continue to take ibuprofen. On my second visit, she asked me about stressors in my life. I ran through the litany—personnel challenges at work, evening meetings and out-of-town travel demands of my job, my mother's decline and the resulting need to manage her financial affairs, my father's recent death, the Sunday morning children's music program at church, weekly rehearsals of the community Gospel choir, committee meetings at church and in Laurel Park, home maintenance and up-keep chores, driving Jody to his karate lessons, picking Jesse up from cross-country practice, keeping up to date on the run with Beth. Naming the list exhausted me.

She then asked a question that panicked me: "Now, Tom, are there any of these stressors you can drop or delegate to someone else?" I kept my knee-jerk reaction—"None of them! I'm the only one who can do them and do them right!"—to myself. What came out was, "I'll have to give that some thought." I went home and wrote down the list of activities and responsibilities that were contributing to my existential logjam. The list totaled sixteen items. I had a claustrophobic dream one night that I was being buried in an avalanche of snow. One day I was explaining to Beth and Jody that they wouldn't see much of me the next day because of a one-hour commute each way to a day-long meeting for work, a church music committee meeting, and then a Laurel Park finance meeting. Jody looked at me and said, "Y'know what? I think you're on too many committees!"

I began to look for ways to reduce my long list without pulling the rug out from under everything all at once. I turned the children's music program over to others at the end of the Sunday school season in June 2000, freeing me from attending two monthly committee meetings. After two years singing in the community Gospel chorus, I knew it was time to let it go, and I did so after the spring concert. And when my term expired on the Laurel Park finance committee, I turned down a request to continue.

In late June 2000, Jody and I drove to Roanoke for a small get-together of family and friends to celebrate Mom's eightieth birthday; Jesse and Beth's work commitments again prevented them from making the trip. By this time, Mom's decreasing physical and cognitive abilities had led to her move into the nursing home at Brandon Oaks. All three of my sisters, my brother-in-law Brad, and nephew Ben came for the event. Amy arranged the use of a guest dining room at the nursing home. Judi brought several presents for Mom to unwrap. Kelly chose a special birthday cake at the grocery store, and she and Ben set up an attractive photo display of Mom's life.

A small group of Mom's friends from Brandon Oaks and her church joined us on a Sunday afternoon in a sun-filled room in the nursing home. It was a friendly, lively celebration, highlighted by the singing of "Happy Birthday" with harmonies on the last line. With help from her two grandsons, Mom blew out the candles. After about an hour and a half, Mom stood up and said, "It's getting older," which was her way of saying, "This party's over, folks!" Later in the evening I noticed with gratitude how well-organized it had been and how little I had done to make it so.

During the course of that weekend in Roanoke, my sisters took responsibility for some tasks that I had looked after for the past four years. Judi became the key contact with Mom's social worker. Amy lived the closest to Roanoke, and we all agreed it made sense for her to be the first contact person for Brandon Oaks nursing staff. Kelly was willing to take over most of Mom's financial matters. A small sign that letting some of my responsibilities go was working was that the supply of ibuprofen I had packed remained untouched all weekend. I had no idea what might take the place of these commitments, but I was willing to find out. In light of my health concerns, I had to trust that I was making the right decisions. Here I was, the former "slogan cynic," practicing in tangible ways the bumper sticker advice to "Let go and let God."

IN SEPTEMBER 2000, Jesse, Jody, Beth, and I packed up the car and headed for Wolfville, Nova Scotia, where Jesse was set to begin his first year of post-secondary schooling at Acadia University. Jesse's choice of a Canadian school did not come out of the blue. Ever since the topic of choosing a college had come up a few years before, we had encouraged him to look north of the border where post-secondary education costs were significantly less than in the United States. The night before we left, I located a shoebox full of family slides. I pulled out my old Kodak carousel projector, and we had a two-hour family history slide show. Bowls of popcorn, hilarious tales, and lots of belly laughs made it a memorable final evening together at home.

We helped Jesse move into his dorm room at Acadia. Later that evening in our motel room, Jody listened as Beth and I talked, sometimes through our tears, about this momentous transition in our lives. Our older son was "leaving the nest," "testing his wings." What would become of him? What would become of *us*? In his inimitable ability to capture in a few words the essence of a moment, Jody reassured us, "We're not losing Jesse. We're just loaning him."

Around the same time, a new topic began to grab my attention. In February 2000, two men I admired—Tom Landry, the highly successful coach of the National Football League Dallas Cowboys, and Charles Schultz, the cartoonist who created the comic strip *Peanuts*—died on the same day. Death became something I started to notice.

I was shopping in a home center store for a new hanging lamp for our kitchen one day. The lighting section was near the large plate glass windows in the front of the store facing the parking lot. The clerk who was helping me looked out through the windows. He began to tell me about the day in the spring when he watched as a young boy rode his bicycle down a small hill from the neighboring housing project into the parking lot. A car moving in the parking lot did not have time to stop for him, and the little boy was killed. The incident clearly left a strong impression on the clerk. I was left to wonder what unseen hand had placed me in that store at that time with that clerk to hear a tale that so closely resembled my own brother's final moments.

After we had left Jesse at Acadia, we visited several historical sites in Nova Scotia. I noticed myself especially drawn to sites that recounted stories of sudden, unexpected tragedy. The 1917 collision in Halifax harbor of two ships, one of them fully loaded with wartime explosives, caused an explosion that instantly killed 2,000 people and injured 9,000 more. The Grand Pre National Historic Site commemorates the expulsion of the Acadians from Nova Scotia in the mid-eighteenth century. The American poet Henry Wadsworth Longfellow composed the epic poem *Evangeline*, a fictional dramatization of the deportation and the tragic separation of Evangeline and her beloved Gabriel. At Peggy's Cove on the southern shore of Nova Scotia, the Swissair 111 Memorial remembers the 229 lives lost in the 1998 crash of a flight from New York to Geneva. De-cluttering my life was opening up space that had not been available before, space that, inexplicably, was being filled with death and tragedy.

This new interest mirrored the melancholy tone of my customary outlook and demeanor. I felt like I was allergic to happiness, incapable of joy or exuberance, because I instinctively told myself never to forget that sudden tragedy could strike anyone, anytime, anywhere.

The Zink family gathered in Cleveland for their parents' fiftieth anniversary in June 1992. Left to right, they are Tom, Amy, Judi, Kelly, Charlotte, and Al.

Tom, Jesse, Jody, and Beth, with Sparky, on the steps of their home in Laurel Park in Northampton in 1999.

10 Opening Up

NORTHAMPTON'S LOCATION in western Massachusetts placed it squarely in the path of so-called "nor'easters," major snow storms that could, over the course of a winter, dump close to ten feet of snow on the region, as happened during the winter of 1995–1996. For me, a child of winter, the snow falling, the drifts growing, and schools and businesses closing gave me that indescribable feeling of home. The small patio on the south side of our house in Laurel Park disappeared under the blanket of white. But spring did come, and by late April, the snow was nearly gone, and the patio had reappeared.

I woke up one morning, however, after an unusually cold night to find the patio covered once again with a thin dusting of snow. I'd had my fill of shoveling, so I decided to let the sun do the work of clearing it. As the sun moved across the sky, the snow melted, and the puddles evaporated. With delight, I watched the sunshine turn winter into spring. Several years later, I thought back to that morning's sunshine as a harbinger of my own personal melting of grief.

Beth, our two sons, and I made our annual trip to Niagara-on-the-Lake, Ontario, to celebrate Canadian Thanksgiving in October 2000 with Beth's extended family. Jesse and Jody looked forward to these Hewson family weekends and the special bond they shared with their cousins, Sean and Sandy, who were close in age to our boys.

During the weekend, family members scattered in many directions to window-shop, ride bicycles, play soccer and Frisbee, or hit golf balls at the driving range. One event that brought all eighteen of us together was the Sunday service at St. Mark's Anglican Church, the oldest Anglican church in continuous use in Ontario. The church is nestled in a park-like setting in Niagara-on-the-Lake. Built in the early 1800s of native stone quarried from the nearby Niagara Escarpment, the footprint of the church is in the shape of a cross. Rising above the heavy wooden entry doors sits a squat, square bell tower with crenellations at the top, like a guard tower on a medieval castle.

The church was filled to capacity on this holiday Sunday, so our large extended family wasn't able to sit all together. Our sons were seated with their cousins several rows in front of Beth and me. There's a point in the

Anglican service after the sermon has been preached, beliefs have been proclaimed in the Creed, and sins confessed and forgiven that the priest stands up and intones the words of Christian fellowship, "The peace of the Lord be always with you." The congregation responds, "And also with you." The priest then offers the invitation to "Greet one another in the name of Christ." What follows is a medley of handshakes, pats on shoulders, hugs, and air kisses near the cheek.

In the midst of the greetings going on around me, I caught a glimpse of Jesse and Jody, Sean and Sandy. Their teenaged-boy hugs, laughter, and high-fives, showed how much they were enjoying one another during this brief intermission in the service. As I watched their special camaraderie, instead of feeling the gift of their connection to each other, I suddenly felt completely alone in that packed church with my memories of Steve, my great, unrevealed burden of loss. I realized that my boys and their cousins were now the same age that Steve and I were when he was killed. Jesse and Jody and their cousins were enjoying developments in their relationships that I had never had the opportunity to enjoy with Steve. In that quick moment, I saw the enormity of what had been taken away from me. It was a blinding ray of light that, like the sunshine on our Laurel Park patio, began to thaw forty years of snow covering my grief.

After the service, I walked alone through the church's cemetery, where the shadowed shapes of tall evergreens fell on weathered tombstones. I pushed open the wrought-iron gate at the back of the cemetery and made my way down to the Lake Ontario waterfront, where I found a quiet spot to gather my thoughts and try to make sense of what just happened. I was astounded to discover that my grief over Steve had not dissipated by now, worn down over the years by some natural process of emotional erosion. One look at my tear-soaked handkerchief laid to rest the myth that I had gotten over his death.

On our return to Northampton after the Canadian Thanksgiving weekend, I felt myself pivoting in a 180-degree reversal to look back into the years of living the fiction that the safest route for me was to ignore the loss of my brother. I was turning back to face that moment when time stopped in my soul, frozen by the police officer's words that my big brother was dead. My angst over my father's alcoholism, my recurrent headaches, and this new revelation were all coalescing into a directive that I pay some attention to my past.

THE CRASH THAT ENDED STEVE'S LIFE took him away so swiftly, I sometimes thought of him as vaporized. After Steve said to me, "There's another bundle out there," and rode off to deliver his papers, I never saw him again. I knew full well Steve had not simply vanished. So then, what actually did happen to him on that morning in October 1961? I was transported back to that time, and over the next several weeks, questions came to mind that I had never considered asking back then because I was afraid of stirring up emotions in myself or others I was not prepared to handle. I considered Steve's point of view: Did he see the car coming? Did he know his own fate? And the legal angles: Were there records available that could help me find answers? I thought, too, about the driver of the car: Was he running late for work? Was he arrested at the scene?

While the questions were now clear to me, I was not sure about how I would find answers or the ultimate destination of my new quest. So I once again relied on the tai chi practice of stepping empty. When an idea for a step forward came to mind and scared the hell out of me, I knew it was probably the next thing I needed to do. These stepping stones began breathing new life into my relationship with Steve, which I'd long ago given up for dead. I expected, and was prepared to feel, the pain and grief of the loss of my brother, but I was surprised to discover how often my path to recovery opened me to laughter and lightness. I thought of the line in Victor Hugo's *Les Miserables* that captured the changes in attitude and outlook in Jean Valjean: "Laughter is sunshine; it chases winter from the human face."

My first step was to attend a grief support group held at a local church, something I had never done before. I sat with other people who had lost someone close, all of them more recently than me. I was surprised how refreshing it was to be with people who were familiar with death and were willing to talk about it. Keeping company with the memories shared and the tears shed, were the anecdotes of unexpected funeral humor, ironic twists, and seeing ourselves in others' words that sparked laughter in the group. I was learning to speak the language of death.

One day in mid-November, bothered by one of my recurrent headaches, I tried something completely different. I sat down at the computer and, for the first time in my life, I wrote out the story of the morning Steve died, capturing every detail I could remember. Several times I had to stop typing to wipe tears off the keyboard. By the time I'd finished, two hours later, my headache was gone. I printed out the narrative I'd written and sent it to a couple close friends in Northampton to read. It was a rare, but significant, exception to the rule of keeping my personal pain to myself.

A week later, a long phone conversation with my sister Judi in Chicago about these early stepping stones lightened my spirit. Before I went to bed that night, I stepped outside. Under a clear night sky, I searched for familiar constellations I had studied years ago for my high school science fair project. Then

I noticed the crescent moon with its curved tips pointed upward in the shape of a celestial smile. In my journal that night, I noted, "Each time I talk about this to another person, I become more sure that this is the key to my heart opening up without fear of judgment or ridicule or sympathy from others."

In these months of recovering memories and thinking about Steve, I found myself drawn to cemeteries, where the language of death is engraved in stone, bracketed by dates. The gravestones in the Hill Cemetery in the farming town of Hatfield near our house dated back over two hundred years. I walked among the weathered grave markers, reading inscriptions, wondering about the stories in the stones. I took special notice of families like Silas and Mary Billings, who had three children die before the age of two. Rufus and Lucy Cowles lost two teenaged sons within six weeks of each other in 1822. Every stone held a story. These stones in western Massachusetts made me mindful of the stories held inside Steve's bronze marker in Elmhurst Park Cemetery in Ohio.

One night on my way home from the grief support group, I stopped at St. Mary's Cemetery in Northampton. I stood by the car under the stars, looking over the large field of gravestones in the light of the waxing moon. Through the open car window, the stirring trumpet opening of Aaron Copland's "Fanfare for the Common Man" on the tape player brought me to tears, thinking of Steve and his trumpet. Then I did something I had never done before: I talked to Steve. I told him how my life had changed since 1961, that Dad had died three years before, and that Mom's health was in decline. I told him about my love for Beth and our sons, Jesse and Jody. "You'd be Uncle Steve to them, you know," I said. For once, I allowed myself the freedom to feel the warm flood of grief that welled up inside me. I had nothing to lose in that solitary cemetery setting. With my tears that night I began to see that, in the interminable winter of my grief, I might soon notice the first crocus shoots of spring.

The more I spoke with others about death, wrote about my own memories of Steve's death, and thought about his grave marker in Ohio, the more I thought about my own death. I found myself wondering how, when, and where it might happen, and where I wanted to be buried. I was burdened by the many years I had ignored my memories of Steve. We were not close in life at the time of his death. But I felt I wanted to be close to him after mine.

I MADE SEVERAL TRIPS to Roanoke to visit my mother during this time when Steve's death had become a new focus for me. On one visit, I found time to look through some of the boxes of papers Mom and Dad had kept over the years. I thumbed through the file folders they had maintained for each of their children's school memorabilia and found grade school report cards and class photos. There was a large manila envelope with all my letters from the Peace Corps.

Then I found a folder of news clippings from the time Steve died. A faint new hope flickered that I might yet be able to discover answers to some of my questions. Westlake's weekly newspaper, *West Life*, ran an editorial a week after Steve's funeral:

> The Stephen Zink accident has set off a series of police and newspaper reappraisals of the entire bicycling-after-dark situation... The accident was the result of a number of unfortunate circumstances rather than the fault of an individual driver... The cards were stacked against Stephen Zink [as they are] against any kid who rides his bicycle on the road in the dark, carrying dim headlight and small reflector.

The editorial noted also that the police chiefs in Westlake and the neighboring town of Bay Village were urging cyclists to ride on sidewalks "to change the odds before another tragedy occurs." The Bay Village chief took a proactive role on the issue of bicycle safety: he began stopping all cyclists he found riding at night without reflectors and lights.

I was determined to press forward in my search for answers about what happened to Steve and decided to start with the police department in Westlake. In a November 2000 letter to the police chief, I asked how I could get in touch with officers who were on the police force in 1961, and how I could obtain copies of records that might still exist. The chief's reply noted that to protect former officers' privacy, he would send them a copy of my letter and leave them the option of contacting me.

The chief also suggested other agencies to contact, and he provided me with some basic facts of the case. On October 31, 1961, a grand jury indicted the driver for second degree (involuntary) manslaughter. He was arrested on November 3, 1961, brought to the Cuyahoga County (Cleveland) jail, and released on $1,000 bail. A reply I received from the Cuyahoga County Archives told me that after consultations between the prosecutor and my father over the next few months, the indictment was "nolled" in January 1962, meaning the prosecution decided not to press charges in the case. Evidence of excessive speed was inconclusive.

Early in 2001, an envelope arrived in the mail from the Cuyahoga County Coroner's Office, containing the report of the autopsy conducted a few hours after Steve died. Even with the help of a dictionary, I found it difficult to make the connection between the anatomical detail on the page and what actually happened to Steve. But I could not simply fold up the report and forget about it. The answers contained in the report still puzzled me. I needed to talk with someone who could explain the medical language without mincing words yet be sensitive to the emotions dancing in the wings. I talked with Beth about what to do next. Almost with the same breath, we both said the name "Dr. Abel" as the physician I could approach.

Dr. Jim Abel was our son's pediatrician at the Health Services clinic at the University of Massachusetts, and Beth and I first met him when I was a doctoral student in the 1980s. Often decked out in mismatched shirt and tie under his lab coat, Dr. Abel moved nimbly around the clinic, whistling as he went. His whistling was like a sonar signal—a dead giveaway of his location within the clinic. He was physically fit, brisk, and lively.

With her Canadian roots, Beth felt a special connection with Dr. Abel, who spent his summer vacations leading wilderness canoe trips on the Yukon River in Canada's far north. He was the pediatrician who attended at Jody's birth in 1987. He took Jody's Apgar scores, then placed Jody snug up against Beth's cheek and quipped, "Okay, you two, it's epoxy time—time to start bonding." With my letter to Dr. Abel asking for his help, I enclosed a copy of the autopsy report and *The Cleveland Press* article of October 19, 1961, which included photos of the crash scene and Steve's high school yearbook picture.

While I was waiting to hear back from Dr. Abel, a call came one day at work from a staff person at the coroner's office. She told me that Steve's file contained two photos, one of his leg and one of his head. She discouraged me from ordering them, saying, "You want to have nice memories." I felt ambivalent. I knew the photos would not be pretty; I knew that Dad and Mom had good reason for keeping Steve's casket closed. Yet I still felt a deep longing to see him once more, to say good-bye, and to close the aching circle left open at his death. I discussed my quandary with Beth, one of my sisters, and a couple of friends. I decided to ask Dr. Abel's advice as well.

I walked into Dr. Abel's office a couple weeks later, and the first thing he said to me was, "You do look a lot alike. I can see the resemblance." We shared a laugh when I joked about the family trait Steve and I shared of big noses and big ears. Dr. Abel's brief observation brought to life my link to Steve that I thought was lost forever. His casual remark, tossed in as we began the interview, was a turning point, a solid, new stepping stone that alerted me to expect the unexpected as I moved forward. I recorded Dr. Abel's direct, thoughtful words that helped me better understand the autopsy report. He strongly advised me against ordering the coroner's photos.

ALL THROUGH THE YEARS since 1961, "before" people who knew Steve and had experienced the shock of his sudden death were the ones with whom I was most uncomfortable broaching the subject of Steve. But now I began to seek them out—cousins, high school friends, teachers, aunts and uncles. Several schoolmates responded to a notice I placed in the Lutheran High School West alumni newsletter asking friends to share memories. Some remembered Steve as "bright, quiet, and shy" and "pretty reserved and serious and not one to make a big splash." One recalled Steve's appearance as "angelic." I couldn't help but chuckle that these friends were describing the same Steve I knew as anything but shy, reserved, or angelic.

Steve's two best school buddies, Wayne Peters and Tim Fangmeier, recalled a boy who was much more like the older brother I knew. They remembered Steve as a character and a rascal, full of energy and nearly always upbeat. Tim remembered Steve's "winning personality" and that he always "had a twinkle in his eye."

My cousins Kathy and Conrad Ziegler both shared memories with me in 2002. They are children of my mother's older sister, Dorothy Ziegler. Our family had visited the Zieglers on our 1961 summer vacation just two months before Steve died.

Kathy, who was fourteen at the time, recalled her mother telling her the sad news as they were carrying something down the basement stairs. Kathy wrote that her tears "just sprang out of my eyes and poured down my cheeks." She remembered Steve as "tall, handsome, happy, clean-cut, and seeming to enjoy life." Along with her sad memories were more lighthearted moments. Her story of riding in our car on that 1961 family visit made me laugh: "Steve and Tom were giggling and making fart jokes about the 'Do Not Pass' signs on the highway. The wit, wisdom, and good times of vacations with the Zinks!"

A couple months later, Kathy told me that she was heartbroken when she was not allowed to travel with her mom to Steve's funeral. It warmed my heart to read Kathy's reflections, to learn that someone else had pain I had not known about.

Kathy's younger brother Conrad was eight years old at the time Steve died. He remembered the day clearly:

> I had a bad spill that day riding home on my bicycle. A car turned out of a side street, I overreacted to move to the curb, and fell over the front of my bicycle. When I went home to tell Mom and get patched up, it was then that she sat me down and told me about Steve's fatal accident that morning while delivering newspapers on his bicycle. The news was shocking enough, but the circumstances involving this pair

of bicycle accidents seemed uncanny (and still do) and I suppose this might have made an even deeper impression on me.

I also learned that when Conrad and his wife, Anne, had their first child twenty-seven years later, they named him Stephen. Conrad later wrote to me that he remembered thinking that this seemed a natural choice to honor and remember his cousin Steve.

In July 2001, I took a flight to Chicago, where I met up with my sisters Kelly and Judi and, together, we drove to Valpo to join an eighty-sixth birthday celebration for Dad's older sister, Marlise. My sisters and our three cousins, Rob and John Springsteen and Marlise's daughter Marlise Anne Reidenbach, gathered around a tape recorder one night to reminisce about Steve. As we talked, we were able, for the short time we had together, to alter our families' history of silence about Steve.

We all laughed a lot, swapping memories of childhood antics. John remembered a scene one morning in the bedroom Steve and I were sharing with Rob and John. All four of us were awake and goofing around. From my lower bunk, I started kicking Steve's bunk above me in retaliation for his irritating jokes. There was a slight creaking sound, then a louder one, then something snapped. One side of the top bunk suddenly broke loose and slipped down onto the bottom bunk from which I'd rolled out a split second before. Rob and John were laughing. I was relieved I'd escaped, and Steve said, "Now look what you did! I'm telling!" "C'mon, we can fix it," Rob said. Very soon, we had the upper bunk back in place.

Marlise Anne shared a memory that July night in 2001 that surprised me by how incorrect it was and how long it had gone unspoken. "I also remember something," she said, "and this is the first I've spoken of it, and no one spoke of it then and no one has spoken of it all of your life. We all were concerned about you, Tom."

"No one has ever told me that," I responded with a rueful laugh.

"You were with him when he died. Nobody knew what you saw or what you felt or what you were thinking. Did anybody ever, ever talk to you?"

"No one ever has," I said, correcting the misinformation that, unbeknownst to me, had been held in silence for so long: I was indeed the last to see Steve alive and the first in the family to learn he was dead. But I did *not* witness the crash nor did I see his body afterwards.

After a year of gathering memories about Steve from "before" people and finding out what I could about the crash that took his life, I knew that my next stepping stone was to return to the place on Columbia Road where I had first learned Steve was dead. Part of me was still that boy, standing alone in the middle of the road, unable to move on or to forgive myself for choosing to hide the story that came to define my identity.

I ARRANGED TIME OFF from work in early June 2002 for a trip to Cleveland to give myself time alone in places Steve and I had been together so I could remember who I was in relation to him. Ahead of my trip, I wrote to the current owners of our former homes on Riverview Avenue and Columbia Road to ask if I could stop by for a look at the house. I contacted Steve's and my good friend Wayne Peters about my upcoming visit, and he and his wife, Karen, extended a dinner invitation. When my sister Judi heard of my plans and asked if she could join me for the weekend, I replied that I welcomed her company. The Westlake Police Department informed me that the retired police chief from 1961 was willing to talk with me and that their accident reconstruction officer could arrange time to meet with me.

I put my bicycle on the car, packed a suitcase, camping gear, and bicycle helmet and left Northampton on a Wednesday morning. I stopped overnight to camp at Letchworth State Park in western New York, a place we visited on our family vacation in August 1961, two months before Steve died. Before I set up camp in the park, I found a pay phone and called Beth to let her know where I was, and tell her about my day's travels. On this journey into the past, the sound of Beth's voice was a reassuring reality check. I kept in touch with home on a daily basis while I was away.

From photos taken by my father and images still scrapbooked in my mind, I remembered places and kinesthetic feelings that I couldn't express in words. When I reached a spot that had left its mark years ago, I exhaled a single word, "Yes." This was the place where Steve and I stood with Kelly, Amy, and Judi, on the top of a cliff, looking down into the Genesee River Gorge on a day that was bright and sunny, unlike this day, which was overcast and humid. Dad took one of his stair-step photos of the five of us.

On my visit in 2002, I left that high spot above the gorge and walked down the stone steps to the Genesee River, crashing its raucous, outraged water through the narrow ravine. In 1961, I was the younger brother, shorter, more cautious, and less hasty than Steve. Now, as I descended the hundreds of wet granite steps, I could feel the boy I was back then still alive inside my skin. Yet now, I was the only older Zink brother, the one who lived, the one who got married and became a father. And as my feet stepped back in time, I knew that I was both the boy I was then and the man I had become: the younger brother who lived long enough to seek these places of memory and to slip between then and now.

I ARRIVED IN WESTLAKE on Thursday afternoon. My motel was located on Columbia Road, a couple miles north of our house at 3250. I checked in, unloaded my gear, and then drove to 19517 in Rocky River. When I introduced myself to the young man who greeted me at the door, he recognized my name from my letter. He explained that he was the grandson of the couple who bought the house from Dad and Mom in 1957. He said he was heading out shortly, but invited me in to have a look around.

I was forty-five years older and fifteen inches taller than the last time I had stood in these rooms. They seemed to have shrunk. I now understood my parents' reasons for moving to the larger house in Westlake. I went upstairs to get a quick look at the bedroom Steve and I shared. I thanked my host and exited by the side door onto the gravel driveway. I was excited to see that the garage was still the same. It was fifty years since Dad had the bottom half of the back wall knocked out and an extra eighteen inches added to accommodate the nineteen-foot-long DeSoto Suburban. I walked around back and was thrilled to see that the addition was not only still there, but its sloping narrow roof appeared to have been recently re-shingled. I was certain that, were Steve still alive, he and I would be the only two people in the universe who knew the story behind this mini-renovation on this sturdy old garage.

Filled with memories of Steve and stories from 19517, I drove back to the motel for my phone call with the retired police chief. I was taken aback when he began our conversation by asking if I was a partner with a law firm. Did he suspect a lawsuit, I wondered, after all these years? Feeling immediately on the defensive, I tried to reassure him that I was simply trying to find out what happened to my brother. He said he didn't think he could tell me anything I didn't already know, but our conversation proved otherwise. I learned there was a similar bicycle-automobile crash in the neighboring suburb of Bay Village about the same time as Steve's. As a result of these crashes involving their paper boys, the *Plain Dealer* started providing reflective vests to their carriers. The chief also assured me that my father and the judge in the case were both very satisfied with his department's accident report. I thanked him for contacting me and for sharing what he remembered.

That evening, with plenty of daylight left, I got on my bicycle and rode south on Columbia Road from the motel to do some field research, to ride and remember. I took note of differences between the bicycle Steve rode and my 2001 Trek 7200 hybrid with twenty-four speeds. Steve had a one-speed Schwinn bike with coaster brakes and balloon tires. Steve's bike had simple handlebars with a single C-cell battery-powered headlight. My handlebars had gear shifters, levers for the caliper brakes and a digital odometer. I wore a helmet, cycling gloves, and a riding jacket with reflective stripes.

On the ride to our old house at 3250, the fragrance of lilac hedges in full bloom filled the late spring air. I could hear lawn mowers at work and catch whiffs of the aroma of freshly-mown grass. The current owners of 3250 had told me they were out of town so I stopped on the edge of the road to have a look. The house looked the same, but much had changed. The willow tree where Steve had nailed a piece of wood into a crotch in the tree to help our sisters climb was gone. So was the basketball hoop where Steve and I played out our sibling rivalry. The blue spruce and mountain ash trees that were close to the road had been displaced by sidewalk. A monster loomed just behind the house. This was the pin oak tree that Dad, Steve, and I had transplanted in 1960, hauling its root ball from the Back Acres in a wheelbarrow. The tree was now three times taller than the house.

I turned my bike around and started riding north with the traffic up Columbia Road. It was the same route I had taken forty years earlier on an October morning to find out why Steve had not come home. My odometer calculated the distance from 3250 Columbia to 2929 Columbia, where the collision occurred, at one-third of a mile. So much for my youthful skepticism years ago about the article I'd read in the *Plain Dealer* that a large majority of traffic crashes happened close to home. Although the road still had thin gravel shoulders, no curbs, and a narrow tree lawn, sidewalks set back about ten feet now ran parallel to the roadway.

When I reached 2929, I made a right turn into the driveway. A row of red and white impatiens blooms highlighted the dark green shades of the neatly-trimmed arbor vitae hedge in front of the house. Straddling my bike, I looked back at the roadway and the double yellow line down the center. I thought about those early Sunday mornings when Steve and I would dash out to the road in front of 3250, check that no cars were in sight, and lie down on the yellow line, feigning nonchalance. I remembered the summer mornings in 1960, when I delivered Steve's Columbia Road route while he was away at Philmont Scout ranch in New Mexico. Then I began to try and visualize Steve's final morning.

When Steve and his bicycle were in this same driveway on that Thursday morning in October 1961, he was in haste to get his job done. We'd gotten up late. Customers would be looking for their papers. He'd have placed Mrs. Brown's paper inside her front door, hopped back onto his bike, and pedaled down the driveway. Behind the wheel of his 1953 Pontiac, Mr. Johnson may have been running late that day as well, on his way to work at the Ford Motor Company plant in a nearby suburb. As he moved out into the opposite lane to overtake the vehicle ahead of him, Steve came wheeling out of Mrs. Brown's driveway.

In his defendant's claim to the police afterwards, Mr. Johnson wrote this:

> I was going south on Columbia Road, and I was passing that guy up. I was going about thirty to thirty-five to forty miles an hour, somewhere in there. The kid came out of the driveway right in front of me, and I hit him with my front left. Then I stopped and waited for the police. I didn't move the car a muscle.

The accident reconstruction officer at the Westlake Police Department had earlier described the scenario for me. He had read Mr. Johnson's claim and looked over The Cleveland Press photos on the day of the crash, showing Steve's broken bike and the location of the damage to the Pontiac, all of which were consistent with Mr. Johnson's statement. His detailed technical description of accident reconstruction—laws of inertia, driver's reaction time, and the coefficient of friction of the roadway—confused me. It all became clear, however, when he stood up his mobile police radio on the metal table top. To illustrate the effect of an impact on the upper half of an object, he poked his pencil at the upper half of his radio. It toppled backwards, clattering on the table top.

"I hope I didn't break the thing," he said, laughing, as he picked up the radio and stood it back up. "It's a matter of simple physics, Tom," he said to me.

"What happened to your brother was this." He poked his pencil at the radio again, this time undercutting it close to the bottom with a sharp jab. The radio fell forward with a rattle. When the car's left front fender and headlight undercut Steve on his bike, he told me, Steve's momentum propelled his body forward head first into the car's windshield. His bicycle flew out from under him backwards, smacking into the large tree where I saw it that morning lying in two pieces.

My visit with Dr. Abel a year earlier had given me an idea about the cause of death. After reviewing the coroner's autopsy report ahead of time, Dr. Abel told me that Steve had died from a very serious head injury and that his death had to be "absolutely, totally immediate." Given the circumstances, neither a bright bicycle headlight nor a helmet nor reflective clothing would have changed the outcome, he said. Steve was in the wrong place at the wrong time, plain and simple.

Forty years before, I had straddled my bike on the other side of Columbia Road, looking on in silent shock at Steve's broken bicycle in Mrs. Brown's driveway. On this June evening, as I straddled my bike in that same driveway, memories washed over me of the deep connection Steve and I shared, often characterized as much by friction as by friendship and brotherly love.

From all the evidence I'd been able to gather, I believe that Steve did not suffer in pain but died the instant the car struck him. I grieved the fact that he had to die so suddenly and so alone. Squeezed in beside my regret that we missed the chance to say good-bye was a lurking annoyance with Steve for going and getting himself killed because his constant haste did not allow him to slow down for five seconds in Mrs. Brown's driveway, check for oncoming cars, and watch Mr. Johnson's car whiz past.

I got back on my bike, rolled down the driveway, checked for traffic, and turned north onto Columbia Road as Steve would have been expecting to do to bring the newspaper to his next customer, the Fangmeiers, who lived just one house beyond 2929 Columbia.

In March 2002, three months before my trip to Cleveland, I went to Charlotte, North Carolina, to visit with Tim Fangmeier and, for the first time in forty years, we talked together about Steve. Tim remembered as vividly as I did the October morning when Steve died. I learned for the first time that his experience was almost a carbon copy of mine. My mother and Tim's father had expressed concern that something might be wrong. They each asked us to go and find out what had happened. I rode my bike to the scene, heard that Steve was dead, then was driven home in the police car. Not long after that, Tim walked through the neighbor's yard to the scene. He saw the broken bicycle up against the big oak tree as I had, papers spilled on the driveway. Tim remembered asking the policeman, "Is he alive?" and the policeman, shaking his head, said, "No."

Tim went to school that day and recalled that the news "put the school into a state of shock. It was a spiritual time where you thought about death because hardly anybody had experienced the death of someone that age."

Tim became a Lutheran pastor and, during the 1980s at spiritual retreats, he gave talks on the theme of grace in the lives of Christians. The key point of his talk was that the day of death was the most sacred of the grace-filled days of a Christian's life; Tim illuminated that point by telling the story of his experience of Steve's death. During the years when I was coping with Steve's death by closing down the story, hundreds of retreat participants were profoundly moved by Tim's telling of the story.

I pedaled my bicycle as far as Tim's boyhood home and stopped to reflect. With so many details, truths, and stories falling into place, some of the mysteries were also unraveling. I now understood why the ambulance that passed me on Rose Road had its siren silent; why I heard the dead-on-arrival message on the police radio from the hospital where Steve's body was taken. I understood what Dad meant when he said that Steve "really took a beating."

As I rode back to the motel, I realized that in some crazy, mystifying way, the circumstances that led to Steve's sudden death now made sense to me.

WITH THE SOLITARY PARTS of my Cleveland visit behind me, I was ready for some company. I was happy to see Judi when she arrived at the motel Friday evening. On Saturday evening, we made our way to the Rocky River home of Wayne and Karen Peters for dinner. As we finished dessert, Wayne and I brought out our collections of photographs, high school yearbooks, and newspaper articles. In the photo of Steve and Wayne's confirmation day in May 1959, Judi pointed out that Steve was the only boy wearing a white bow tie. Wayne looked at Steve's tilted head and the smirk on his face and said, "There he is, just being his rascally self."

The custom at our high school was to have your friends sign their picture in your yearbook. We each kept our own tally: the more signatures you snagged, the more friends you had. Paging through Wayne's yearbook, Karen found the words Steve had written to Wayne. "To the best friend I've had all these years at West Shore [Lutheran elementary school] and at Lutheran [high school] West," a true testimony to their friendship.

Earlier that day, Judi had joined me on an unusual excursion around the city. In my determined efforts to record and document everything I could while in Cleveland, I wanted to photograph all the stops on Steve's final journey from the scene of the collision, all the way to Elmhurst Park Cemetery where he was buried four days later. For me, following the route I was not able to follow in 1961 was a way to pay respects to Steve's memory. As we related the story to Wayne and Karen, the somber tone of the excursion was lightened a number of times by touches of irony and humor.

I got out of the car to take a photo at Fairview Park Hospital, where the ambulance had taken Steve's body. I framed the scene and set the exposure only to see in my viewfinder a security guard jogging towards me. "Snap!" went the shutter.

"Hey, you can't take pictures here," he called out.

"Too late," I said, closing my camera case and hopping back into the car.

We drove across to the east side of the city to the county coroner's office. No security guards here tried to interfere with my photographic duties, but Judi remarked with a laugh that we very likely were the only people in the known world who would drive across town just to take a picture of the sign at the coroner's office.

Karen's religious upbringing was Catholic, so she brought a different perspective when our conversation shifted back to 1961. Recalling the mood at school the day Steve died, Wayne said, "I remember it being so sad and so somber, walking through it like a zombie. The whole school was just in shock." With sincere concern, Karen then asked Wayne if he talked about it at home with his mother and father.

Wayne replied with a rising, almost jocular, tone in his voice, "I'm sure I did, but you know how Lutherans are!"

His response triggered an unexpected burst of nervous, knowing laughter from both Wayne and me which continued as Karen replied, "No, I don't know. How are they?"

"They keep quiet about that," I said.

"They don't talk about that life-and-death stuff," added Wayne.

But now, forty-one years later, we were at last doing just that.

Karen then pointed out that when Steve died, "Your thoughts and your memories went with him. You couldn't turn around and ever say to him, 'Remember when we did this?' because he wasn't there to say, 'Yeah, I remember.'"

The next morning, Judi and I went to church at St. Thomas Lutheran, our childhood church. It was much the same as it had been years ago. The same Lutheran hymnal, the same wooden pews, the same bright colors of the stained-glass windows. The large wooden cross, dedicated to Steve's memory, still hung above the altar in the front of the church. When I left Cleveland for the Peace Corps in 1968, I felt like I was also leaving behind this church and what it represented in my life. Standing with Judi for the opening hymn, I felt gratitude that the spiritual faith that was nurtured in me here had far outlasted my disillusionment with the restrictive religiosity St. Thomas had come to represent.

After the service, I was surprised and overwhelmed by the warm, friendly reception Judi and I received from family friends we had not seen in years. It was an odd feeling for me. I had moved around so much over the years that my new-kid-on-the-block complex was taken by surprise to be recognized and welcomed with such affection. As I did when Dr. Abel remarked that he could see Steve's resemblance to me, I felt a connection to a past I had mostly ignored. It led me for perhaps the first time in my life to recognize the love in this church community for me and my family. I sensed that my blindness to all this good will and positive regard contributed to my long-standing emotional and spiritual disconnect from this home of my childhood and youth. That I could even consider my hometown to once again be a safe haven for me was an unexpected gift of this trip.

Judi returned to Chicago on Monday, and I packed up to leave on Tuesday morning. My last act in Cleveland was to say my farewells to Dad and Steve and to place bouquets of bright yellow flowers at their graves. As I turned onto Interstate 90 and headed east, my familiar headache returned. I wondered why. The visit to Cleveland felt like a success. Wayne, Karen, Judi, and I had enjoyed our evening together, sharing photos, memories, and laughter. I had connected my present back to my past in clear, honest, visceral ways. I knew a lot more about the story of Steve's life and death than I had two years before. But my habit of trying to guard that story waged a continuing duel with a growing need to tell it. The resulting ambivalence manifested itself in these occasional headaches.

FOR MANY YEARS, I distanced myself from "before" people to avoid the topic of Steve's death. The conscious effort I began in early 2001 to reconnect with "before" people reached a high point during this Cleveland visit. It was a wonderful relief and reassurance to be able to spend so much of my time in Cleveland with them—my sister Judi, Wayne and Karen Peters, the retired Westlake police chief, and old friends at our church—to whom I didn't have to provide any background to my story.

Now, I was returning to western Massachusetts where, with only a few exceptions, all the folks I knew were "after" people who knew nothing about Steve. As I made my way home to Northampton on that June afternoon, it occurred to me that the distinct line creating this "before-after" dichotomy had begun to dissolve ever so slightly. Starting with Angie and José, the Saipanese teenagers I told about Steve just before I left the Peace Corps, there were people whom I had come to understand as "between" people. "Between" people did not suddenly become "before" people after learning about Steve as they had neither experienced the shock of his sudden death nor did they know me as a younger brother. But they were also not truly "after" people: They were friends with whom I could bring Steve's life back into the light. By the time I got home, I saw clearly that my opening up in the past two years about my brother had turned many friends from "after" people into "between" people.

The first time I talked about Steve at an Al-Anon meeting, about a year before my Cleveland trip, three people approached me afterwards to say that they also had lost a sibling in adolescence. That connection led to an ongoing conversation with one of the women over the next few years; together, we explored in more depth the experience of surviving the loss of an older brother.

One day in early summer 2001, I had lunch with Judson Brown, a Laurel Park neighbor, friend, and fellow member of St. John's church. Judson knew of my efforts to recover memories of my brother, and wanted to know how I was doing. He listened with interest as I described my outreach to the police, the courts, the coroner's office, and my high school friends.

Hearing about the two photos at the coroner's office had left me feeling deeply ambivalent. I was fortunate to be able to seek the advice of friends who were at ease talking about death. I took occasional walks around the Smith College campus in Northampton with Priscilla Lane, another St. John's church member, whose comfort with the topic of death allowed us to speak freely of loved ones who had died. She empathized with my uncertainty about the autopsy photos without telling me what I should do.

I spent an afternoon in the summer of 2001 describing my discoveries about Steve with my UMass faculty advisor, Janine Roberts, who first learned about Steve when I worked on the *Ordinary People* project. She helped me consider the issue of the photos from a variety of perspectives and understood the ambiguity I experienced being a second-born oldest child.

I also sought out organizations in which speaking the language of death was part of the program to help give further voice to my grief. The local chapter of Compassionate Friends, a national voluntary organization that provides grief support after the death of a child, sponsored an annual candle-light vigil on December 6, 2002, to remember children who had died. Beth and Jody accompanied me to the ceremony on a cold, winter night. Each family present took a turn remembering the child who had died. When my turn came, I said words I had never before been able to say aloud to a group of complete strangers: "My brother died just short of his sixteenth birthday. Today is his birthday, and he'd have been fifty-seven today. He is still missed, and, because of events like this, he is still remembered."

But I still had moments when I hesitated to mention Steve, even when opportunities did appear. One day I sat in the lunchroom with a handful of colleagues at work. We were talking about children and parenting and how we were raised and how we learned to get along with others because we had siblings and how birth order influenced our development. As others talked about their birth order in their own families of origin, I felt a growing apprehension: Do I mention Steve, or do I stick with the safer, partial truth? When asked how many siblings I had, I instinctively chose the latter. "I have three sisters, all younger than me," I said. I regretted the silence I kept about Steve that felt like a disservice to his memory.

MOM'S MENTAL DECLINE continued from the time of our small celebration of her eightieth birthday in June 2000. Kelly, Amy, Judi, and I had arranged our schedules so that at least one of us could make the trip to visit her every month or two. We also hired a woman for about fifteen hours a week to be Mom's companion and advocate in the nursing home.

My sisters and I made special plans for all of us to be together to celebrate Christmas with Mom in Roanoke in 2004. One evening that week, I was sitting with Mom when a staff person brought Mom's supper on a tray. Mom sat in her wheelchair, head bent forward, hands in her lap, as though she were in prayer. I told her that dinner had come, and she lifted her head. She whispered something unintelligible—a series of breathed consonants—and then fell silent again. We carried on a conversation of sorts while I fed her supper.

"I'm gonna go get you a bib," I told her.

She replied, "Oh!" I returned with the bib, and began feeding her the meal.

"Let's have a little more to drink, Mom."

"Yeah."

"I'm going to give you some more iced tea."

"Well, yeah, the first time... (trails into gibberish)."

"Want some sour cream with your baked potato?"

"Mm-hmmh. I don't know about that."

"I have more potato for you."

"Oh, you did! Good!"

She was alert with her eyes open for the whole meal and never needed a single prompt to open her mouth. She actually started talking by herself several times, all in gibberish. The only words I could understand were those she said in response to something I said.

The Lettermen, a pop vocal music trio in the 1960s, had a hit song, "Softly, As I Leave You." I thought of that song as I watched this tail end of my mother's long life. We were losing her, bit by bit, her decline so soft, gradual, and slow as to go almost unnoticed.

Softly is how Mom did leave us, in her sleep, less than two months later, in the early morning hours of the day after Valentine's Day 2005. Her doctor believed she may have had several transient ischemic attacks (TIAs or "mini-strokes") in the past few years that contributed to her cognitive decline. There was life in her body still, but the mother we had known so well for so long became difficult to recognize, even as she lost her ability to recognize us.

Mom's love of music was one of her enduring legacies to us, a gift she shared with us throughout her years. The music my sisters and I chose for her funeral a few days later harked back to her comforting voice on the night of the Mother's Day windstorm in Cleveland in 1956. The opening hymn was "O God, Our Help in Ages Past," the hymn we'd also sung at Dad's memorial service six years before. The service concluded with the very simple melody of

"Now the Day is Over," reminiscent of our family road trips to Valpo as the evening darkness fell. At a later date, we interred Mom's remains at Elmhurst Park Cemetery in the same burial plot as Dad's. A single bronze grave marker bearing both of their names was placed at the site, immediately to the right of Steve's grave marker.

THE FOLLOWING TWO YEARS saw a succession of significant changes in our families. One month after my mother's death in February 2005, Beth's father, Geale, passed away in Sudbury at the age of 83. That summer, Jesse packed up and moved to Nome, Alaska, to work as a news reporter at KNOM, a radio station serving the many Inuit villages in western Alaska.

Beth had long desired to move to Ontario to be close to her mother's home in Sudbury. About the time of Jody's high school graduation in June 2006, I found a job in my field of public health tobacco control in North Bay, a city of 55,000 located less than one hundred miles from Sudbury. In September, Jody departed for his first year of university. A few days after seeing him off at the airport, Beth and I packed our empty nest into a U-Haul truck and moved to North Bay. Our twenty-three years in Northampton and seventeen years in the same Laurel Park house were the longest settled periods in either of our lives.

Steve's lifelong friend Wayne Peters and Tom, when they met in Cleveland in June 2002 to tell stories and remember Steve.

Zink family grave markers, side by side in Elmhurst Park Cemetery.
(Photo credit: Mike Kemper)

Epilogue

ELMHURST PARK CEMETERY, Avon, Ohio, November 2012. After an eight-hour drive from North Bay to Cleveland, I arrive the next morning to meet Wayne Peters here at the cemetery, where his parents, my parents, and Steve are all buried. It's been ten years since my solo visit to Cleveland in 2002.

The grave markers here lie flat an inch or two below the level of the grass: finding the one you want can take on the air of a treasure hunt. I do remember that Steve's is not far from the road, so that's where Wayne and I begin our search. Moving among the cemetery plots, we find several markers with German surnames we recall from our days at West Shore Lutheran School. "Remember Kaye Albers?" Wayne calls over to me. "She was in Steve's and my eighth-grade class at West Shore Lutheran. By the date here, these must be her grandparents."

"Here's another. Krone is the last name," I say, swiping away leaves and twigs with my foot. "This must be a relative of Jim Krone. Now there was a good athlete. Played first base. Remember him?"

"I sure do. And look! Right here! I found Steve's grave."

With his foot, Wayne brushes aside some brittle brown leaves. I kneel down to brush the dust off the bronze marker. Looking up at Wayne, I tell him about the time our boys were little, and they helped Dad and me clean the grave with a car key, some Kleenex, and water from Jesse's empty orange juice bottle.

I stand up and hear Wayne say, "Now where'd you say your parents are buried, Tom?"

"Right over here. Both their names are on this one marker. We buried their ashes right next to each other in the same plot."

"Right next to Steve's then?"

"Yeah. They bought four plots back in the 1950s. I think they said something once about a special cemetery offer for Lutherans back then. Expected they'd be the first ones buried here, I figure."

"Boy, I'll say! What a shock that was when he died. I will never forget that day. How many years has it been now?"

"Fifty-one, Wayne." Of the four plots Dad and Mom had purchased, two remain empty.

As Wayne and I walk together towards the back of the cemetery where his parents are buried, Wayne talks about his life after high school, his stint in the military, and how he landed an accounting job at the *Plain Dealer*, where he worked until his retirement. I fill him in on the highlights of how I managed to wind up living in Canada and my retirement from public health work two years earlier. After paying our respects at his parents' graves, we part company with plans to meet for lunch later.

I turn and walk to the cemetery office for the meeting I've planned with the cemetery's family service coordinator. In the past ten years, I have been privately mulling over the idea of being buried in the same plot as Steve. I want to find out how to make that happen. The coordinator tells me that the cemetery designates burial plots by letters: Steve's is Plot A, Mom and Dad's is Plot B. The two open patches of grass to the right of Mom and Dad's are Plots C and D. The cemetery permitted my sisters and me to inter our parents' ashes in a single burial plot with a single marker for a small additional cost. The coordinator tells me, however, that sharing Steve's Plot A with my own separate grave marker creates additional complications.

The new information gives me pause. From the coordinator's office near the back of the cemetery, I walk slowly to our family's plots near the road, rethinking my plans due to this unsettling turn of events. I stand at the foot of Plot B and look down. Focusing on the inscription, I read it out loud: "Albert C. G. Zink 1916–1997 Charlotte Zucker Zink 1920–2005." To the left, Plot A and my brother. I pronounce it slowly: "Stephen Alan Zink 1945–1961." To the right are the two empty untouched plots of grass.

I soften my focus, letting my vision widen to include all four plots. The details on the grave markers blur. These three people whose lives have now ended were my world when my life began. I take in the entirety of the four burial plots, and see two choices; the symbolic differences are stark.

To share Steve's gravesite is an affirmation that we are still the Zink brothers, even if we are together only in death. And yet it also implies being beneath him or behind him, forever dwelling in his shadow. To choose one of the empty plots to the right of my parents creates a certain symmetry that appeals to me. It's an assertion that my life can stand on its own, separate from my brother's and free from that tired old place in his shadow: our parents' original oldest child to one side, their second oldest—the surviving oldest—on the other.

I picture my own bronze marker—"Thomas Christopher Zink 1947—..."

In that brief moment, one thing becomes crystal clear: It is in picturing my own death and final resting place that I can at last step outside of the shadow of Steve's life and his death and accept that, today, I continue to cast shadows of my own and sometimes seek the shadow of others. It seems entirely fitting that this grace moment of at last knowing myself to be separate and distinct from Steve—yet still closely linked—occurs with me looking at grave markers in a cemetery just a few miles from where my brother and I grew up.

MY SEASONED EYES are now more attuned to the presence of grace, both in past events in my life and in the present. Like the old saying, I "keep my eyes peeled," ever on the alert for signs of grace. From this recognition of the grace present in everyday life flows a sense of gratitude. From this seasoned place, I sense that grace has caught up with and overtaken my grief.

I am a child of winter no more.

Al and Charlotte on their 34th anniversary in June 1976.

Acknowledgements

I HAVE BEEN ASKED BEFORE, and expect I will be asked again, "How did you remember all that?" The short answer is, "I didn't." For the countless family letters and photographs, diaries and journals, newspaper articles and obituaries, telephone calls and face-to-face conversations that comprise the long answer, I am first and foremost grateful to my parents, Albert and Charlotte Zink, who not only wrote detailed, timely letters, but also kept all those they had written and received. The hundreds of photographs my father took over the years also recalled stories that might otherwise have been forgotten. After our parents died, each of my three sisters, Kelly Castle, Amy Fowler, and Judi Zink, kept portions of these family archives, and shared them with me when I was doing my research. My sincere thanks, Kelly, Amy, and Judi, for your support.

I also am grateful to many other relatives whose recollections and family history research have informed various parts of the book. Among them are cousins Rob and John Springsteen, Kathy and Conrad Ziegler, Andy Liederley, and Jonathan Matsey; my late aunt and uncle, Anne and Bob Springsteen; and my late aunts Marlise Reidenbach Springsteen and Irene Benson. My heartfelt "Thank you!" goes especially to my dear cousin, Marlise Anne Reidenbach, a fellow logophile who has been a welcome, dependable source of reassurance, light-hearted wordplay, and advice that helps me stay spiritually grounded. We often laugh together, sometimes we cry, but always our phone calls have inspired me to persevere.

I owe a special debt of gratitude to four people, without whose friendship and loyalty to me and to my story, this book could not have happened. Moreen Torpy, Craig Hurst, Elaine Hurst, and my cousin, Janet Springsteen, worked through early drafts with me, chapter by chapter, month by month, for more than a year to help me figure out what I was really trying to say. I am grateful also to Dennis Davis, Tim Fangmeier, Wayne Hill, Teresa Maebori, Jim Munroe, and Heather Topps, all of whom read later drafts and provided insights, guidance, and encouragement.

I am grateful for the inspiration and support I received in the Mourning Reflections writing group in Northampton, Massachusetts, from the facilitators, Becky Jones and Carol Bevan-Bogart, and the group members. My confidence as a writer received a tremendous boost from a summer writing school course at the University of Toronto, called "Writing the Memoir." I am indebted to Marina Nemat, the course instructor, for her clear, enthusiastic feedback, and to my fellow writers in the course, especially to Chris Cameron, who generously offered to read an early draft and provided insightful feedback.

I am most appreciative of friends from Lutheran High School West who shared their memories about my family, about Steve and their experiences of his death, including Tim Fangmeier, Terry Fibich, Don Halter, Rick Hagedorn, Phil Hemke, John Hemsath, Dave Kemp, Roger Luekens, Sue Michael, Wayne Peters, and Donna Slepack. I'm grateful to the many members of Al-Anon in western Massachusetts who shared their experience, strength, and hope, and helped me find the courage to open myself up to the story within these pages. I trust that you know who you are.

Joe "Ping" Limes and Florence Selepeo Kirby, Carolinian friends from Saipan, have played an invaluable role as language informants, helping to ensure that my use of Carolinian and Chamorro terms was accurate. I am very grateful for their continuing support: *si Yu'os ma'ase'*, my friends.

My thanks also to the following for their willingness to discuss my work on this project and to help me fill in details: Dr. James Abel, Eva Black, Judson Brown, Fay Giordano, Priscilla Lane, Marilyn Lindner, Dr. Janine Roberts, and members of the Westlake, Ohio, Police Department.

The skill, sensitivity, and professionalism of my editor, Janice Beetle, are gifts that helped to sharpen, shorten, and sweeten the narrative. Her challenge to go deeper into early interactions with Steve led me to new understandings I had never before considered. Thanks also to Maureen Scanlon, whose creative design talents are responsible for the handsome appearance of the book, and to Steve Strimer, who helped guide me through the self-publishing process at Off the Common Books in Amherst, Massachusetts.

Special thanks to my sons, Jody, my "rainy day people" son, for his attentive listening, wise insights, and convincing hugs, and Jesse, himself the author of three published books, for his readiness to answer my questions about producing a book, to offer advice, and support me on the way forward.

And to you, Beth, my wife, partner, confidante and soul support: You told me so often that I could talk to you anytime about what I was thinking, feeling, and writing about Steve that I came to believe you. Our conversations as you read the full draft opened new windows into the story. I don't say nearly enough how much I love you.

SOURCES

Albers, James W. 2006. "Stories of Lutherans and Race: A Bibliographic Perspective." *The Cresset*, 70 (1): 20–26.

Baepler, Richard. 2002. *Flame of Faith, Lamp of Learning: A History of Valparaiso University*. St. Louis: Concordia Publishing House.

Boyer, David S. 1967. "Micronesia: The Americanization of Eden." *National Geographic*, 131 (5): 702–742.

Funeral Sermon

October 23, 1961
St. Thomas Lutheran Church, Rocky River, Ohio
Reverend Paul W. Streufert

This is the transcript of the sermon preached by
Reverend Streufert at Stephen Zink's funeral.

Much grace, mercy and comfort be unto you from our Lord Jesus Christ. Amen.

The Word of God, which I have chosen for Stephen's burial, I once chose for him at the moment when he knelt at the altar of God. I had chosen for him the words of God to Joshua in his first chapter, in verse nine. There the Lord says to Joshua, "Be strong and of a good courage, be not afraid, neither be thou dismayed; for the Lord, thy God, is with thee withersoever thou goest."

My beloved,

There are many questions being asked this morning by the family and by the congregation and Stephen's friends. And if I should sum up the questions in the heart of every one of us, it would be the one word, Why? Why did it have to be your family? Why in your family did it have to be Stephen? Why in our congregation did it have to be the president of the young people's organization? Why in the high school class should it be one member who seemingly had mental talents that would bring him far in his lifetime? Why among his friends should it be this one who had always demonstrated that there is, in the midst of culture, also a Christianity that goes far deeper than a veneer, superimposed upon a human being? Why? Why this one?

The Lord looks at us, and He says, "Have you been my counsellor? Have you sat in the halls of heaven with Me, the Maker and Creator of the universe, to advise Me how I shall take the universe in My hand and mold it and shape it? And shall I be advised by you, My creatures, how I shall take My children and mold their lives for their good and for a blessed eternity?" There are times, my beloved, when God in our lives simply pulls down the curtain, and He does not let us look upon the stage where He is working out His own design for His people. He had to tell His own apostle Peter one time that Peter should not search too deeply into the ways of God, for Jesus had to tell him on one occasion, "What I do now, thou knowest not, but thou shalt know hereafter." And I'll have to repeat the Savior's words to you, His children, "What I do now, thou knowest not, but thou shalt know hereafter." Here is a promise of God that the time is coming when we will be able to look into His designs. There is a glorious day coming when the haze of our own intellect will be removed, and there will be given to us a wisdom and understanding of God's ways with His children.

And while we are looking forward to that day, let us look to the apostle, who says to us in this hour, "Brethren, I would not have you to be ignorant concerning them which are asleep. That ye sorrow not even as others which have no hope." The apostle pins it down, and he says, "There are those in this world, who if they were standing beside such a casket, and had met such a tragedy in their families, they would have a right to cry and to moan." And he points to the heathen world, and he characterizes it by the one statement, "They that are without hope."

And the hope that you have, and the hope that Steve had is all in his confirmation verse: "Be of good courage, be not afraid; I will be with thee withersoever thou goest." God kept that promise. He made that promise first when you, his parents, brought him in Pilgrim Church as a little babe and laid him as a sinful child into the arms of Jesus in the Sacrament of Holy Baptism. In that moment, all the blessings that Jesus won for us on the cross, the forgiveness of sins, the breaking of the curse of the Law, the whole condemnation and judgment of which Paul spoke in that fifth chapter to the Romans, had all been removed and God gave to him in his own kind, unfathomable way a new heart, a believing heart, a trusting heart. In Baptism, Steve became His child.

By faith. Beloved, you could give him only his body and his life. You transmitted nothing to him but a sinful heart. I didn't say that. Scripture says that. "Behold, I was shapen in iniquity and in sin did my mother conceive me." Nothing else. But from heaven God reached down and took this seed, and He regenerated it, recreated it and gave to it the image of the Son of God Himself, and in that image which God created by Holy Baptism, you, the loving parents, attempted to keep Steve during the days of his childhood. The Savior was not an unknown entity to him. The kingdom of God was not a *terra incognita*, an unknown soil, an unknown country, an unknown territory. Steve was acquainted with his Jesus, he was acquainted with His kingdom, he was acquainted with His power, and he was acquainted with His love.

And as I learned to know Stephen as one of the sheep of Jesus and I, the undershepherd for the Christ, I would say, would to God that we had many such Stephens in our community, many such Stephens in our congregation. He recognized his weaknesses. He recognized his sin, but ever he had those folded hands which went to the Christ, Who had given him the promise, "Be not afraid, be of good courage, I will never leave thee withersoever thou goest." The promise of Baptism was carried by the Savior all through his life.

And you parents, you'd made wonderful plans for Stephen for the future. God wanted you to do that. God wants us to plan as though we'll live forever, but He wants us to live as though we have to go tomorrow. And you, the parents, were not unmindful of this sacred duty. The sacred duty of impressing upon the teenager, yes, he shall prepare himself adequately by the talents of his body, the gifts of his mind, that he may use them for the welfare of this world. But, at the same time, ever to be mindful that he might be called tomorrow. You didn't know that God's clock had run out on Thursday morning when so quickly he got onto his bicycle and went to peddle his papers as he was wont to do, and as you bade him good-bye, and then God said hello. He met him on Columbia Road. God could have said to his angels, "Stop that car." You know what God said? He said to the angels, "Keep your hands off that car. I want that boy—now!" Stephen didn't realize it. God in His power could have accomplished it, but God wanted him. And if you and I say it's a tragedy, it's a mistake, it's an error, it's an accident, we say, "Are you God's counsellor? Have you sat in the halls of heaven to advise God what incident in life He should use to call His children home?" Beloved, here we have one of those evidences of God's love where He has a greater plan to accomplish something in the lives of us all.

Why did it have to be Steve? Maybe God wanted to teach you, his friends, a terrific lesson. Might I ask you a question? Are all you young people sitting in front of me ready to say, "I was as ready as Steve to meet my Maker."? Have you made peace with God? Have you given any thought at all to the next world? Have you given any attention beyond the development of your mind and the talents of your hands to grasp up for the great hope of eternity? And beloved, I assure you, this is not the end for Stephen. His body shall rise out of that grave, not because I said so, but because the Scripture said, "They shall all hear His voice and shall come forth." The day is coming when that body rises out of the grave, and then he will meet Jesus again, clothed in body and soul, and then will come the great question of the judgment of God. And here again comes his confirmation verse: "I will not leave thee, withersoever thou goest." The Lord Jesus had His hand of love on Stephen even in the midst of that accident. And if God decided to remove him quickly to the eternal heavens, we bow in humble submission, and say, "Oh, God, your ways are mysterious, they are past finding out, but Thy ways are always ways of love." Look what Jesus had done for Stephen.

There was a great problem that God had to solve: how to bring a person to heaven. All the world said, "God, we'll try to do the best we can, and maybe You will understand that we are just human, erring sinful people and you'll overlook the bad things we've done." God said, "No." It takes a different price, and that first Christmas He sent His Son, Jesus Christ, that He might be born of a virgin, without a human father, by the miracle of the Holy Spirit, a sinless Son, the only sinless person Who ever lived in the world. Outside of Jesus, all are sinners, the Scripture says. There's not one human being who hasn't offended God, sinned against Him, broken His law, violated His holiness, and that problem had to be solved. And so whom did God send? The only One He could find. Not Moses, not Peter, not Paul, but His Son, Jesus. And he permitted Him to live a perfect and holy life, and that was placed in the balance for our redemption. And then at the end of His life, He had Him nailed to the cross by wicked hands, so that, before God, there could be a sacrifice which would cleanse the whole world of its sin and guilt. And by one justifying act, God, in the death of His Son, declared that the pathway to heaven is open for everyone who believeth. That's what God meant when He said, "I will not leave thee nor forsake thee, withersoever thou goest." As God had created that faith in Stephen, so He kept Stephen in that faith until the hurried moment of his departure.

Stephen attempted to live for that Jesus Who had redeemed him. Oh, how often Stephen knelt here at this altar to receive Christ's body and blood in the blessed Sacrament. How consistently he announced for this Holy Communion that he might again be assured from God Himself that his sins are forgiven. Beloved, isn't that victory? When God calls such a one who stands in the faith and stands in His grace, stands under the forgiving love of God into His eternal home, isn't that one reason for us to sing "Ten Thousand Times Ten Thousand," the victory hymn of the Christian Church? This is not a moment for sadness. This is a moment when God has given to him the fruition of all his hopes.

And for you and me, there is one lesson. One lesson to the parents. Oh, how often have I said from this pulpit, you fathers and mothers, how foolish, when you think these children belong to you. How foolish, when you think you are shaping their destiny and their future. How foolish when you think all the children need is a development of the abilities of their hands and of their mind and leave undone the greater duty of preparing them for the day when they are to meet their Maker. There is a lesson for you. Oh, what if God had come into your home and had taken one of your youngsters and that youngster should stand before the Lord, his Judge!

There's a lesson for you teenagers. I know, when we are young, it's so hard for us to think about dying. We're so busy. We've got so many things to do. So many plans to make—what I'm going to do when I'm eighteen, what I'm going to do when I'm twenty-five, and what I'm going to do when I'm an adult. I've got all these plans as a youngster. And then we forget that God from heaven also has a plan for us. And He has already given us a bank-note for each day. And each day, God turns over the bank-note of time. How big is your stack? God knows now when your last number is coming. He knows now already whether you're going to reach twenty-five or thirty-five or eighty-five. God hasn't revealed it to you because God wants you to know, just like Steve, it can be tomorrow. Oh, beloved, come to the Savior. Come to the Lord Jesus today and don't let Him wait, because in eternity, you will have to meet Him, whether you want Him or not, as the Judge of all. And, oh, God give you teenagers the grace to understand that there is no jewel in life that is worth the precious jewel of faith. The Lord Himself told you, "What does it profit a man if he gain the whole world and yet lose his own soul?"

And, beloved, for our congregation, there is a tremendous lesson in this that we dare lose no opportunity to preach clearly and distinctly at every opportunity that we have the salvation of the sinner through the blood of Jesus Christ. I didn't know that that was the last time I would have a chance to tell Steve how to get to heaven when I stood in this pulpit and preached to the congregation. It's a terrific lesson for me as pastor never to lose an opportunity to share with others the richness of this Gospel that there is but one way to eternal heaven. And I say to you, St. Thomas congregation, get busy, stay at it, don't give up, for the Lord has said to you also as He said to Steve, "Be of good courage, be not afraid; I will be with thee withersoever thou goest."

And now, as we carry his body out to its last resting-place to await the great dawn of eternity, we sink it into the ground as a seed, that is sown in dishonor, but it shall be raised in glory. It has been sown in sin, but it shall be raised by the Savior. And so we come to his last resting-place, truly with burdened hearts. But amid our tears the song of victory that we shall someday, if we remain faithful to the Word of our Lord, see him in that glorious and happy eternity. And now together let us all join in the encouragement each one of us needs as we sing the hymn, "What God Ordains is Always Good."

May God grant it, for Jesus' sake, Amen.

The Trumpeter

*A poem written by Stephen's aunt, Anne Springsteen,
as published in 1962 in* The Cresset, *Valparaiso University's
review of literature, the arts, and public affairs.*

And the trumpet shall sound — and in a moment, in the twinkling of an eye, we shall be changed.

the trumpeter

In memoriam S.A.Z.

By Anne Springsteen

The trumpet sounded through the church:
Do you believe in one God,
    the Father Almighty, Maker of heaven and earth
    and in one Lord Jesus Christ, the only begotten Son of God,
    and in the Holy Ghost, the Lord and Giver of Life?
Do you acknowledge one Baptism for the remission of sins,
and do you look for the resurrection of the dead,
and the life of the world to come?

        The sponsors answered for the child;
        the parents answered silently, "Yes, Lord."

"I baptize you in the name of God the Father,
        God the Son,
        and God the Holy Ghost,
        Amen."

        And the child was called by name.

The parents were thankful,
and full of prayerful thoughts for their firstborn.
They renewed themselves before God,
searching for patience and wisdom and faithfulness.

    The family grew, and became a tumbling, happy assortment of brothers and sisters.

But the child was first.

        He was the first to learn to walk,
        the first to learn a language,
        the first to go to school,
        the first to learn to read and write,
        the first to learn to pray.

And in this learning he found pleasure and pain:

> when the arithmetic problems defied a quick solution,
> the wads of paper covered the desk;
>
> when the snow refused to pack properly for the snowman's head,
> the furious stomp of boots shook the house;
>
> when a small sister, in curiosity and admiration,
> brushed too close to the castle of bricks,
> the cry of rage could be heard from cellar to attic;
>
> when the childish hand brought the hammer down
> on the thumb instead of the nail,
> the scream of anguish electrified the whole family.

The parents and children continued in love and prayer,
and grew stronger in understanding and faith.

The child explored his world with fearlessness and curiosity:

the beetle and the snake in the garden,
the path through the woods,
the campfire in the clearing,
the bridge spanning the river,
the stream in the valley,
the friend two blocks away,
the church of his family

In his exploring he found excitement and joy and impatience:

> no time to hang up the coat,
> no time to waste on girls,
> no time to walk the steps one by one,
> no time to dawdle over perfection.
>
> There were important things to be done.
>
> On the bike and down the road
> to the Scout meeting,
> to the trumpet lesson,
> to the paper route,
> to the church meeting.

And the parents looked to God for help in guiding their sons and daughters.

Again the trumpet sounded through the church.

    "Do you this day, in the presence of God and of this Christian congregation,
    confirm the solemn covenant which at your Baptism you made with the Triune
    God?"

                  The child answered, "Yes, Lord."
                  The parents answered silently, "Yes, Lord."

And the child was called by name again.

    "Be strong and of good courage, be not frightened,
      neither be dismayed, for the Lord your God
      is with you wherever you go."

Tall and straight,
Quick-tempered and loving — He was God's young man.   He did not yet know himself,
                                          but God knew him well,
                                        and gave him His work to do.

    On the bike and up the road   to the Scout meeting,
                                              to the trumpet lesson,
                                            to the paper route
                                            to the church meeting.

And God reached out His hand to the child and touched him

      with patience   as he copied for the family of singers
                                           the harmonies of a favorite hymn;

      with joy   as he walked the hills of New Mexico
                                           with Scout friends;

      with determination   as he created and built the ship model;

      with love   as he helped with the irksome household chores,

      with forgiveness   as he stood at the Lord's table.

The trumpet sounded through the dusk before dawn:

"Child, come home."

    He answered, "Yes, Lord."

    The parents bowed their heads, and answered aloud, "Yes, Lord."

The trumpet sounds again and again:

Be still   and know that I am God.

    Thou shalt also be a crown of glory

    in the hand of the Lord,

    and a royal diadem

    in the hand of thy God.

A Day in Micronesia

A song written by Tom Zink

Lava-lava topless mother husks a coconut on the beach,
A topless, bottomless toddler waddles safely within reach,
The chattering children cheerfully chew a starchy morning feast,
And the palm tree branches sway in the trade winds from the east.
      The sun is low, but it's getting hot,
      The tide is high but it's going out,
      And it's morning-time in Micronesia:
Try to say it in their language and the little children tease ya,
Let them do things their way and their friendliness will please ya,
Turn on to local time 'cause from the clock it frees ya,
And the hours pass by unnoticed, when it's morning-time in Micronesia.

Big boat with no outrigger slowly enters the lagoon,
Due tomorrow with supplies, it's come a bit too soon,
No longer topless T-shirt mother lifts her baby from the sand,
And the chattering children stop and run to watch the big boat land.
      The sun's straight up and it's burning hot,
      The tide is leaving, but the boat is not,
      And it's noon-time in Micronesia:
Teach the kids to say it your way and they'll no longer tease ya,
Then let them see the things you've brought and wide white smiles will please ya,
Show them how your watch works how from being late it frees ya,
Look closely at the minute hand, and it's twelve noon in Micronesia.

The chattering children return from school carrying books made far away,
The office clerks all head for home after another air-conditioned day,
Television programs start this afternoon at half past three,
There's a Coca-cola sale going on, if you buy one case, you get one free.
  The sun is sinking, but it's still quite hot,
  The tide's returning but the morning cannot,
  And it's afternoon in Micronesia:
If their new styles don't look right, don't let it displease ya,
'Cause you know how well that new tube, made in Japan, TVs ya,
Buy a beer in the hotel bar and that'll help to ease ya,
Watch the office workers driving home when it's afternoon in Micronesia.

The chattering children's new diversions are delinquency, dances and drugs,
Grandma minds the baby, a light-bulb calls the bugs.
Waves flop on the beach to lick a littered old beer can,
Drained to prove to someone that the drinker was a man.
  The sun is gone, now the moon is out,
  The tide's returned and without doubt,
  It's now night-time in Micronesia:
Take a look at what's gone on, what you can find to please ya,
Can this be the right road or does each day more displease ya,
Grab the question, try to answer before the morning sees ya,
Something must be done before the morning comes,
For it's night-time in Micronesia:

And the question keeps re-echoing: What will tomorrow bring?
And the question keeps re-echoing: What will tomorrow bring?

What will tomorrow bring...?

Good Enough for Me

A song written by Tom Zink

When Bobby was a little boy, he was really smart in school,
He always got straight A's, and he followed every rule.
One day he proudly showed his Dad the 96 on his math test,
And his dad said, "You could have got a hundred
if you'd only done your best,"
When he could have said,

CHORUS
Oh, you're doin' just fine and I like you like you are,
If you trust your own thinking then you really will go far,
And if someone comes along and says,
"You're not what you should be,"
Just let 'em have a [Bronx cheer!] and say, "I'm good enough for me.
I'm good enough for me, I'm good enough for me,"
Just let 'em have a [Bronx cheer!] and say "I'm good enough for me."

Becky loved to sing and dance when she was only three,
She'd chortle, gallop, and spin around, her voice a singin' free.
When she was five, she went to school, and the teacher taught a song,
When she heard Becky singing, she said,
"My dear, you'd better mouth along,"
When she could have said,

CHORUS
Oh, you're doing just fine and I like the way you sing,
If you trust your own thinking, you can do most anything,
And if someone comes along and says, "You're not what you should be,"
Just let 'em have a [Bronx cheer!] and say, "I'm good enough for me.
I'm good enough for me, oh, I'm good enough for me,"
Just let 'em have a [Bronx cheer!] and say, "I'm good enough for me."

Johnny had it hard in school, he could never get good grades,
And every night his parents let him have the same tirade—
      ("Get your homework done, kid!")
So he struggled hard and sweated blood and he finally got a B,
And his parents said, "Those teachers sure are softer
than they ever used to be,"
When they could have said,

CHORUS
Oh, you're doin' just fine and I like you like you are,
If you trust your own thinking then you really will go far,
And if someone comes along and says,
"You're not what you should be,"
Just let 'em have a [Bronx cheer!] and say, "I'm good enough for me.
I'm good enough for me, oh, I'm good enough for me,"
Just let 'em have a [Bronx cheer!] and say "I'm good enough for me."

About the Author

Tom Zink has degrees from Valparaiso University in Indiana, George Williams College in Illinois, and the University of Massachusetts at Amherst. He served as a Peace Corps volunteer in Micronesia in the late 1960s, and has also been a preschool teacher and director, a child care counselor, a city parks and recreation super-intendent, and a New Games trainer. He worked in public health for twenty-two years up until his retirement in 2010. He is currently *not* retired from being a husband, father, grandfather, brother, cousin, uncle, musician, bicyclist, gardener, and other pursuits yet to be discovered. Tom lives with his wife, Beth Hewson, in North Bay, Ontario.

The Stephen A. Zink Scholarship

Proceeds from the sale of this book will go towards the Stephen A. Zink Scholarship at Steve's alma mater, Lutheran High School West in Rocky River, Ohio. Additional contributions to the fund may be sent by check payable to "CLHSA" to: Alumni & Development Director, Cleveland Lutheran High School Association, 3870 Linden Road, Rocky River, Ohio 44116-4016 USA. Phone: 440-356-7155 ext. 3. Please enclose a note indicating that the contribution is for the Stephen A. Zink Scholarship. For checks drawn on Canadian banks, please write "Payable in U.S. dollars" in the memo line.